The Business Tax Return Handbook

Fifth Edition

The Business Tax Return Handbook

Jack Zuckerman and
Ron Thompson

AMERICAN BAR ASSOCIATION
Family Law Section

Cover design by ABA Design

Printed in the United States of America.

27 26 25 24 23 5 4 3 2 1

ISBN 978-1-63905-344-5

CONTENTS

ABOUT THE AUTHORS

JACK ZUCKERMAN is a founding partner of White, Zuckerman, Warsavsky, Luna, & Hunt, LLP, who are Certified Public Accountants with offices in Los Angeles and Irvine, California. He received his undergraduate degree from the City College of the City University of New York and his J.D. from Southwestern University School of Law. Mr. Zuckerman authored a chapter in 1999 Los Angeles Bar Association Family Law Symposium titled "Interpreting Business Tax Returns for Family Law Purposes." He has also authored the books *Understanding Business Tax Returns: A Lawyers Handbook* (2014, American Bar Association), and previous editions of *The 1040 Handbook.* In addition, Mr. Zuckerman has coedited the book *California Community Property with Tax Analysis* (Matthew Bender), coauthored the articles "Legal Tender" (Appraising Interests in Law Practices, *Los Angeles Lawyer*, May 1995), and coauthored a chapter in the 1994 and 1995 Los Angeles Bar Association Family Law Symposium titled "Tracing and Its Application in Family Law." He has lectured frequently on the subjects of valuation of assets in divorce and tax strategies in divorce. Mr. Zuckerman is accredited in business valuation by the American Institute of Certified Public Accountants. Mr. Zuckerman has served as an expert forensic accounting witness since 1980 and testified in court on more than 300 occasions.

RON THOMPSON is a partner in the Tax and Accounting Department of White, Zuckerman, Warsavsky, Luna, & Hunt, LLP. He received his Bachelor of Arts degree from the University of California at Los Angeles in Economics. He is a Certified Public Accountant and a CERTIFIED FINANCIAL PLANNER™ practitioner. He has served as an accountant for over thirty-five years and is now in charge of the Irvine Tax and Accounting Department responsible for the delivery of tax, estate planning, accounting, and attestation services to clients, which consist principally of small business enterprises and individuals. Mr. Thompson has testified in the Superior Court of California as an expert witness in matter of taxation.

PREFACE

This book is designed to provide practical help for family law practitioners and other lawyers interested in improving their understanding of business tax returns. It can be used as a complete introduction to the family law aspects of business tax returns or as a quick reference for lawyers who want to concentrate on particular areas of business taxation.

A wide variety of common business fact patterns accompanied by explanation and commentary is presented for study and reference. Discussion of fundamental tax issues relevant to family law matters are explored to help lawyers understand the import of the figures shown and statements made on these returns. Explanatory comments for similar line items in all three types of business tax returns have been duplicated in whole or part, where appropriate, to obviate the need for page flipping from one section to the next.

The implications of data relevant to the determination of discretionary cash flow and the evaluation of fair market value are frequently referenced throughout the book. Examples include subject matter such as cash basis versus accrual basis accounting, income versus cash flow, and perquisites. Suggestions for discovery procedures accompany many of the explanatory comments. The book also serves to enhance the practitioner's familiarity with business and tax terminology commonly arising in family law matters.

HYPOTHETICAL FACT PATTERNS

Hypothetical fact patterns for corporations, partnerships, and unincorporated businesses are presented to provide an overview of typical tax reporting for commercial businesses and professional practices. Included are tax returns for two unincorporated businesses, two types of partnerships, and three types of corporations.

The hypothetical unincorporated business reported on the Schedule C of the personal income tax return:

- A sole practitioner, and
- A business involved in product sales.

Partnership hypothetical tax returns:

- A real estate limited partnership, and
- A service-oriented business.

Corporate hypothetical tax returns:

- A service-oriented business ("loan-out corporation"),
- A "C" Corporation for a business involved in product sales, and
- An "S" Corporation involved in product sales.

The extensive variety of examples provided in the above mentioned hypothetical situations will cover many of the most common scenarios lawyers will confront in actual practice. Hopefully, the observations and explanations in the text and the accompanying hypothetical tax returns will prove invaluable to lawyers who wish to gain a greater understanding of business tax returns.

PART ONE: PROPRIETORSHIPS

Schedule C: Profit or Loss from Business

➢ FACT PATTERN FOR SERVICE PROVIDER

Roberta Doctor M.D. operates a medical practice as a sole practitioner. She must report her taxable practice income on Schedule C of her individual income tax return. A copy of her 2022 Schedule C is presented and referenced in this section.

➢ FACT PATTERN FOR BUSINESS INVOLVED IN SALE OF PRODUCTS

Howard Shopowner operates three pet stores. He also must report taxable income on the Schedule C of his individual income tax return. A copy of his 2022 Schedule C is presented and referenced in this section.

➢ PURPOSE OF SCHEDULE C

Anyone who operates a business or a professional practice as a sole proprietorship or a single member LLC must complete Schedule C of the individual income tax return. If individuals operate multiple separate sole proprietorships, a Schedule C is required for each business. Husband and wife may each operate separate sole proprietorships in which case, each must file a separate Schedule C.

➢ SECTIONS OF THE SCHEDULE

Unlike other partnership and corporate income tax returns, the Schedule C does not contain a section for a balance sheet. As a result, a complete financial overview of the business is not available from the tax return itself. Schedule C does, however, provide important information concerning the annual taxable income from the practice or business. Form 4562 of the individual income tax return and supporting schedules may provide data on cost basis and the depreciation history of the fixed assets of a business (note that Internal Revenue Service rules generally do not require that detailed fixed asset schedules be attached to the return).

Schedule C is divided into five sections. The first section, Lines A through J, contains questions such as the type of accounting method used and whether the taxpayer "materially participated" in the business. Part I: Income, Part II: Expenses, Part III: Cost of Goods Sold, Part IV: Information on Your Vehicle, and Part V: Other Expenses comprise the remaining sections of the Schedule C.

First Section: Accounting Methods and Material Participation

Lines C and E: The name under which the practice is conducted is indicated on this line. Most unincorporated professional practices do not use a "DBA" (Doing Business As) and simply leave this line blank to signify that the practitioner's name is the business's name. If the practice is located outside the home, its address is listed separately.

Line D: The taxpayer's employer I.D. number is generally required if the taxpayer files an employment tax return. The appearance of the number also suggests the possibility of a Keogh plan. Confirmation of this fact may be obtained by looking at Page 2, Line 16 of the Schedule 1 attached to Form 1040 (not included in this book) titled "Self-employed SEP, SIMPLE, and Qualified Plans." The absence of an entry on this line does not necessarily mean a plan does not exist; it indicates only that no contribution was made in 2022.

Line F: The two most common accounting methods are known as the "cash basis" and "accrual basis." When a business is on a cash basis, revenue is reported in the year in which it is actually or constructively received in the form of currency, checks, credit card payments, or electronic fund transfers. Under the "cash basis" deductions are taken for expenses actually paid during the year. In contrast, accrual basis businesses report revenue when it is earned (when the right to receive that revenue occurs). Thus, if a customer was billed for an item that it received on December 30, 2022 but did not pay for until February 1, 2023, the business reporting on an accrual basis would still record the income in 2022 even though the service or merchandise was paid for in the subsequent year. On the accrual basis, expenses may be deducted when incurred, whether paid or not in the tax year.

In many businesses with income-producing inventories, such as automobile dealerships or hard and soft goods retailers, the Internal Revenue Service will not allow cash basis accounting because of the enhanced possibility of material manipulation of income. Delaying the reporting of income or advancing the payment of costs distorts annual income when the cash method is used. However, the Tax Cut and Jobs Act enacted in 2017 provided that most sole proprietorships are allowed to utilize the cash method even if they have inventories.

Cash basis accounting is particularly common to service businesses and professional practices. When the cash basis of accounting is used, inquiry as to the amount of accounts receivable is advisable. The receivables are not shown on the Schedule C but determining the value of the collectible receivables is essential for valuation purposes because receivables often represent one of the largest assets of the business or practice.

Accounts receivables present an interesting problem when cash basis businesses are valued in family law matters when the spouse charged with the receivables will also be required to pay child and/or spousal support based partially on the income related to the collection of these same receivables. The perceived "double-dip" may appear particularly inequitable in property divisions where one party is receiving the business and paying support while assets of equal stated value are awarded to the other spouse. Nevertheless, a recent California appellate court decision determined that it is proper to include earnings as income available for support from those same receivables the spouse received in the property division.

The "double-dip" effect, while appearing inequitable, can be better understood in terms of accrual basis accounting. On an accrual basis, the paying spouse is actually providing support from current accrual basis earnings. This can be illustrated by the following hypothetical. Assume that the business or practice is terminated at date of separation and the owner/spouse finds a job as an employee immediately after separation. In this situation, there is no "double-dip" because the spousal and/or child support will be based on wages that the paying spouse will be receiving and on only half of the accounts receivable. The receivables from the business would be shared equally by both spouses when collected (and considered part of each spouse's income). The resulting income of each spouse that is considered available for support will include one-half of the receivables. As a result, no double-dip occurs.

Another manner of reporting revenue and expense is known as "Percentage of Completion." Used primarily in construction type businesses. Motion picture projects generally utilize a similar method of accounting known as the "Income Forecast Method." These methods dictate that revenue and expenses be recognized in conjunction with the progress of the construction project(s). Cash paid in advance is set up as a liability rather than recorded as revenue under this method.

Line H: If the business or practice was started in 2022, the net profit or loss shown may not represent the true income potential of the business because only the results for a partial year are reflected on Schedule C in this situation. Furthermore, the expenses for the business may be greater than will be experienced in future years because of start-up costs generally associated with the first year of operations.

Part I: Income

Line 1: Gross Receipts or Sales Gross receipts, commonly stated as what the business "grosses," is usually significant for valuation purposes. Non-accountants frequently use the terms "Income," "Revenue," and "Gross Income" interchangeably. This is an area ripe with confusion that lawyers should understand. The gross cash receipts are synonymous with revenue for a business that operates on a cash basis. If the business operates on an accrual basis, gross cash receipts and revenue may be totally different amounts. In the case of accrual businesses, the revenue represents what the business has billed or sold, but not necessarily collected, while the cash receipts are entirely collections on accounts receivable or services performed for which payment is received during the period.

On the other hand, "Income" is the difference between revenue and expenses. It is synonymous with the terms "Profit" or "Bottom Line."

The "Gross" is an important element of tax return analysis. Often, a business or practice is sold on the basis of multiples of gross receipts. On Roberta Doctor's Schedule C, $454,200 of gross receipts is reported. Comparison with prior years "Gross" will provide information for a historical trend analysis of patient fees. If a material decrease in revenue occurred in 2022, the cause for the reduction should be ascertained through interviews, depositions, or document inspections. The concern in such instances generally focuses on whether the decrease was caused by the psychological effects of the divorce or by a willful slowdown on her part. If so, the other spouse's attorney can argue that the decrease in current income is a non-recurring event that is not representative of the party's true earning ability.

A trend analysis is also appropriate for Howard Shopowner's business. Revenue and income trends are important factors to consider in appraising a commercial business. Divorce needs may induce the owner spouse to manipulate the revenue of the business once the parties have separated.

In some service businesses, the owners do not deposit checks received in December until January of the following year and do not report the income from the held checks even though they are required to do so. If a sole proprietor has just begun this practice of holding checks in December 2022, the "Gross" of the business will be understated by the amount of the held checks. The result is a lower tax and a lower apparent income for that spouse. If the practice of holding checks has been consistently followed for years, an analysis of the amounts involved for the prior versus the current year will provide the most accurate representation of the true gross receipts for the year in question.

The opportunity not to report revenue is present in businesses that handle cash, particularly retail businesses such as restaurants. Analysis of cash register tapes and other business records may be helpful in determining the amount of unreported income that results in those circumstances.

When information relevant to such an analysis is unavailable, other procedures are employed by forensic accountants to assist in quantifying the unreported income.

One such analysis uses statistical gross profit information for the industry to suggest appropriate levels of gross receipts. The quantification of what the "Gross" should be is achieved by dividing the actual "Cost of Goods Sold" of the subject business by the industry percentage for "Cost of Goods Sold." The comparison of the gross profit ("Revenue" less "Cost of Goods Sold"—also known as "Gross Margin") of the subject business to industry statistical information provides a quick method for determining the probability of unreported income and deciding if incurring the cost of further inspection of the business records is warranted.

An analysis of the mark-up on the company's merchandise may also be revealing. If the typical mark-up is 25% (let's say $1.25 on goods that cost $1.00), then the gross profit to be expected is 20% ($.25 divided by $1.25). Enhanced scrutiny is advisable if the tax return reflects "Gross Profit" that is materially lower than industry statistical norms. But the value of this type of analysis is substantially reduced where there is a large product mix or merchandise is frequently discounted.

Another approach, more time-consuming and costly than those mentioned previously, is the lifestyle analysis. A disparity between the parties' lifestyle and their reported income for the tax year may provide a reasonable estimate of the unreported income. The lifestyle approach requires an accounting for all sources and uses of cash for the year including deposits to the parties' personal accounts that may have come from gifts, inheritance, borrowing, or prior year loan repayments.

Classification by category of the type of expenditures by the parties during the particular period under scrutiny may reveal expenditures well in excess of reported income. Additionally, such classification may disclose either small or nonexistent expenditures for known costs of living such as housekeeper costs and grocery expenses. Such expenditures are often paid with cash and do not show up on bank or credit card statements. An estimate of the reasonable monthly cost of such expenditures may then be added to the reported cost of living obtained from bank, brokerage, and credit card statements to arrive at the total lifestyle of the parties.

Many retail businesses are cash and carry. In those cases, the business owner should be questioned about how cash receipts are recorded, to what extent payment is received in cash, and the procedure for depositing the receipts into the business bank account. Inquiry into barter transactional activity is also recommended. The inquiry may be informally conducted by a forensic accountant but if the owner refuses to cooperate voluntarily, the above questions should be asked at the owner's deposition.

Line 2: Returns and Allowances Returns and Allowances represent sold merchandise that has been returned or, in the case of a personal service business or practice, a refund of an overpayment. While seemingly similar, "Returns and Allowances" should not be confused with an "Allowance for Bad Debts or Uncollectible Accounts." The "Allowance" or "Reserve for Bad Debts," as it is sometimes called, is an expense taken by accrual based businesses to recognize that certain accounts receivable will probably not be collected.

Line 4: Cost of Goods Sold Professional practice and service businesses typically report nothing on this line (although some report professional wages here). Commercial businesses with inventories report the cost relating to the products sold on this line. In Part III of the Schedule C, the Internal Revenue Service requests additional information relative to "Cost of Goods Sold." A more detailed explanation of this area starts at the explanation of Part III, Line 33, presented later in this chapter.

Line 5: Gross Profit The gross profit is the difference between "Gross receipts or sales" ("Revenue") and the cost of merchandise sold. Reference to the percentage of "Gross Profit" to "Revenue" is an important indicator of business trends. A decline in the gross profit percentage may indicate greater price competition in the industry or higher raw material costs. Howard Shopowner's gross profit percentage is about 60% ($1,489,362 gross profit divided by $2,502,588 in sales). Gross profit variances in the year of divorce warrant concern and scrutiny. Both "Revenue" and "Cost of Goods Sold" may affect this percentage. As mentioned previously, a divergence from industry norms may signify that the subject business is not reporting revenue. More on "Gross Profit" (also known as "Gross Margin") is presented starting at Part III, Line 33.

Line 6: Other Income "Other Income" is taxable income that is not considered "Gross receipts or sales." It also does not include capital gains, recapture of depreciation, or ordinary income from sale of assets. Unusual business receipts that are not in the ordinary course of business are reported on this line. One example of such income is proceeds from a lease termination whereby the lessor has paid the business owner consideration in exchange for the owner's consent to move prior to the lease termination date. Such unusual income should be analyzed to determine whether it is recurring or not. Non-recurring sources of income are usually not considered as cash available for the determination of current and future support.

Line 7: Gross Income The amount shown is usually less significant than "Gross Profit" because it is either the same as "Gross Profit" or is greater than the "Gross Profit" by the amount of nonrecurring income sources.

Part II: Expenses

Certain lines within this part have been skipped because the line description is self-explanatory and the expense represented is one that is not frequently analyzed in family law matters. This is not to say that such expenses may not be extremely important in some cases. For that reason, expenses should be converted into percentages and compared with prior years. Anomalies and deviations can be more easily identified through use of this type of analysis (also known as "Common Size" comparative income statements).

Line 9: Car and Truck Expenses Automobile expenses are frequently overstated both in terms of amount and degree of business versus personal use involved. In either case, the actual business-related auto expenses should be investigated. Overstated expenses or the cost of personal use is one of the most common perquisites found on business tax returns. Inquiry of the owner, either through interview or deposition, is the starting point for this analysis. The nature of the business activity should dovetail with the owner's explanations. Where such is not the case, forensic accountants frequently estimate a reasonable business use percentage based on the available evidence. Part IV of Schedule C reflects the IRS's concern that only legitimate vehicle expenses be deducted. Part IV is not filled out on the hypothetical tax returns in this book because it is only to be completed if no Form 4562 is included in the tax return. There is a Form 4562 included for both Roberta Doctor and Harold Shopkeeper.

Line 13: Depreciation and Section 179 Expense Deduction Reported depreciation is a non-cash expense in the sense that it usually does not mirror the actual cash outlays for business capital assets. Most small-business operators do not maintain cash replacement reserve accounts to equal depreciation write-offs. Frequently, the depreciation written off represents available income for child support or alimony if the historical capital expenditures exceed the prospective future investment in new capital assets.

Analysis of depreciation and asset history may be provided either wholly or partially on Form 4562 and supporting schedules of the individual income tax return. More information may be obtained from a business's internal depreciation schedules or the work papers maintained by its independent certified public accounting firm.

Proprietorships are not required to provide the Internal Revenue Service with balance sheets in their tax returns; accordingly, little information on balance sheet items (assets, liabilities, and net worth) are available. However, a fixed asset depreciation schedule is often included in the tax return although as noted earlier it is generally not required. Probative information concerning the assets of the business, including date of acquisition and original cost, are provided on the depreciation schedule. Assets may be identified that have been written off but still have value. In addition to providing relevant data for determining the fair market value of the fixed assets, the depreciation schedule is also useful for evaluating claimed income needs of the business for investment in new equipment.

Immediate expensing of capital assets in the current year is available under IRC Section 179 as well as the somewhat redundant "Bonus Depreciation" provisions of IRC Section 168(k). The current depreciation for the full cost of assets under Sections 179 and 168(k) were enacted as a tax incentive for investment in plant and equipment. Most small businesses can expense up to $1,080,000 of new equipment purchases in 2022 (the limitation on the amount that can be expensed in 2023 is $1,160,000). When purchases of equipment reach the $2,700,000 million level for 2022, the Section 179 deduction gives way to "Bonus Depreciation" for certain qualified property in which new equipment over the $2.7 million threshold may be depreciated at 100% of cost (this percentage will drop to 80% for assets placed in service in tax year 2023 and will be phased down in subsequent years until it becomes zero for purchases in tax year 2028 and thereafter). One advantage to the bonus provisions over Section 179 is that they may be utilized on certain qualified used property, whereas Section 179 is exclusively for new property. In addition, Section 179 depreciation may not be deducted if the business does not have net income, while the bonus deduction may be utilized whether or not the business has income. IRC Section 179 expense is shown in Part I of Form 4562 while bonus depreciation is shown in Part II. Typically, when Section 179 and bonus depreciation are material, there is a commensurate material understatement of profit for that year. A frequent adjustment to profit for the year in which material Section 179 and bonus expense are deducted is the amortization of the expense over the useful life of the acquired capital assets. Restatement of profit to make profit more representative is an important procedure in the analysis of income available for alimony and child support.

A business may choose not to take advantage of Section 179 if it is losing money and wants to defer most of the depreciation deduction into future years when the business may be profitable and can better take advantage of the depreciation tax deduction. Thus, there are situations in which the current depreciation expense related to personal property acquisitions may indeed be a non-cash expense when a business had in fact made major non-recurring capital asset acquisitions in the past and decided not to elect Section 179. If the foregoing fact pattern exists, depreciation in excess of a normalized amount should be added back to income to arrive at the true profitability of the business.

An add back of depreciation is also warranted if the business owns real property that is being depreciated. The cash outlay for all or part of the purchase of the real property may have occurred in prior years. As a result, current year depreciation expense represents a reduction in profit without a commensurate reduction in cash flow available to the owner. That is why forensic accountants frequently add back such depreciation in determining income available for support. In such circumstances, the forensic accountant will also evaluate cash outflows that do not reduce profit. One such use of cash that is not deductible is the payment of principal on the note secured by the real property. Adjusting income for inflows and outflows of cash not readily apparent on a tax return is a standard part of the forensic accountant's analysis when preparing reports of income available for support.

Rapid depreciation write-offs under Section 179 and the bonus provisions usually result in an overstatement of operating costs for that year and a corresponding understatement of value for the business (especially when a capitalization of earnings method is used to value the business or its goodwill).

Form 4562 for Howard Shopowner depicts the kind of information typically found on this schedule. A supporting schedule with greater detail is presented on the following page of the hypothetical form to illustrate the limitations of the usefulness of Form 4562 in the absence of supplementary support schedules.

LINE 14: EMPLOYEE BENEFIT PROGRAMS Employee benefits, other than retirement benefits reported elsewhere, include life and health insurance, dental insurance, and dependent care assistance programs. Health insurance for the owner should be reported on Part II, Line 17 of Schedule 1 attached to Form 1040. If employee benefits are claimed, a careful investigation should be made to determine whether the employer is benefiting from these payments or if non-employee friends or relatives are being used to divert funds. In other words, the opportunity to disguise personal expenditures as a business expense is present.

LINE 15: INSURANCE (OTHER THAN HEALTH) To the extent that any insurance premium payments charged to the business personally benefit the owner, that perquisite or personal benefit should be noted when dealing with issues of need and ability to pay support.

Insurance policies should be inspected to obtain information on assets not otherwise disclosed. Liability riders on such items as artwork and special equipment may be uncovered through this process. The amount of insurance coverage may also be evidence of the value of inventory or capital assets.

LINES 16A AND 16B: INTEREST: MORTGAGE/OTHER An interest expense deduction on the Schedule C denotes the existence of either secured or unsecured loans. The existence of business borrowing may warrant requests for the production of loan applications files. Loan application files obtained from the lenders may uncover probative evidence of financial information not previously known. For example, the loan application may uncover or help to confirm the existence of certain marital assets not otherwise disclosed. Opinions of value are also found in loan applications. While the owner's opinion of the value of the business may carry little weight at trial, it may be useful for settlement purposes. Opinions of value, either from the owner or an expert, may also exist for marital real property. This information may promote settlement and save expert witness appraisal costs.

In summary, loan files may contain application forms and other informative documents that provide a cross-reference relative to the accuracy of marital asset values. The loan application usually includes a sworn statement of earning ability, an amount that can be compared with the income reported for the same period on the party's tax return. The spouse's credibility as a witness may be impaired by presenting evidence of major inconsistencies between the income shown on the loan application and the tax return income.

LINE 17: LEGAL AND PROFESSIONAL SERVICES Payment of legal or other professional services should be investigated to determine if personal benefits are being derived. It is not unusual to find that the business owner in a dissolution action may be deducting his or her attorneys' fees, accountants' fees, appraisal fees and other divorce-related professional fees as a business cost. Comparison with prior years' tax returns may disclose a significant variance in this expense that may indicate that the spouse is writing off divorce-related professional fees.

LINE 18: OFFICE EXPENSES "Office Expense" is a line item that provides a convenient slot to bury a multitude of personal expenses. The materiality of the amount expensed should first be determined before undertaking a thorough investigation. Typically, a brief analysis of the company's general ledger and journals may indicate whether an in depth investigation is warranted. Payments to "cash" and personal expenses are often improperly deducted in this category.

LINE 19: PENSION AND PROFIT-SHARING PLANS An entry on this line suggests the existence of a retirement plan. The amount shown represents payments made on behalf of employees, not the owner. As previously noted, Part II, Line 16 of Schedule 1 attached to Form 1040 will contain the annual contribution for the owner or practitioner. Determination of the value of the marital portion of the plan is essential for property division purposes.

Qualified plans (those that meet IRS standards for deductibility) usually require the annual filing of IRS Forms in the 5500 series. An exception exists with respect to plans having only one participant and containing less than $250,000 in assets. These tax returns, when required, generally reveal substantial probative information of trust value. Participant statements for the owner can usually be obtained from the retirement plan administrator or from the spouse if the plan is self-directed.

The funding of nonqualified plans (nondeductible because they allow discrimination, i.e., non-inclusion of employees other than the business owner) will not be reported on the individual income tax return. If business records are properly maintained, the nonqualified plan balances should appear on the business balance sheet as an asset.

LINE 20: RENT OR LEASE Inquiry should be made concerning the identity of the lessor and the fair market value of the rental payment. If the lessor is a friend or relative, the probability of overstated rent, which in turn reduces profitability, is enhanced. Examination of the facility lease is generally an integral part of the appraisal process. A bargain lease has the effect of overstating profitability; accordingly, business appraisers often make an adjustment to restate the annual rental expense to fair market rental value.

A bargain lease suggests an asset with value that typically will not be disclosed in any discovery material. Real estate experts are able to render opinions of value for leases whose stated rent is lower than market.

LINE 21: REPAIRS AND MAINTENANCE Items deducted as "Repair and Maintenance" expenses may contain payments of personal home repairs and improvements. Vendors who provide goods or services to the business may also provide additional personal goods or services. The "out-spouse" may be helpful in identifying non-business related repairs.

Capital expenditures that are written off as an expense of the period are often found in this category. The effect of expensing the entire acquisition cost of an asset was considered above in the depreciation section in our discussion of Section 179 depreciation. A review of that section will highlight the distortion of income available for support that may occur because of the immediate expensing of assets that have a useful life of more than one year.

LINE 23: TAXES AND LICENSES Real estate, personal property, and payroll taxes should be included on Line 23. Tax bills and other supporting documentation may disclose unreported assets or misstated values. Payroll tax returns are typically requested if there is knowledge or suspicion that friends or relatives are on payroll.

LINE 24: TRAVEL AND MEALS Travel and meals (T&M; note that with the passage of the Tax Cut and Jobs Act in 2017, business entertainment is no longer deductible) is another category under which personal expenditures may be hidden. It is common practice for forensic accountants to investigate the charges to this account for the existence of perquisites. The process usually includes the examination of supporting documentation, such as credit card statements and expense reports, in conjunction with interviews with and/or deposition testimony of the owner. The relationship of the underlying business activity, or lack thereof, associated with the "Travel and Meals" expenditures is the pivotal element in distinguishing between what is personal and what is business. Business value and income available for support may be understated if no adjustment is made to increase profits for the personal portion of T&M expenses improperly deducted on a tax return.

Line 25: Utilities Sometimes business owners deduct the payment of their personal residence utility charges as a business expense. While this may be appropriate in cases where the home is the true business location, generally Form 8829 (Expenses for Business Use of Your Home) should be used to report this expense if the home is the true business location. Investigation of the underlying utility bills should confirm the propriety of the amount deducted as "Utilities."

Line 26: Wages "Wages" does not include salary paid to the owner because the owner's income is the profit of the business. However, wages could include salary paid to a spouse.

Are friends and relatives who do not really perform full services for compensation received on payroll? Inspection of payroll tax returns and, where available, payroll journals will identify those persons on payroll. To the extent that "Wages" may be overstated, conclusions as to the value of the enterprise and income available for support are understated.

Forensic accountants often include an adjustment to reduce the profit of a business for the cost of replacing a spouse who has worked in the business without salary but who is compelled to discontinue working at the business as a result of the separation of the parties. The payroll expense associated with the new employee will make the business less profitable because the efforts of the spouse who left the business was not quantifiable as a deduction. In such cases, a historical analysis of profitability should be performed and adjustments should be made for valuation and income available purposes to reflect the true cost of operations.

Closely related, but not included in "Wages," are payments to independent contractors. Businesses are required to file IRS Form 1099 to report all payments to unincorporated independent contractors paid in excess of $600 per year. Scrutiny of the payees listed on the 1099 forms may disclose payments to friends or relatives.

Line 30: Expenses for Business Use of Your Home If an amount appears on this line, IRS Form 8829 should be included with the return. The appearance of that deduction on a Schedule C suggests a possibility that personal residence expenses are being paid through the business. Investigation of the facts and circumstances should be undertaken with a view toward determining whether the office space in the home is "regularly and exclusively" used for business. Failure to meet IRS guidelines for deductibility suggest that this expense item is not a proper business expense and should be added back to income.

Line 31: Net Profit or Loss The net profit or loss is the starting point for the analysis of profitability. Adjustments to profit for perquisites and other forensic accounting adjustments result in "true profitability," the more relevant profit concept used for valuation and income available analyses. Historical analysis of true profitability is mandatory for valuation purposes under IRS Revenue Ruling 59-60.

Schedule Cs that have consistently shown losses over the last few years suggest the possibility that the business is, in fact, a hobby. The IRS disallows losses for businesses whose primary purpose is not the production of income. If a business loss is not bona fide, the loss should not be considered as a reduction of that spouse's income. Frequently, business owners continue to run loss businesses in the hopes that the businesses can recover. A difficult judicial decision exists if the business can be liquidated readily without extensive liability. The point at which a losing business needs to be shut down is a difficult issue to resolve.

The "Net Profit" amount is subject to "Self-Employment Tax." A self-employed individual (sole proprietor or partner actively participating in a business or professional practice) must fill out a Schedule SE if their net earnings are $400 or more. Each self-employed person must file his or her own Schedule SE. In our example, both Roberta and Howard are self-employed. Even though they are filing a joint return, each must file a separate Schedule SE in which they report their self-employment income.

Line 2 of Schedule SE reflects the $185,183 profit Howard reported on his Pets Are Us Schedule C. The amount on Line 13 of Schedule SE ($11,594) is an adjustment that reduces gross taxable income and is reported on Part II, Line 15 of Schedule 1 attached to the individual tax return.

There is a cap on the amount of income subject to the self-employment Social Security tax of 12.4% but no cap on the self-employment Medicare tax of 2.9%. In 2022, the cap on income subject to the self-employment Social Security tax of 12.4% is $147,000, as shown on Line 7 of Schedule A. It had been $142,800 for 2021and will rise to $160,200 in 2023.

Income from self-employment can be reduced by a loss from another business or farm owned and actively operated by the taxpayer. The amount of tax is also affected by wages earned by the same person whose income is reflected on the Schedule C. If the wages are in excess of the 2022 cap of $147,000 for social security, no additional social security tax from business income is computed on Schedule SE.

Part III: Cost of Goods Sold

Line 33: Methods Used to Value Closing Inventory The method by which inventory is valued may significantly affect a business valuation. Inventories are frequently undervalued in order to report lower taxable profit. Greater motivation to manipulate inventory exists in divorce cases because lower profitability from reporting lower than actual inventory benefits the partner/spouse via a lower business valuation and less income available for support.

Inventory valuation methods are important factors in accurately and reliably determining the value of a business' inventory. The method used to value inventory must conform to the best accounting practice in the particular trade or business. Inventory may be valued using a "Lower of cost or market" method. Under this method, the cost of inventory, on an item by item basis, is compared to respective market value. "Cost" means the price paid for the inventory. If the market value (the sales price) of an item of inventory is lower than its cost then the lower of the two values is used.

Determining the cost of inventory is a prerequisite to the "Lower of cost or market" method. LIFO (last-in, first-out) and FIFO (first-in, first-out) are terms often used in connection with the determination of the cost of inventory subject to valuation. If a LIFO method of costing inventory is used in an inflationary period, book value and profitability will tend to be understated because inventory purchased at the highest price is expensed first. On the other hand, the FIFO method of costing inventory provides a more accurate representation of the actual market value of the inventory because ending inventory is "costed" by reference to the most recent purchases of inventory.

Changes to or from LIFO to FIFO after the parties separate and/or in subsequent tax years may warrant additional scrutiny.

Many businesses take a physical inventory at their fiscal year-end. Requests for documents detailing the actual inventory count and the manner in which the counted inventory is valued may lead to different perspective on viewing the true profitability of a business. Such facts as the method used to value the inventory will usually be revealed on the inventory work papers.

Line 35: Inventory at Beginning of Year This is the starting point for analyzing the cost of goods sold. The amount should match the ending inventory reported in the prior year's tax return. If it does not, an explanation of the reason why should be sought.

Reporting a higher than actual opening inventory will understate profit. It is good practice to analyze prior years' returns and accompanying supporting documentation to verify the reliability of the opening inventory.

Line 36: Purchases Less Cost of Items Withdrawn for Personal Use Inventory purchased by retailers and wholesalers during the tax year appears on this line. If a business manufactures goods, the cost of materials and supplies is entered on Line 38.

Timing of expense is an important factor in determining the reliability of the amount shown. Typically, businesses with inventories report on the accrual basis; accordingly, the date of payment for the goods is not as relevant as the date of purchase. Remember, as noted with the enactment of the Tax Cut and Jobs Act many businesses with inventory are now able to report on the cash basis. In this case although inventory is to be treated as "non-incidental material and supplies," in practice it is often expensed when acquired. Criteria for determining the date of purchase follow legal guidelines reflected in the Uniform Commercial Code. The contractual time at which goods change hands determines when goods are considered purchased under the accrual basis of accounting.

Consistency in the manner in which transactional activity with regular vendors is recorded generally indicates reliability in the timing of the expense. Inconsistency indicates less reliability and merits further analysis of transactional detail.

Testing of year-end transactions to determine appropriate reporting of purchases at the cut-off date, December 31 for all Schedule C filers, is another accounting technique available for determining the reliability of the amount reported.

The business's "Accounts Payable" is a balance sheet item closely associated with the recordation of purchases. A balance sheet is a listing of the assets, liabilities, and net worth of a business as of a particular point in time. An accounts payable journal is maintained in many businesses. Monthly summations of additions to accounts payable for purchases of goods or raw materials constitute the "Purchases" account reflected on the general ledger and, ultimately, the tax return. The general ledger summarized by category all of the transactions of a business for the period it covers. The categories used in the general ledger are either directly related to the line item description of income, expense, assets, or liabilities shown on the financial statement or they are grouped to form those categories. For example, a general ledger will identify the basis for the telephone expense deducted on a tax return by detailing all of the transactions that comprise the total expense. In most small businesses the general ledger will show each of the telephone expense transactions, such as payments to the providers, during the year.

Inspection of the accounts payable journal and the cash disbursement journal may disclose personal items paid by the business and improperly deducted as business expenses. As stated in the line description, the IRS requires that personal use items be withdrawn. But small scale evasion of tax is common practice. For example, Howard Shopowner's pet store provides him with an opportunity to bury personal pet expenses. Examples of other businesses that warrant investigation of personal use of inventory not properly disclosed on the tax return are restaurants, electronics retailers, computer stores, and clothing outlets.

Line 37: Cost of Labor Generally, this line is filled in by manufacturing businesses. Only direct labor costs of manufacturing are included. Indirect labor costs may be partially included depending on the type of overhead allocation formula used by the business to incorporate indirect expenses into the cost of producing the product.

As pointed out in the discussion of Line 26, "Wages," obtaining the names of all employees is advisable to ascertain whether friends and relatives who do not really perform full services for compensation received are on payroll. Inspection of payroll tax returns and, where available, payroll journals will identify those persons on payroll. To the extent that "Wages" may be overstated, conclusions as to the value of the enterprise and income available for support are understated.

Line 38: Materials and Supplies The same recommendation provided for "Purchases" that are input on Line 36, apply here. An improper deduction for expenses incurred in connection with improvements to the personal residence may appear as part of the amount shown. The possibility of materials and supplies purchased for third parties who pay with unreported cash is another scenario by which a business owner may wrongfully understate profit.

LINE 39: OTHER COSTS On many tax returns "Other Costs" refer to overhead, also known as indirect costs of manufacturing. An entire area of accounting, known as "Cost Accounting," is devoted to the study of allocating overhead expenses not directly related to the manufacture of the product to the determination of the total cost of the product. Portions of the rent, utilities, administrative labor, and property taxes are examples of types of indirect manufacturing expenses that are allocated to the cost of manufactured goods.

LINE 41: INVENTORY AT END OF YEAR Relevant documentation for reliable research and analysis of the value of ending inventory as of the appraisal date is usually readily available when the year-end for which ending inventory is determined is close to the time at which the appraisal is performed. If an actual inventory count is taken, the forensic accountant usually requests copies of the supporting detail to confirm reliability of the amount shown. A memo regarding inventory procedures performed may be included within the requested documentation. A lower level of scrutiny of procedures and valuation methodology is required if the inventory was observed by certified public accountants in conjunction with a certified audit than if the financial statements are prepared on a compilation basis. Audited financial statements engagements require the CPA to perform rigorous procedures, such as the observation of the taking of the physical inventory.

Unreported sale of inventory during the post-separation period is a frequent allegation made by non-operating spouses. Irregularity of gross profit ratios with industry percentages and against prior years' figures for the business may give rise to such allegations. Testing mark-up percentages against gross profit is another tool used in some cases to spot irregularities in inventory value.

LINE 42: COST OF GOODS SOLD Cost of Goods Sold is carried forward to Part 1, Line 4 of Schedule C.

Part IV: Information on Your Vehicle

Please refer to the discussion of Part II, Line 9.

Part V: Other Expenses

"Other Expenses" include deductible transactions for which no line items were provided in Part II. The expense categories that may be included here are numerous and vary with the type of business or practice. Examples of expenses that appear in this section are credit card service charges, outside services for independent contractors, security, uniforms, collection expenses, continuing education, and dues and subscriptions. These various and sundry expenses are frequently analyzed by inspecting the business's general ledger. Most businesses use accounting software to maintain their books and records and perform typical business transactions like writing checks. Obtaining the digital computer accounting file will facilitate the inspection of the business's financial activity. Financial statements and underlying reports like general ledgers are usually easily accessed if the forensic accountant firm has the same accounting software on its network. Computer generated reports represent the first layer of documents supporting tax returns and/or financial statements. Drilling down from that point to specific underlying areas of investigation is traditionally the manner in which a typical forensic investigation is performed. So, for example, if payees listed in a general ledger account appear suspicious, the forensic investigation may focus on inspection of underlying supporting documentation, such as canceled checks and vendor's invoices to determine the legitimacy of the deduction.

The Schedule C for Roberta Doctor and Howard Shopowner contain line-item entries for income and expenses that are typical of their industry.

12/31/22

2022 FEDERAL DEPRECIATION SCHEDULE

PAGE 1

HOWARD SHOPOWNER AND ROBERTA DOCTOR

NO.	DESCRIPTION	DATE ACQUIRED	DATE SOLD	COST/ BASIS	BUS. PCT.	CUR 179 BONUS	SPECIAL DEPR. ALLOW.	PRIOR 179/ BONUS/ SP. DEPR.	PRIOR DEC. BAL DEPR.	SALVAG /BASIS REDUCT	DEPR. BASIS	PRIOR DEPR.	METHOD	LIFE	RATE	CURRENT DEPR.
	SCHEDULE C - ROBERTA DOCTOR															
	AUTO / TRANSPORT EQUIPMENT															
2	AUTOMOBILE **	6/01/21		40,000	80.00			14,560			17,440		200DB HY	5	.32000	5,581
	TOTAL AUTO / TRANSPORT EQUIP			40,000		0	0	14,560	0	0	17,440	0				5,581
	MACHINERY AND EQUIPMENT															
3	MEDICAL EQUIPMENT **	6/30/22		50,000		50,000					0		200DB HY	5		0
	TOTAL MACHINERY AND EQUIPME			50,000		50,000	0	0	0	0	0	0				0
	TOTAL DEPRECIATION			90,000		50,000	0	14,560	0	0	17,440	0				5,581
	SCHEDULE C - PET ARE US															
	FURNITURE AND FIXTURES															
6	RACKS AND SHELVING **	9/01/22		23,250		23,250					0		200DB HY	7		0
8	STORE DISPLAYS **	1/02/20		16,475							16,475	6,384	200DB HY	7	.17490	2,881
9	SIGNAGE **	3/01/20		45,000							45,000	6,525	150DB HY	15	.08550	3,848
	TOTAL FURNITURE AND FIXTURE			84,725		23,250	0	0	0	0	61,475	12,909				6,729
	MACHINERY AND EQUIPMENT															
4	KENNELS & CAGES **	3/01/22		45,000		45,000					0		200DB HY	7		0
5	COMPUTER EQUIPMENT **	6/01/22		10,600		10,600					0		200DB HY	5		0
7	CASH REGISTER **	2/05/20		8,875							8,875	4,615	200DB HY	5	.19200	1,704

12/31/22

2022 FEDERAL DEPRECIATION SCHEDULE

PAGE 2

HOWARD SHOPOWNER AND ROBERTA DOCTOR

NO.	DESCRIPTION	DATE ACQUIRED	DATE SOLD	COST/ BASIS	BUS. PCT.	CUR 179 BONUS	SPECIAL DEPR. ALLOW.	PRIOR 179/ BONUS/ SP. DEPR.	PRIOR DEC. BAL DEPR.	SALVAG /BASIS REDUCT	DEPR. BASIS	PRIOR DEPR.	METHOD	LIFE	RATE	CURRENT DEPR.
	TOTAL MACHINERY AND EQUIPME			64,475		55,600	0	0	0	0	8,875	4,615				1,704
	TOTAL DEPRECIATION			149,200		78,850	0	0	0	0	70,350	17,524				8,433
	GRAND TOTAL DEPRECIATION			239,200		128,850	0	14,560	0	0	87,790	17,524				14,014

**ASSET INCLUDED IN UNADJUSTED BASIS IMMEDIATELY AFTER ACQUISITION FOR THE QBI CALCULATION.

SCHEDULE C (Form 1040)
Department of the Treasury Internal Revenue Service

Profit or Loss From Business
(Sole Proprietorship)

Go to *www.irs.gov/ScheduleC* for instructions and the latest information.
Attach to Form 1040, 1040-SR, 1040-NR, or 1041; partnerships must generally file Form 1065.

OMB No. 1545-0074
2022
Attachment Sequence No. **09**

Name of proprietor: ROBERTA DOCTOR
Social security number (SSN): 321-56-4898

A Principal business or profession, including product or service (see instructions): PHYSICIAN/MEDICAL SERVICE
B Enter code from instructions: 621111

C Business name. If no separate business name, leave blank.
D Employer ID number (EIN) (see instr.): 95-1234567

E Business address (including suite or room no.): 33 BEVERLY DRIVE
City, town or post office, state, and ZIP code: BEVERLY HILLS CA 90201

F Accounting method: **(1)** [X] Cash **(2)** [ ] Accrual **(3)** [ ] Other (specify)
G Did you "materially participate" in the operation of this business during 2022? If "No," see instructions for limit on losses. [X] **Yes** [ ] **No**
H If you started or acquired this business during 2022, check here [ ]
I Did you make any payments in 2022 that would require you to file Form(s) 1099? See instructions [ ] **Yes** [X] **No**
J If "Yes," did you or will you file required Form(s) 1099? [ ] **Yes** [ ] **No**

Part I Income

1	Gross receipts or sales. See instructions for line 1 and check the box if this income was reported to you on Form W-2 and the "Statutory employee" box on that form was checked [ ]	1	454,200.
2	Returns and allowances	2	
3	Subtract line 2 from line 1	3	454,200.
4	Cost of goods sold (from line 42)	4	
5	**Gross profit.** Subtract line 4 from line 3	5	454,200.
6	Other income, including federal and state gasoline or fuel tax credit or refund (see instructions)	6	
7	**Gross income.** Add lines 5 and 6	7	454,200.

Part II Expenses. Enter expenses for business use of your home **only** on line 30.

8	Advertising	8		18	Office expense (see instructions)	18	
9	Car and truck expenses (see instructions)	9	2,517.	19	Pension and profit-sharing plans	19	1,650.
				20	Rent or lease (see instructions):		
10	Commissions and fees	10		a	Vehicles, machinery, and equipment	20a	
11	Contract labor (see instructions)	11		b	Other business property	20b	60,000.
12	Depletion	12		21	Repairs and maintenance	21	
13	Depreciation and section 179 expense deduction (not included in Part III) (see instructions)	13	55,581.	22	Supplies (not included in Part III)	22	775.
				23	Taxes and licenses	23	325.
				24	Travel and meals:		
14	Employee benefit programs (other than on line 19)	14		a	Travel	24a	
15	Insurance (other than health)	15	15,100.	b	Deductible meals (see instructions)	24b	
16	Interest (see instr.):			25	Utilities	25	4,950.
a	Mortgage (paid to banks, etc.)	16a		26	Wages (less employment credits)	26	33,000.
b	Other	16b	1,280.	27a	Other expenses (from line 48)	27a	16,919.
17	Legal and professional services	17	1,580.	b	**Reserved for future use**	27b	

28	**Total expenses** before expenses for business use of home. Add lines 8 through 27a	28	193,677.
29	Tentative profit or (loss). Subtract line 28 from line 7	29	260,523.
30	Expenses for business use of your home. Do not report these expenses elsewhere. Attach Form 8829 unless using the simplified method. See instructions. **Simplified method filers only:** Enter the total square footage of (a) your home: ______ and (b) the part of your home used for business: ______. Use the Simplified Method Worksheet in the instructions to figure the amount to enter on line 30	30	
31	**Net profit or (loss).** Subtract line 30 from line 29. • If a profit, enter on both **Schedule 1 (Form 1040), line 3,** and on **Schedule SE, line 2.** (If you checked the box on line 1, see instructions.) Estates and trusts, enter on **Form 1041, line 3.** • If a loss, you **must** go to line 32.	31	260,523.

32 If you have a loss, check the box that describes your investment in this activity. See instructions.

• If you checked 32a, enter the loss on both **Schedule 1 (Form 1040), line 3,** and on **Schedule SE, line 2.** (If you checked the box on line 1, see the line 31 instructions.) Estates and trusts, enter on **Form 1041, line 3.**
• If you checked 32b, you **must** attach **Form 6198.** Your loss may be limited.

32a [ ] All investment is at risk.
32b [ ] Some investment is not at risk.

Schedule C (Form 1040) 2022 ROBERTA DOCTOR 321-56-4898 Page **2**

Part III **Cost of Goods Sold** (see instructions)

33 Method(s) used to value closing inventory: **a** ☐ Cost **b** ☐ Lower of cost or market **c** ☐ Other (attach explanation)

34 Was there any change in determining quantities, costs, or valuations between opening and closing inventory? If "Yes," attach explanation ☐ **Yes** ☐ **No**

35 Inventory at beginning of year. If different from last year's closing inventory, attach explanation	35	
36 Purchases less cost of items withdrawn for personal use	36	
37 Cost of labor. Do not include any amounts paid to yourself	37	
38 Materials and supplies	38	
39 Other costs	39	
40 Add lines 35 through 39	40	
41 Inventory at end of year	41	
42 **Cost of goods sold.** Subtract line 41 from line 40. Enter the result here and on line 4	42	

Part IV **Information on Your Vehicle.** Complete this part **only** if you are claiming car or truck expenses on line 9 and are not required to file Form 4562 for this business. See the instructions for line 13 to find out if you must file Form 4562.

43 When did you place your vehicle in service for business purposes? (month/day/year) ________

44 Of the total number of miles you drove your vehicle during 2022, enter the number of miles you used your vehicle for:

a Business ________ **b** Commuting (see instructions) ________ **c** Other ________

45 Was your vehicle available for personal use during off-duty hours? ☐ **Yes** ☐ **No**

46 Do you (or your spouse) have another vehicle available for personal use? ☐ **Yes** ☐ **No**

47a Do you have evidence to support your deduction? ☐ **Yes** ☐ **No**

b If "Yes," is the evidence written? ☐ **Yes** ☐ **No**

Part V **Other Expenses.** List below business expenses not included on lines 8-26 or line 30.

ACCOUNTING		1,100.
BILLING SERVICE		5,000.
LABORATORY		6,310.
TELEPHONE		4,509.
48 **Total other expenses.** Enter here and on line 27a	48	16,919.

Schedule C (Form 1040) 2022

FDIZ0112L 07/18/22

SCHEDULE C (Form 1040)

Department of the Treasury Internal Revenue Service

Profit or Loss From Business
(Sole Proprietorship)

Go to *www.irs.gov/ScheduleC* for instructions and the latest information.
Attach to Form 1040, 1040-SR, 1040-NR, or 1041; partnerships must generally file Form 1065.

OMB No. 1545-0074

2022

Attachment Sequence No. **09**

Name of proprietor: HOWARD SHOPOWNER

Social security number (SSN): 321-56-4899

A Principal business or profession, including product or service (see instructions): PET STORE

B Enter code from instructions: 459910

C Business name. If no separate business name, leave blank.: PET ARE US

D Employer ID number (EIN) (see instr.)

E Business address (including suite or room no.): 13000 VENTURA BOULEVARD

City, town or post office, state, and ZIP code: SHERMAN OAKS CA 91423

F Accounting method: **(1)** [X] Cash **(2)** [ ] Accrual **(3)** [ ] Other (specify)

G Did you "materially participate" in the operation of this business during 2022? If "No," see instructions for limit on losses. [X] **Yes** [ ] **No**

H If you started or acquired this business during 2022, check here [ ]

I Did you make any payments in 2022 that would require you to file Form(s) 1099? See instructions. [ ] **Yes** [X] **No**

J If "Yes," did you or will you file required Form(s) 1099? [ ] **Yes** [ ] **No**

Part I Income

1	Gross receipts or sales. See instructions for line 1 and check the box if this income was reported to you on Form W-2 and the "Statutory employee" box on that form was checked [ ]	1	2,502,588.
2	Returns and allowances	2	
3	Subtract line 2 from line 1	3	2,502,588.
4	Cost of goods sold (from line 42)	4	1,013,226.
5	**Gross profit.** Subtract line 4 from line 3	5	1,489,362.
6	Other income, including federal and state gasoline or fuel tax credit or refund (see instructions)	6	
7	**Gross income.** Add lines 5 and 6	7	1,489,362.

Part II Expenses. Enter expenses for business use of your home **only** on line 30.

8	Advertising	8	47,219.	18	Office expense (see instructions)	18	13,405.
9	Car and truck expenses (see instructions)	9	1,880.	19	Pension and profit-sharing plans	19	
10	Commissions and fees	10		20	Rent or lease (see instructions):		
11	Contract labor (see instructions)	11			**a** Vehicles, machinery, and equipment	20a	7,690.
					b Other business property	20b	147,562.
12	Depletion	12		21	Repairs and maintenance	21	6,415.
13	Depreciation and section 179 expense deduction (not included in Part III) (see instructions)	13	87,283.	22	Supplies (not included in Part III)	22	
				23	Taxes and licenses	23	342,796.
				24	Travel and meals:		
14	Employee benefit programs (other than on line 19)	14			**a** Travel	24a	
15	Insurance (other than health)	15	65,994.		**b** Deductible meals (see instructions)	24b	2,500.
16	Interest (see instr.):			25	Utilities	25	77,752.
	a Mortgage (paid to banks, etc.)	16a	21,324.	26	Wages (less employment credits)	26	264,843.
	b Other	16b		27a	Other expenses (from line 48)	27a	194,272.
17	Legal and professional services	17	23,244.		**b Reserved for future use**	27b	

28	**Total expenses** before expenses for business use of home. Add lines 8 through 27a	28	1,304,179.
29	Tentative profit or (loss). Subtract line 28 from line 7	29	185,183.
30	Expenses for business use of your home. Do not report these expenses elsewhere. Attach Form 8829 unless using the simplified method. See instructions. **Simplified method filers only:** Enter the total square footage of (a) your home: ______ and (b) the part of your home used for business: ______. Use the Simplified Method Worksheet in the instructions to figure the amount to enter on line 30	30	
31	**Net profit or (loss).** Subtract line 30 from line 29. • If a profit, enter on both **Schedule 1 (Form 1040), line 3,** and on **Schedule SE, line 2.** (If you checked the box on line 1, see instructions.) Estates and trusts, enter on **Form 1041, line 3.** • If a loss, you **must** go to line 32.	31	185,183.
32	If you have a loss, check the box that describes your investment in this activity. See instructions. • If you checked 32a, enter the loss on both **Schedule 1 (Form 1040), line 3,** and on **Schedule SE, line 2.** (If you checked the box on line 1, see the line 31 instructions.) Estates and trusts, enter on **Form 1041, line 3.** • If you checked 32b, you **must** attach **Form 6198.** Your loss may be limited.	32a / 32b	[ ] All investment is at risk. / [ ] Some investment is not at risk.

Schedule C (Form 1040) 2022 HOWARD SHOPOWNER 321-56-4899 Page 2

Part III Cost of Goods Sold (see instructions)

33 Method(s) used to value closing inventory: **a** ☐ Cost **b** ☒ Lower of cost or market **c** ☐ Other (attach explanation)

34 Was there any change in determining quantities, costs, or valuations between opening and closing inventory? If "Yes," attach explanation ☐ Yes ☒ No

35 Inventory at beginning of year. If different from last year's closing inventory, attach explanation	35	560,662.
36 Purchases less cost of items withdrawn for personal use	36	926,851.
37 Cost of labor. Do not include any amounts paid to yourself	37	
38 Materials and supplies	38	
39 Other costs	39	
40 Add lines 35 through 39	40	1,487,513.
41 Inventory at end of year	41	474,287.
42 **Cost of goods sold.** Subtract line 41 from line 40. Enter the result here and on line 4	42	1,013,226.

Part IV Information on Your Vehicle. Complete this part **only** if you are claiming car or truck expenses on line 9 and are not required to file Form 4562 for this business. See the instructions for line 13 to find out if you must file Form 4562.

43 When did you place your vehicle in service for business purposes? (month/day/year) ________

44 Of the total number of miles you drove your vehicle during 2022, enter the number of miles you used your vehicle for:

a Business ________ **b** Commuting (see instructions) ________ **c** Other ________

45 Was your vehicle available for personal use during off-duty hours? ☐ Yes ☐ No

46 Do you (or your spouse) have another vehicle available for personal use? ☐ Yes ☐ No

47a Do you have evidence to support your deduction? ☐ Yes ☐ No

b If "Yes," is the evidence written? ☐ Yes ☐ No

Part V Other Expenses. List below business expenses not included on lines 8-26 or line 30.

CREDIT CARD FEES		40,864.
DUES AND SUBSCRIPTIONS		1,312.
MISCELLANEOUS		1,500.
OUTSIDE SERVICES		7,974.
SECURITY		114,708.
SECURITY		4,195.
TELEPHONE		19,215.
UNIFORMS		4,504.
48 **Total other expenses.** Enter here and on line 27a	48	194,272.

Schedule C (Form 1040) 2022

FDIZ0112L 07/18/22

SCHEDULE SE (Form 1040)

Department of the Treasury Internal Revenue Service

Self-Employment Tax

Go to *www.irs.gov/ScheduleSE* for instructions and the latest information.
Attach to Form 1040, 1040-SR, or 1040-NR.

OMB No. 1545-0074

2022

Attachment Sequence No. **17**

Name of person with self-employment income (as shown on Form 1040, 1040-SR, or 1040-NR): HOWARD SHOPOWNER

Social security number of person with **self-employment** income: 321-56-4899

Part I — Self-Employment Tax

Note: If your only income subject to self-employment tax is **church employee income,** see instructions for how to report your income and the definition of church employee income.

A If you are a minister, member of a religious order, or Christian Science practitioner **and** you filed Form 4361, but you had $400 or more of **other** net earnings from self-employment, check here and continue with Part I ☐

Skip lines 1a and 1b if you use the farm optional method in Part II. See instructions.

1a	Net farm profit or (loss) from Schedule F, line 34, and farm partnerships, Schedule K-1 (Form 1065), box 14, code A			1a	
b	If you received social security retirement or disability benefits, enter the amount of Conservation Reserve Program payments included on Schedule F, line 4b, or listed on Schedule K-1 (Form 1065), box 20, code AH			1b	
	Skip line 2 if you use the nonfarm optional method in Part II. See instructions.				
2	Net profit or (loss) from Schedule C, line 31; and Schedule K-1 (Form 1065), box 14, code A (other than farming). See instructions for other income to report or if you are a minister or member of a religious order			2	185,183.
3	Combine lines 1a, 1b, and 2			3	185,183.
4a	If line 3 is more than zero, multiply line 3 by 92.35% (0.9235). Otherwise, enter amount from line 3			4a	171,017.
	Note: If line 4a is less than $400 due to Conservation Reserve Program payments on line 1b, see instructions.				
b	If you elect one or both of the optional methods, enter the total of lines 15 and 17 here			4b	
c	Combine lines 4a and 4b. If less than $400, **stop;** you don't owe self-employment tax. **Exception:** If less than $400 and you had **church employee income,** enter -0- and continue			4c	171,017.
5a	Enter your **church employee income** from Form W-2. See instructions for definition of church employee income	5a			
b	Multiply line 5a by 92.35% (0.9235). If less than $100, enter -0-			5b	0.
6	Add lines 4c and 5b			6	171,017.
7	Maximum amount of combined wages and self-employment earnings subject to social security tax or the 6.2% portion of the 7.65% railroad retirement (tier 1) tax for 2022			7	147,000.
8a	Total social security wages and tips (total of boxes 3 and 7 on Form(s) W-2) and railroad retirement (tier 1) compensation. If $147,000 or more, skip lines 8b through 10, and go to line 11	8a			
b	Unreported tips subject to social security tax from Form 4137, line 10	8b			
c	Wages subject to social security tax from Form 8919, line 10	8c			
d	Add lines 8a, 8b, and 8c			8d	
9	Subtract line 8d from line 7. If zero or less, enter -0- here and on line 10 and go to line 11			9	147,000.
10	Multiply the **smaller** of line 6 or line 9 by 12.4% (0.124)			10	18,228.
11	Multiply line 6 by 2.9% (0.029)			11	4,959.
12	**Self-employment tax.** Add lines 10 and 11. Enter here and on **Schedule 2 (Form 1040), line 4**			12	23,187.
13	**Deduction for one-half of self-employment tax.** Multiply line 12 by 50% (0.50). Enter here and on **Schedule 1 (Form 1040), line 15**	13	11,594.		

Part II — Optional Methods To Figure Net Earnings (see instructions)

Farm Optional Method. You may use this method **only** if **(a)** your gross farm income(1) wasn't more than $9,060, **or (b)** your net farm profits(2) were less than $6,540.

14	Maximum income for optional methods	14	6,040.
15	Enter the **smaller** of: two-thirds (2/3) of gross farm income(1) (not less than zero) **or** $6,040. Also, include this amount on line 4b above	15	

Nonfarm Optional Method. You may use this method **only** if **(a)** your net nonfarm profits(3) were less than $6,540 and also less than 72.189% of your gross nonfarm income,(4) **and (b)** you had net earnings from self-employment of at least $400 in 2 of the prior 3 years. **Caution:** You may use this method no more than five times.

16	Subtract line 15 from line 14	16	
17	Enter the **smaller** of: two-thirds (2/3) of gross nonfarm income(4) (not less than zero) **or** the amount on line 16. Also, include this amount on line 4b above	17	

(1) From Sch. F, line 9; and Sch. K-1 (Form 1065), box 14, code B.

(2) From Sch. F, line 34; and Sch. K-1 (Form 1065), box 14, code A — minus the amount you would have entered on line 1b had you not used the optional method.

(3) From Sch. C, line 31; and Sch. K-1 (Form 1065), box 14, code A.

(4) From Sch. C, line 7; and Sch. K-1 (Form 1065), box 14, code C.

BAA For Paperwork Reduction Act Notice, see your tax return instructions. FDIA1101L 09/07/22 **Schedule SE (Form 1040) 2022**

SCHEDULE SE (Form 1040)
Department of the Treasury Internal Revenue Service

Self-Employment Tax

Go to *www.irs.gov/ScheduleSE* for instructions and the latest information.
Attach to Form 1040, 1040-SR, or 1040-NR.

OMB No. 1545-0074
2022
Attachment Sequence No. **17**

Name of person with self-employment income (as shown on Form 1040, 1040-SR, or 1040-NR): ROBERTA DOCTOR
Social security number of person with **self-employment** income: 321-56-4898

Part I Self-Employment Tax

Note: If your only income subject to self-employment tax is **church employee income,** see instructions for how to report your income and the definition of church employee income.

A If you are a minister, member of a religious order, or Christian Science practitioner **and** you filed Form 4361, but you had $400 or more of **other** net earnings from self-employment, check here and continue with Part I . . . ☐

Skip lines 1a and 1b if you use the farm optional method in Part II. See instructions.

1 a	Net farm profit or (loss) from Schedule F, line 34, and farm partnerships, Schedule K-1 (Form 1065), box 14, code A	1a	
b	If you received social security retirement or disability benefits, enter the amount of Conservation Reserve Program payments included on Schedule F, line 4b, or listed on Schedule K-1 (Form 1065), box 20, code AH	1b	
	Skip line 2 if you use the nonfarm optional method in Part II. See instructions.		
2	Net profit or (loss) from Schedule C, line 31; and Schedule K-1 (Form 1065), box 14, code A (other than farming). See instructions for other income to report or if you are a minister or member of a religious order	2	260,523.
3	Combine lines 1a, 1b, and 2	3	260,523.
4a	If line 3 is more than zero, multiply line 3 by 92.35% (0.9235). Otherwise, enter amount from line 3	4a	240,593.
	Note: If line 4a is less than $400 due to Conservation Reserve Program payments on line 1b, see instructions.		
b	If you elect one or both of the optional methods, enter the total of lines 15 and 17 here	4b	
c	Combine lines 4a and 4b. If less than $400, **stop;** you don't owe self-employment tax. **Exception:** If less than $400 and you had **church employee income,** enter -0- and continue	4c	240,593.
5 a	Enter your **church employee income** from Form W-2. See instructions for definition of church employee income . . . 5a		
b	Multiply line 5a by 92.35% (0.9235). If less than $100, enter -0-	5b	0.
6	Add lines 4c and 5b	6	240,593.
7	Maximum amount of combined wages and self-employment earnings subject to social security tax or the 6.2% portion of the 7.65% railroad retirement (tier 1) tax for 2022	7	147,000.
8 a	Total social security wages and tips (total of boxes 3 and 7 on Form(s) W-2) and railroad retirement (tier 1) compensation. If $147,000 or more, skip lines 8b through 10, and go to line 11 . . . 8a		
b	Unreported tips subject to social security tax from Form 4137, line 10 . . . 8b		
c	Wages subject to social security tax from Form 8919, line 10 . . . 8c		
d	Add lines 8a, 8b, and 8c	8d	
9	Subtract line 8d from line 7. If zero or less, enter -0- here and on line 10 and go to line 11	9	147,000.
10	Multiply the **smaller** of line 6 or line 9 by 12.4% (0.124)	10	18,228.
11	Multiply line 6 by 2.9% (0.029)	11	6,977.
12	**Self-employment tax.** Add lines 10 and 11. Enter here and on **Schedule 2 (Form 1040), line 4**	12	25,205.
13	**Deduction for one-half of self-employment tax.** Multiply line 12 by 50% (0.50). Enter here and on **Schedule 1 (Form 1040), line 15** . . . 13 12,603.		

Part II Optional Methods To Figure Net Earnings (see instructions)

	Farm Optional Method. You may use this method **only** if **(a)** your gross farm income(1) wasn't more than $9,060, **or (b)** your net farm profits(2) were less than $6,540.		
14	Maximum income for optional methods	14	6,040.
15	Enter the **smaller** of: two-thirds (2/3) of gross farm income(1) (not less than zero) **or** $6,040. Also, include this amount on line 4b above	15	
	Nonfarm Optional Method. You may use this method **only** if **(a)** your net nonfarm profits(3) were less than $6,540 and also less than 72.189% of your gross nonfarm income,(4) **and (b)** you had net earnings from self-employment of at least $400 in 2 of the prior 3 years. **Caution:** You may use this method no more than five times.		
16	Subtract line 15 from line 14	16	
17	Enter the **smaller** of: two-thirds (2/3) of gross nonfarm income(4) (not less than zero) **or** the amount on line 16. Also, include this amount on line 4b above	17	

(1) From Sch. F, line 9; and Sch. K-1 (Form 1065), box 14, code B.
(2) From Sch. F, line 34; and Sch. K-1 (Form 1065), box 14, code A — minus the amount you would have entered on line 1b had you not used the optional method.
(3) From Sch. C, line 31; and Sch. K-1 (Form 1065), box 14, code A.
(4) From Sch. C, line 7; and Sch. K-1 (Form 1065), box 14, code C.

BAA For Paperwork Reduction Act Notice, see your tax return instructions. FDIA1101L 09/07/22 **Schedule SE (Form 1040) 2022**

Form **4562**

Department of the Treasury
Internal Revenue Service

Depreciation and Amortization
(Including Information on Listed Property)

Attach to your tax return.

Go to *www.irs.gov/Form4562* for instructions and the latest information.

OMB No. 1545-0172

2022

Attachment Sequence No. **179**

Name(s) shown on return: HOWARD SHOPOWNER AND ROBERTA DOCTOR

Identifying number: 321-56-4899

Business or activity to which this form relates: PART I - SUMMARY

Part I — Election To Expense Certain Property Under Section 179

Note: If you have any listed property, complete Part V before you complete Part I.

1	Maximum amount (see instructions)	1	1,080,000.
2	Total cost of section 179 property placed in service (see instructions)	2	128,850.
3	Threshold cost of section 179 property before reduction in limitation (see instructions)	3	2,700,000.
4	Reduction in limitation. Subtract line 3 from line 2. If zero or less, enter -0-	4	0.
5	Dollar limitation for tax year. Subtract line 4 from line 1. If zero or less, enter -0-. If married filing separately, see instructions	5	1,080,000.

6 (a) Description of property	(b) Cost (business use only)	(c) Elected cost
SEE STATEMENT 1		128,850.

7	Listed property. Enter the amount from line 29	7	0.		
8	Total elected cost of section 179 property. Add amounts in column (c), lines 6 and 7			8	128,850.
9	Tentative deduction. Enter the **smaller** of line 5 or line 8			9	128,850.
10	Carryover of disallowed deduction from line 13 of your 2021 Form 4562			10	0.
11	Business income limitation. Enter the smaller of business income (not less than zero) or line 5. See instrs			11	574,556.
12	Section 179 expense deduction. Add lines 9 and 10, but don't enter more than line 11			12	128,850.
13	Carryover of disallowed deduction to 2023. Add lines 9 and 10, less line 12	13	0.		

Note: Don't use Part II or Part III below for listed property. Instead, use Part V.

Part II — Special Depreciation Allowance and Other Depreciation (Don't include listed property. See instructions.)

14	Special depreciation allowance for qualified property (other than listed property) placed in service during the tax year. See instructions	14	
15	Property subject to section 168(f)(1) election	15	
16	Other depreciation (including ACRS)	16	

Part III — MACRS Depreciation (Don't include listed property. See instructions.)

Section A

17	MACRS deductions for assets placed in service in tax years beginning before 2022	17	
18	If you are electing to group any assets placed in service during the tax year into one or more general asset accounts, check here ☐		

Section B – Assets Placed in Service During 2022 Tax Year Using the General Depreciation System

(a) Classification of property	(b) Month and year placed in service	(c) Basis for depreciation (business/investment use only — see instructions)	(d) Recovery period	(e) Convention	(f) Method	(g) Depreciation deduction
19a 3-year property						
b 5-year property						
c 7-year property						
d 10-year property						
e 15-year property						
f 20-year property						
g 25-year property			25 yrs		S/L	
h Residential rental			27.5 yrs	MM	S/L	
property			27.5 yrs	MM	S/L	
i Nonresidential real			39 yrs	MM	S/L	
property				MM	S/L	

Section C – Assets Placed in Service During 2022 Tax Year Using the Alternative Depreciation System

(a) Classification of property	(b) Month and year placed in service	(c) Basis for depreciation	(d) Recovery period	(e) Convention	(f) Method	(g) Depreciation deduction
20a Class life					S/L	
b 12-year			12 yrs		S/L	
c 30-year			30 yrs	MM	S/L	
d 40-year			40 yrs	MM	S/L	

Part IV — Summary (See instructions.)

21	Listed property. Enter amount from line 28	21	
22	**Total.** Add amounts from line 12, lines 14 through 17, lines 19 and 20 in column (g), and line 21. Enter here and on the appropriate lines of your return. Partnerships and S corporations — see instructions	22	
23	For assets shown above and placed in service during the current year, enter the portion of the basis attributable to section 263A costs	23	

BAA For Paperwork Reduction Act Notice, see separate instructions. FDIZ0812L 06/28/22 Form **4562** (2022)

Form **4562**

Department of the Treasury
Internal Revenue Service

Depreciation and Amortization
(Including Information on Listed Property)
Attach to your tax return.
Go to *www.irs.gov/Form4562* for instructions and the latest information.

OMB No. 1545-0172
2022
Attachment Sequence No. **179**

Name(s) shown on return: HOWARD SHOPOWNER AND ROBERTA DOCTOR
Identifying number: 321-56-4899
Business or activity to which this form relates: SCHEDULE C - ROBERTA DOCTOR

Part I Election To Expense Certain Property Under Section 179
Note: If you have any listed property, complete Part V before you complete Part I.

1	Maximum amount (see instructions)	1	1,080,000.
2	Total cost of section 179 property placed in service (see instructions)	2	
3	Threshold cost of section 179 property before reduction in limitation (see instructions)	3	2,700,000.
4	Reduction in limitation. Subtract line 3 from line 2. If zero or less, enter -0-	4	
5	Dollar limitation for tax year. Subtract line 4 from line 1. If zero or less, enter -0-. If married filing separately, see instructions	5	

6	(a) Description of property	(b) Cost (business use only)	(c) Elected cost
7	Listed property. Enter the amount from line 29	7	

8	Total elected cost of section 179 property. Add amounts in column (c), lines 6 and 7	8	
9	Tentative deduction. Enter the **smaller** of line 5 or line 8	9	
10	Carryover of disallowed deduction from line 13 of your 2021 Form 4562	10	
11	Business income limitation. Enter the smaller of business income (not less than zero) or line 5. See instrs	11	
12	Section 179 expense deduction. Add lines 9 and 10, but don't enter more than line 11	12	50,000.
13	Carryover of disallowed deduction to 2023. Add lines 9 and 10, less line 12	13	

Note: Don't use Part II or Part III below for listed property. Instead, use Part V.

Part II Special Depreciation Allowance and Other Depreciation (Don't include listed property. See instructions.)

14	Special depreciation allowance for qualified property (other than listed property) placed in service during the tax year. See instructions	14	
15	Property subject to section 168(f)(1) election	15	
16	Other depreciation (including ACRS)	16	

Part III MACRS Depreciation (Don't include listed property. See instructions.)

Section A

17	MACRS deductions for assets placed in service in tax years beginning before 2022	17	
18	If you are electing to group any assets placed in service during the tax year into one or more general asset accounts, check here ☐		

Section B – Assets Placed in Service During 2022 Tax Year Using the General Depreciation System

(a) Classification of property	(b) Month and year placed in service	(c) Basis for depreciation (business/investment use only – see instructions)	(d) Recovery period	(e) Convention	(f) Method	(g) Depreciation deduction
19a 3-year property						
b 5-year property						
c 7-year property						
d 10-year property						
e 15-year property						
f 20-year property						
g 25-year property			25 yrs		S/L	
h Residential rental property			27.5 yrs	MM	S/L	
			27.5 yrs	MM	S/L	
i Nonresidential real property			39 yrs	MM	S/L	
				MM	S/L	

Section C – Assets Placed in Service During 2022 Tax Year Using the Alternative Depreciation System

(a) Classification of property	(b) Month and year placed in service	(c) Basis for depreciation	(d) Recovery period	(e) Convention	(f) Method	(g) Depreciation deduction
20a Class life					S/L	
b 12-year			12 yrs		S/L	
c 30-year			30 yrs	MM	S/L	
d 40-year			40 yrs	MM	S/L	

Part IV Summary (See instructions.)

21	Listed property. Enter amount from line 28	21	5,581.
22	**Total.** Add amounts from line 12, lines 14 through 17, lines 19 and 20 in column (g), and line 21. Enter here and on the appropriate lines of your return. Partnerships and S corporations – see instructions	22	55,581.
23	For assets shown above and placed in service during the current year, enter the portion of the basis attributable to section 263A costs	23	

BAA For Paperwork Reduction Act Notice, see separate instructions. FDIZ0812L 06/28/22 Form **4562** (2022)

Form 4562 (2022) HOWARD SHOPOWNER AND ROBERTA DOCTOR 321-56-4899 Page **2**

Part V **Listed Property** (Include automobiles, certain other vehicles, certain aircraft, and property used for entertainment, recreation, or amusement.)

Note: For any vehicle for which you are using the standard mileage rate or deducting lease expense, complete **only** 24a, 24b, columns (a) through (c) of Section A, all of Section B, and Section C if applicable.

Section A – Depreciation and Other Information (Caution: See the instructions for limits for passenger automobiles.**)**

24a Do you have evidence to support the business/investment use claimed? [X] **Yes** [ ] **No** **24b** If 'Yes,' is the evidence written? [X] **Yes** [ ] **No**

(a) Type of property (list vehicles first)	(b) Date placed in service	(c) Business/ investment use percentage	(d) Cost or other basis	(e) Basis for depreciation (business/investment use only)	(f) Recovery period	(g) Method/ Convention	(h) Depreciation deduction	(i) Elected section 179 cost
25 Special depreciation allowance for qualified listed property placed in service during the tax year and used more than 50% in a qualified business use. See instructions						**25**		
26 Property used more than 50% in a qualified business use:								
AUTOMOBILE	6/01/21	80.00	40,000.	17,440.	5.0	200DB HY	5,581.	
27 Property used 50% or less in a qualified business use:								
28 Add amounts in column (h), lines 25 through 27. Enter here and on line 21, page 1						**28**	5,581.	
29 Add amounts in column (i), line 26. Enter here and on line 7, page 1							**29**	0.

Section B – Information on Use of Vehicles

Complete this section for vehicles used by a sole proprietor, partner, or other 'more than 5% owner,' or related person. If you provided vehicles to your employees, first answer the questions in Section C to see if you meet an exception to completing this section for those vehicles.

	(a) Vehicle 1		(b) Vehicle 2		(c) Vehicle 3		(d) Vehicle 4		(e) Vehicle 5		(f) Vehicle 6	
30 Total business/investment miles driven during the year (**don't** include commuting miles)	12,000											
31 Total commuting miles driven during the year	2,000											
32 Total other personal (noncommuting) miles driven	1,000											
33 Total miles driven during the year. Add lines 30 through 32	15,000											
	Yes	**No**	**Yes**	**No**	**Yes**	**No**	**Yes**	**No**	**Yes**	**No**	**Yes**	**No**
34 Was the vehicle available for personal use during off-duty hours?	X											
35 Was the vehicle used primarily by a more than 5% owner or related person?	X											
36 Is another vehicle available for personal use?		X										

Section C – Questions for Employers Who Provide Vehicles for Use by Their Employees

Answer these questions to determine if you meet an exception to completing Section B for vehicles used by employees who **aren't** more than 5% owners or related persons. See instructions.

	Yes	No
37 Do you maintain a written policy statement that prohibits all personal use of vehicles, including commuting, by your employees?		
38 Do you maintain a written policy statement that prohibits personal use of vehicles, except commuting, by your employees? See the instructions for vehicles used by corporate officers, directors, or 1% or more owners		
39 Do you treat all use of vehicles by employees as personal use?		
40 Do you provide more than five vehicles to your employees, obtain information from your employees about the use of the vehicles, and retain the information received?		
41 Do you meet the requirements concerning qualified automobile demonstration use? See instructions		

Note: If your answer to 37, 38, 39, 40, or 41 is 'Yes,' don't complete Section B for the covered vehicles.

Part VI **Amortization**

(a) Description of costs	(b) Date amortization begins	(c) Amortizable amount	(d) Code section	(e) Amortization period or percentage	(f) Amortization for this year
42 Amortization of costs that begins during your 2022 tax year (see instructions):					
43 Amortization of costs that began before your 2022 tax year				**43**	
44 **Total.** Add amounts in column (f). See the instructions for where to report				**44**	

FDIZ0812L 06/28/22 Form **4562** (2022)

Form **4562** | **Depreciation and Amortization** **(Including Information on Listed Property)** | OMB No. 1545-0172

Attach to your tax return.

Department of the Treasury Internal Revenue Service | **Go to *www.irs.gov/Form4562* for instructions and the latest information.** | **2022** Attachment Sequence No. **179**

Name(s) shown on return: HOWARD SHOPOWNER AND ROBERTA DOCTOR | **Identifying number** 321-56-4899

Business or activity to which this form relates: SCHEDULE C - PET ARE US

Part I Election To Expense Certain Property Under Section 179

Note: If you have any listed property, complete Part V before you complete Part I.

1	Maximum amount (see instructions)	1	1,080,000.
2	Total cost of section 179 property placed in service (see instructions)	2	
3	Threshold cost of section 179 property before reduction in limitation (see instructions)	3	2,700,000.
4	Reduction in limitation. Subtract line 3 from line 2. If zero or less, enter -0-	4	
5	Dollar limitation for tax year. Subtract line 4 from line 1. If zero or less, enter -0-. If married filing separately, see instructions	5	

6	(a) Description of property	(b) Cost (business use only)	(c) Elected cost

7	Listed property. Enter the amount from line 29	7	
8	Total elected cost of section 179 property. Add amounts in column (c), lines 6 and 7	8	
9	Tentative deduction. Enter the **smaller** of line 5 or line 8	9	
10	Carryover of disallowed deduction from line 13 of your 2021 Form 4562	10	
11	Business income limitation. Enter the smaller of business income (not less than zero) or line 5. See instrs	11	
12	Section 179 expense deduction. Add lines 9 and 10, but don't enter more than line 11	12	78,850.
13	Carryover of disallowed deduction to 2023. Add lines 9 and 10, less line 12	13	

Note: Don't use Part II or Part III below for listed property. Instead, use Part V.

Part II Special Depreciation Allowance and Other Depreciation (Don't include listed property. See instructions.)

14	Special depreciation allowance for qualified property (other than listed property) placed in service during the tax year. See instructions	14	
15	Property subject to section 168(f)(1) election	15	
16	Other depreciation (including ACRS)	16	

Part III MACRS Depreciation (Don't include listed property. See instructions.)

Section A

17	MACRS deductions for assets placed in service in tax years beginning before 2022	17	8,433.
18	If you are electing to group any assets placed in service during the tax year into one or more general asset accounts, check here ☐		

Section B – Assets Placed in Service During 2022 Tax Year Using the General Depreciation System

(a) Classification of property	(b) Month and year placed in service	(c) Basis for depreciation (business/investment use only – see instructions)	(d) Recovery period	(e) Convention	(f) Method	(g) Depreciation deduction
19a 3-year property						
b 5-year property						
c 7-year property						
d 10-year property						
e 15-year property						
f 20-year property						
g 25-year property			25 yrs		S/L	
h Residential rental property			27.5 yrs	MM	S/L	
			27.5 yrs	MM	S/L	
i Nonresidential real property			39 yrs	MM	S/L	
				MM	S/L	

Section C – Assets Placed in Service During 2022 Tax Year Using the Alternative Depreciation System

(a)	(b)	(c)	(d)	(e)	(f)	(g)
20a Class life					S/L	
b 12-year			12 yrs		S/L	
c 30-year			30 yrs	MM	S/L	
d 40-year			40 yrs	MM	S/L	

Part IV Summary (See instructions.)

21	Listed property. Enter amount from line 28	21	
22	**Total.** Add amounts from line 12, lines 14 through 17, lines 19 and 20 in column (g), and line 21. Enter here and on the appropriate lines of your return. Partnerships and S corporations – see instructions	22	87,283.
23	For assets shown above and placed in service during the current year, enter the portion of the basis attributable to section 263A costs	23	

BAA For Paperwork Reduction Act Notice, see separate instructions. FDIZ0812L 06/28/22 Form **4562** (2022)

PART TWO: PARTNERSHIPS

Form 1065: U.S. Partnership Return of Income

➢ FACT PATTERN FOR REAL ESTATE PARTNERSHIP

Hudson Grey Properties, L.P. is a limited partnership consisting of two partners, Mr. Hudson, the general partner, and Mr. Grey, the limited partner. The partnership invested in an apartment building in 2004 and has operated it for the last 34 years.

➢ FACT PATTERN FOR A PROFESSIONAL PRACTICE PARTNERSHIP

Dealmaker & Codehead, a law firm operating as a general partnership, consists of three partners, Mr. Dealmaker, Mr. Codehead, and a new partner, Grant A. Herring, P.C.

➢ OVERVIEW OF PARTNERSHIP TAXATION

Persons who share profits and losses from unincorporated businesses are required to report their income on a partnership tax return, IRS Form 1065. The partnership itself is not subject to income taxes. Rather the income of the partnership flows through to the individual partners who must report their share of partnership income on their individual income tax return, Schedule E, Page 2.

The partnership tax return is a combination income statement, balance sheet, and information report for the partnership. A reconciliation format within the return is used to denote differences between taxable income and financial statement income (also known as "Book Income"). As a result, a very thorough financial overview of a business or practice is usually available from the tax return itself.

The 2022 Form 1065 contains five pages plus as many K-1s as there are partners. The K-1 Form is titled "Partner's Share of Income, Credits, Deductions, Etc." and reflects the taxable income and deductible expenses allocable to each partner.

Income from a trade or business is reported on the first page. Page 2 and 3 consists of Section B in which 30 questions concerning the attributes of the partnership are contained. Page 4 requires reporting a summary of the amounts shown on all of the partnership K-1s. Page 4 generally contains additional income or expense items that do not appear on Page 1 because tax law requires special treatment for those items. Page 5 contains comparative balance sheets for the current and prior year-ends. Also reported on Page 5 are the reconciliation of taxable income to book income, and the analysis of partners' capital accounts. The capital account analysis reconciles the prior year-end partners' capital balances with the current year-end balances.

Additional supporting schedules are required to report other partnership activity. Examples of such schedules are Form 1125-A, used to report cost of goods sold, Form 8825, where real estate rental activity is reported, and Form 4562, the depreciation detail summary. Examples of supporting partnership tax forms are presented in the hypothetical tax returns included at the end of this section.

Page 1: U.S. Partnership Return of Income

Generally, a partnership of individuals reports on a calendar year basis because, as a rule, it must conform to the tax year of the majority of its partners unless the partnership can establish a business purpose for adopting another fiscal year. Certain partnerships may elect a fiscal year-end other than December 31 because the alternative year-end coincides with the partnership's business cycle. Form 8716 is used to elect a fiscal year other than the required tax year.

Greater complexity in the preparation of income available for child support and spousal support (which the IRS and many states call "alimony") is more likely to exist where substantial income, loss, or cash flow is derived from activities of a partnership that reports on a fiscal year other than December 31. The complexity arises because income from a partnership is reflected on the personal income tax return based on the results of operation for the partnership's fiscal year-end. Note that a partnership return for a fiscal year ending November 30, 2023 is considered a 2022 partnership tax return because the fiscal year began in 2022, however, the partner will report the income on their 2023 individual income tax return. To illustrate, a partnership with a November 30, 2023 year-end reflects income for eleven months of 2023 and one month of 2022. When that income is reported on the personal income tax return for 2023, the taxable income shown on the personal income tax return will not only reflect income earned in 2023 but also includes 2022 earnings. Similarly, partnership distributions for 2022 cannot be obtained with reference to the 2022 partnership tax return with a November 30 fiscal year-end because some or all of the withdrawals indicated on the partner's K-1 may have substantially or entirely occurred in 2023. Careful analysis of underlying financial information is necessary in order to avoid misstating income for a specific period. An error resulting from overlooking the timing problems associated with non-calendar fiscal years will distort perceived earnings and cash flow.

FORM 1065: PAGE 1

Lines A and B: Examples of how these boxes for "Principal Business Activity" and "Principal Product or Service" are completed appear in the tax returns at the end of this section. For example, the hypothetical tax return of Dealmaker & Codehead indicates their principal business activity is "Legal" and that it is a "Services" partnership.

Line C: Business code numbers are used by the government to compile statistical economic information. A listing of such codes can be accessed through the IRS website containing the instructions for Form 1065 at (www.IRS.gov./instructions/i1065/ar03).

Line D: A partnership obtains an "Employer ID Number" by filing Form SS-4. The ID number is reflected on all payroll tax forms the partnership is required to file.

Line F: "Total Assets" shown here should be exactly the same as the total assets on Page 5,

Schedule L, Line 14. A quick idea of the size of the business may be gleaned from this number.

Line G: The "Initial return" and "Final return" boxes alert the reader to important basic information. If the business or practice was started or terminated in 2022, the net profit or loss shown may not be indicative of the true income potential of the business because only the results for a partial year are reflected. Furthermore, the expenses for the business may be greater than will be experienced in future years because of start-up costs generally associated with the first year of operations. Other considerations apply if a business was terminated during the year. Inquiry should be made whether the business has continued to operate as a different legal entity or whether it has ceased operations. If the business was incorporated during the year, the partial income and cash flow for the partnership's final year must be added to the partial corporate income and cash flow to arrive at representative earnings. As mentioned throughout this book, representative, or "true" earnings, is a critical factor in appraising businesses and providing meaningful income analyses.

Line H: The two most common accounting methods are the "cash basis" and the "accrual basis." Both of the hypothetical partnership tax returns presented at the end of the section use the cash basis. When a partnership is on a cash basis, revenue is reported in the year in which it is actually or constructively received in the form of cash. Deductions are taken only for expenses actually paid during the year. In contrast, accrual basis partnerships report revenue when it is earned (when the right to receive it occurs). Thus, if a customer was billed for an item shipped on December 31, 2022, but the customer did not pay for the item until February 1, 2023, the business reporting on an accrual basis would still record the income in 2022 even though the merchandise was paid for in the subsequent year. On the accrual basis, expenses may be deducted when incurred, whether or not the expense is paid in that tax year.

If the accounting method changes from cash to accrual or vice versa between two tax years, adjustments to taxable income resulting from the change should have no effect on income available for support. The accounting transition is merely a change in form that does not change the underlying economic reality.

Partnerships whose business activity includes the sale of inventory must use the accrual basis of accounting unless their average annual gross receipts do not exceed $27 million. Service partnerships, such as professional practices, generally are on a cash basis. A cash basis partnership generally does not report accounts receivables on its Schedule L. As a result, for purposes of business appraisal, forensic accountants must obtain this information from the partnership's accounting records. Discovery of the net realizable value of accounts receivable is important for valuation purposes as it is often one of the largest assets of the business or practice.

Accounts receivables present an interesting problem when cash basis partnerships are valued in family law matters if the spouse charged with the receivables will also be required to pay child or spousal support based on cash basis income derived from the collection of some or all of the accounts receivable that existed at the date the business or practice was appraised. The perceived "double-dip" may appear particularly inequitable in property divisions where one party is receiving the partnership interest and paying support while assets of equal stated value are apportioned to the other spouse. Nevertheless, California law support the proposition that it is proper to include earnings as income available for support even is some of those same receivables the spouse received in the property division will be used to pay support.

The "double-dip" effect, while appearing inequitable, can be better understood in terms of accrual basis accounting. On an accrual basis, the paying spouse is actually providing support from current accrual basis earnings. This can be illustrated by a hypothetical in which it is assumed that the business or practice is terminated at date of separation and the partner/spouse finds a job as an employee. In this situation, no apparent inequity exists if the spousal support is based on wages that are received currently because the accounts receivable can be shared by both spouses equally when collected. Similarly, although it may be that the paying spouse is using cash flow from accounts receivable collected prior to the appraisal valuation date, the accrual basis earnings, not yet collected, are the actual earning base from which support is derived. In essence, the problem is one of a timing difference rather than a "double dip."

If accounts receivable are awarded one-half to each spouse in the marital property division, the spouse who earned the receivables will still be taxed on all of the post separation receivables collected in the tax year. Filing a joint return, assuming the parties were still legally married at year-end, is one way both spouses can equally share the tax liability associated with the collection of the post separation accounts receivable. The partner/spouse cannot assign 50% of the taxable income earned from the collection of the account receivable to the non-partner spouse when separate returns are filed. If a joint return is not an option, reimbursement for the additional taxes paid by the partner/spouse, or other property offsets, may be employed to equalize the property division. The non-operating spouse's share of taxes on the accounts receivable is often recognized in the property division by virtue of "deferred income tax" calculations included in the appraisal of the practice or business at the date of separation.

Another manner of reporting revenue and expense is known as "Percentage of Completion." The percentage of completion method is used primarily in the construction industries. Motion picture projects generally utilize a similar method of accounting known as the "Income Forecast Method." Under these methods, revenue and expenses are recognized in conjunction with the progress of the construction project(s). Advance payments in anticipation of completion of a certain percentage of a project are recorded as liabilities (often called "Unearned Revenue" on a balance sheet) rather than as revenue considered in determining profits for the period. When each phase of construction is completed, the revenue associated with that phase is considered earned. At that point, the liability is extinguished and the revenue earned in connection with that phase of construction is recognized.

The completed contract method is another accounting method for reporting income and expenses in the construction industry. Under this method, income and expenses of a project are reported in the year that a contract is completed. However, the percentage of completion method is more often used for tax purposes.

Line I: "Number of Schedules K-1" The line item is self-explanatory.

Line J: "Check if Schedules C and M-3 attached" Large partnerships, those with over $10 million in assets or $35 million in total receipts, must file a Schedule M-3. The form requires a more in depth disclosure of the partnership's possible book/tax differences. The hypothetical partnerships included in this book do not file Schedule M-3 because they are not large enough. Few family law scenarios include appraisals of large partnerships because it is rare for a spouse to have control over the income of larger entities. Usually, a spouse's interest in a large partnership represents a small fraction of the total ownership. The most common example is the partnership interest of an individual attorney in a large law firm.

INCOME

Line 1a: Gross Receipts or Sales Gross receipts, commonly referred to as the business's "Gross," is usually one of the most significant statistics for valuation purposes. Non-accountants frequently use the terms "Income," "Revenue," and "Gross Income" interchangeably. This is a common area of confusion that lawyers should avoid. The gross cash receipts are synonymous with revenue for a partnership that operates on a cash basis. If the partnership operates on an accrual basis, gross cash receipts and revenue usually differ. In the case of accrual partnerships, the revenue represents what the business has billed or sold while the cash receipts are merely collections on accounts receivable. "Income" is the difference between revenue and expenses. It is synonymous with "Profit" or the "Bottom Line."

The "Gross" is an important element of tax return analysis. Often, a business or practice is sold on the basis of multiples of gross receipts. On the Dealmaker & Codehead hypothetical partnership, $3,405,694 is reported as gross receipts. Comparison with prior years' "Gross" will provide information for a historical trend analysis of client fees. If a decrease in revenue in 2022 has occurred, the cause for the reduction should be ascertained through interview, deposition, or document inspection. The concern generally focuses on whether the decrease was the result of lower productivity engendered by the divorce or just market conditions. Whether this decrease was caused by the psychological effects of the divorce or by a willful slowdown are possibilities requiring investigation.

A trend analysis is also appropriate for partnership income analysis. Revenue and income trends are important factors to consider in appraising a commercial business. The effects of a divorce on income may be highlighted by reference to such analyses.

In some cash basis service partnerships, client checks received in December are not deposited into the business bank account until January of the following year. If a partnership has just begun this practice of holding checks in December of 2022, the "Gross" of the business is understated by the amount of the held checks. This results in a lower amount of partnership taxable income allocable to the partner/spouse and a lower apparent income for that spouse. If this practice of holding checks has been consistently followed for years, an analysis of the amounts involved for the prior versus the current year will provide the most accurate representation of annual gross receipts.

Unusually low amounts of reported gross in partnerships that handle cash, particularly retail businesses such as restaurants, may indicate unreported income. Comparing cash register tapes to bank deposits and other business records may be helpful in determining the amount of unreported income in some circumstances. When information required for such an analysis is unavailable, other procedures are employed by forensic accountants to assist in quantifying the unreported income.

One such procedure relies upon statistical gross profit information for the industry to suggest appropriate levels of gross receipts. The quantification of what the "Gross" should be is achieved by dividing the actual "Cost of Goods Sold" of the subject business by the industry percentage for "Cost of Goods Sold." The comparing of the gross profit ("Revenue" less "Cost of Goods Sold"—also known as "Gross Margin") of the subject business to industry statistical information provides a quick method for determining the probability of unreported income.

An analysis of the mark-up on the company's merchandise may also be revealing. If the typical mark-up is 25% (let's say $1.25 selling price on goods that cost $1.00), then the gross profit to be expected is 20% ($.25 divided by $1.25). If the partnership tax return reflects a materially lower "Gross Profit" enhanced scrutiny is advisable. The value of this type of approach is substantially reduced in partnerships that have a large product mix or in cases where merchandise is frequently discounted.

Another way of proving unreported income exists, albeit more time consuming and costly than those mentioned previously, is the lifestyle analysis. A disparity between the parties' lifestyle and their reported adjusted gross income for the period may provide a reasonable estimate of unreported income under certain circumstances. If the unreported income is stored in a safe deposit box and not exhausted on living expenses, the lifestyle analysis will not prove very useful. The lifestyle approach requires an accounting for all sources and uses of cash for a particular period. The accounting should include deposits to the parties' personal accounts that may have emanated from gifts, inheritance, borrowing, or prior year loan repayments. Cash balances at both the beginning and the end of the period need to be ascertained in order to calculate the amount of income funded by savings on hand at the beginning of the period. Classification of recorded expenditures by the parties during the particular period under scrutiny may reveal expenditures well in excess of reported income. Additionally, such classification may disclose either small or nonexistent expenditures for known costs of living such as housekeeper costs and grocery expenses. An estimate of the reasonable monthly cost of such expenditures may then be added to the reported cost of living to arrive at the total lifestyle of the parties.

Note that no gross receipts are reported on the Hudson Grey hypothetical partnership tax return. Because Hudson Grey is involved in real estate rental activities, the receipts and expenses of the business are shown on Form 8825, not on Page 1.

When a partnership has income or loss from rental real estate, the amount is passed through pro rata to each partner on the K-1. The allocation is required because of limitations on deductibility of rental losses. Partners who actively participate in rental activity and report less than $150,000 in adjusted gross income on their personal return may be entitled to deduct up to $25,000 in losses for the year. Otherwise, rental activity is considered to be a passive activity subject to passive loss limitations.

As in the case of Hudson Grey, Rental revenue and expenses are listed on supplemental schedules in partnership tax returns. Cash flow to the partnership from rental real estate is generally derived by adding depreciation back to rental income or loss and subtracting principal payments on mortgages. Note that the Internal Revenue Service generally does not require the inclusion of detailed fixed asset schedules with the return so you may need to acquire them separately. Whether this cash flow is relevant to a specific partner may depend on the degree to which that partner controls his or her withdrawals from the partnership.

Line 1b: Returns and Allowances Returns and Allowances includes sold merchandise that has been returned or, in the case of a personal service partnerships, a refund of an overpayment. While seemingly similar, "Returns and Allowances" should not be confused with "Bad Debts" discussed later.

Line 2: Cost of Goods Sold Professional practices, rental real estate, and service partnerships typically report nothing on this line. The two hypothetical partnership tax returns at the end of this section are examples of these kinds of partnerships. Commercial businesses with inventories report the cost relating to the products sold on this line. Form 1125-A is the partnership tax return form in which additional information relative to "Cost of Goods Sold" is reported. Perquisites may be buried here. Detailed information regarding Cost of Goods Sold is presented on Form 1125-A.

FORM 1125 A: SCHEDULE A: COST OF GOODS SOLD

Line 1: Inventory at Beginning of Year This is the starting point for analyzing the cost of goods sold. The amount should match the ending inventory reported in the prior year's tax return. If it does not, the matter should be investigated.

Reporting a higher than actual opening inventory will understate profit. As a result, analysis of last year's return and accompanying supporting documentation to verify the reliability of the opening inventory is recommended.

Line 2: Purchases The cost of inventory items purchased for sale by retailers and wholesalers appears on this line. If a partnership manufactures goods, the amount shown will represent raw material purchases.

Timing of expense is an important element in determining the reliability of the amount shown. Typically, businesses with inventories report on the accrual basis; accordingly, the date of payment for the goods is not as relevant as the date of purchase. Criteria for determining the date of purchase follow legal guidelines reflected in the Uniform Commercial Code. The contractual time at which goods change hands determines when goods are considered purchased under the accrual basis of accounting.

Consistency in reporting transactional activity with regular vendors is indicative of reliability in the timing of the expense. Inconsistency merits further analysis.

Accountants preparing audited or reviewed financial statements will test year-end transactions to determine appropriate reporting of purchases at the cut-off date, December 31 for all calendar year partnerships. This accounting technique provides enhanced reliability of the amount reported.

The partnership's "Accounts Payable" is a balance sheet item that is closely associated with the recordation of purchases. In many businesses an accounts payable journal or purchases journal is maintained. Monthly summations of additions to accounts payable for purchases of goods or raw materials constitute the "Purchases" account reflected on the general ledger and, ultimately, the tax return.

Inspection of the accounts payable or purchases journal and the cash disbursement journal is recommended when suspicion exists that personal items have been paid for by the business. As stated in the line description, the IRS requires that personal use items be withdrawn. Examples of partnerships that warrant analysis for inventory used personally are restaurants, electronics retailers, computer stores, and clothing outlets.

Line 3: Cost of Labor Generally, this line is use by businesses that manufacture goods. Only direct labor costs of manufacturing are included. Indirect labor costs may be partially included depending on the type of overhead allocation formula used by the business to incorporate indirect expenses into the cost of producing the product.

Administrative salaries should not be included in this area of the return. As pointed out in the discussion of Line 9 of Page 1, "Salaries and Wages," obtaining the names of all employees is advisable to ascertain whether friends and relatives who do not really perform full services for compensation received are on payroll. Inspection of payroll tax returns and, where available, payroll journals will identify those persons on payroll. To the extent that there is an overstatement of "Wages," conclusions as to the value of the enterprise and income available for support are understated.

Line 4: Additional Section 263A Costs Businesses that manufacture or resell a product are subject to "Uniform Capitalization Rules." (Resellers with gross receipts of less than $27 million on average in the last three years are exempt from this rule). Under IRS regulations, indirect costs such as overhead (e.g., warehouse rent, freight in, certain salaries, etc.) attributable to the cost of inventory are added to inventory. This type of cost is rarely an issue in marital dissolution matters because it generally does not arise in those partnerships where manipulation of income is an issue.

Line 5: Other Costs Generally, this refers to overhead (e.g., warehouse rent, freight in, certain salaries, etc.), also known as indirect costs of manufacturing. An entire branch of accounting, known as "Cost Accounting," is devoted to the study of allocating overhead expenses not directly related to the manufacture of the product. Portions of the rent, utilities, administrative labor, and property taxes are examples of types of indirect manufacturing expenses that are allocated to the cost of manufactured goods.

Line 7: Inventory at End of Year Because the year-end for which ending inventory is determined is often close to the time at which the appraisal is performed, the relevant documentation for intensive research and analysis of this account is usually readily available. If an actual inventory count is taken, copies of the supporting detail should be obtained and reviewed. The procedures employed to make the count should be analyzed. Less scrutiny of procedures and valuation methodology is required if the inventory was observed by certified public accountants in conjunction with a certified audit.

Unreported sale of inventory during the post-separation period is a frequent allegation made by non-partner spouses. Testing of gross profit ratios with industry percentages and against prior years' percentages for the partnership may support such allegations. Testing mark-up percentages against gross profit is another tool available in some cases to spot irregularities in inventory value.

LINE 8: COST OF GOODS SOLD Cost of goods is carried forward to Page 1, line 2.

LINE 9A TO F: METHODS USED TO VALUE CLOSING INVENTORY The method by which inventory is valued may significantly affect the partnership valuation. Inventories are frequently undervalued in order to report lower taxable profit. Greater motivation to manipulate inventory exists in divorce cases because lower profitability from lower inventory benefits the partner/spouse via a lower business valuation and less income available for support.

Inventory valuation methods are important factors in determining the appropriate amount of inventory. The method must conform to the best accounting practice in the particular trade or business. "Cost" means that the inventory is valued at the price paid. "Lower of cost or market" means that the cost of inventory, on an item by item basis, is compared to its respective market value. The lower of the two values is used.

LIFO (last-in, first-out) and FIFO (first-in, first-out) are terms often used in connection with inventory valuation. If a LIFO method of costing inventory is used in an inflationary period, book value will tend to be understated. The FIFO method of costing inventory provides a more accurate representation of actual market value of the inventory because ending inventory is "costed" by reference to the most recent purchases.

Any changes in inventory accounting between prior years and the year of separation and the subsequent period should be carefully investigated. Unusually large negative adjustments to inventory also warrant research.

LINE 3: GROSS PROFIT The gross profit is the difference between "Gross receipts or sales" ("Revenue") and the cost of merchandise sold. Reference to the percentage of "Gross Profit" to "Revenue" is an important indicator of partnership economic trends. A decline in the gross profit percentage may indicate greater price competition in the industry or higher raw material costs. Variances in the year of divorce warrant concern and scrutiny. Both "Revenue" and "Cost of Goods Sold" may impact this percentage. As mentioned previously, a divergence from industry norms may signify that the subject partnership is not reporting revenue. More on "Gross Profit" (also known as "Gross Margin") is presented in the discussion of Schedule A.

LINE 4: ORDINARY INCOME (LOSS) FROM OTHER PARTNERSHIPS, ESTATES, AND TRUSTS The amount shown on this line item reflects taxable income from other entities in which the partnership has an interest. A partnership may be a partner in another partnership. This type of business structure is often seen in connection with syndicated businesses in which one partnership is comprised of promoters who solicit different groups of people to invest in the same kind of business at different geographical locations. A partnership may also be a beneficiary of an estate or trust in which case income derived from such entities is reported here.

LINE 5: NET FARM PROFIT (LOSS) The result of operations from farming ventures in which the partnership is engaged is presented on Schedule F of the Form 1040. Although Schedule F is an individual income tax form, it is also used to provide details on partnership farm revenue and expenses. The profit is then shown here on Page 1. Farming losses in particular should be carefully investigated to ascertain whether the underlying activity is being conducted for profit or as a hobby. Depreciation expenses deducted in connection with livestock and equipment impact cash flow analyses. Depreciation should be added back if continual annual outlays of cash for new purchases are not needed to maintain the business's level of profitability.

Line 6: Net Gain or (Loss) from Form 4797 The ordinary income from disposition of real or personal property used in the business activity conducted by the partnership is reflected here. An entry on this line indicates that a sale of assets has taken place during the year. For income purposes, a sale of capital assets generally is not a recurring business activity. Consequently, a representative income analysis for the year should exclude these proceeds. Form 4797 is used to determine the capital gain versus ordinary income portion of gain from sale of business assets.

Line 7: Other Income This line reflects income that is not considered "Gross receipts or sales." Unusual sources of taxable income that are not in the ordinary course of business are reported on this line. For example, proceeds from a successfully litigated lawsuit are unusual and non-recurring taxable receipts that should be reported here. Non-recurring sources of income are usually not considered cash available for support; however, large amounts of cash generated by such income that remain within the partnership will result in an increase in investment income that should be taken into consideration as a source of additional income to the partner.

Not included in this category are rental income, capital gains, recapture of depreciation, or ordinary income from sale of business assets included on Form 4797. The foregoing are flow-through items that require special tax treatment on the individual partner's tax return. As a result, income from these sources must be separately stated and allocated on the K-1 of each partner. Careful review of the K-1 or Schedule K should be undertaken to determine all sources of income.

Line 8: Total Income (Loss) Total income (loss) is merely the summation of all of the Page 1 income and, standing alone, is not as significant from an analytical perspective as its components.

DEDUCTIONS

For income or appraisal purposes, forensic accountants often convert expenses into percentages and compare these to percentages for prior years to highlight variations. Anomalies and deviations can be more easily identified through use of analysis of comparative percentages (also known as "Common Size" comparative income statements).

Line 9: Salary and Wages Are friends and relatives on payroll who do not really perform full services for compensation received? Inspection of payroll tax returns and, where available, payroll journals will identify those persons on payroll. To the extent that "Salary and Wages" are overstated, conclusions as to the value of the enterprise and income available for support are understated.

Closely related, but usually not included in "Salary and Wages," are payments to independent contractors. A partnership is required to file IRS Form 1099 to report all payments to unincorporated independent contractors in excess of $600 per year. Observation of the payees listed on the 1099 forms may disclose payments to friends or relatives. From a practical standpoint, it is important to note that failure to adhere to this requirement is common. Consequently, analysis of general ledgers and journals may still be required to identify independent contractors hired by the partnership.

Line 10: Guaranteed Payments to Partners Partners may receive payments that are deductible in arriving at partnership income. The payments are known as "Guaranteed Payments." A partner's "Guarantees Payments" are reported on his or her K-1 separately from the partner's share of partnership income. The combination of guaranteed payments to the partner and the partner's share of ordinary typically constitute the self-employment tax portion of the partner's share of partnership income. Guaranteed payments are often paid to a managing partner or to other partners who provide more labor or other skill to the partnership activity then the other partners.

Line 11: Repairs and Maintenance In partnerships where some or all of the partners are relatives, closer scrutiny of this expense item is advised. Frequently, personal residence repairs and improvements are run through this account. Vendors who provide goods or services to the partnership may also provide additional *personal* goods or services. The "out-spouse" may be helpful in identifying companies or individuals who have provided good or services for the parties personally that have been paid for out of the partnership.

Capital expenditures that are written-off as an expense of the period are often classified as repair expense. The effect of improper recording of capital assets is the understatement of business income. If the asset was purchased outright (and not with borrowed funds), actual income for the period is properly reflected; however, cash available reports prepared for support hearings should contain an adjustment for this item (pro rata based on the partner's share of income). Appropriate adjustment to income requires that the amount of capital expenditures charged to expense be added back. By this means, projected future income does not include the non-recurring costs of asset acquisitions. If, on the other hand, it is common practice for the partnership to regularly upgrade and replace assets, no adjustment, or only a partial adjustment, may be necessary.

Line 12: Bad Debts Accrual basis partnerships must use the specific charge-off method to deduct business bad debts. Only direct write-offs are allowed. In terms of income or business value, this means that receivables reported on the partnership return may be overvalued and income overstated because a bad debt deduction pursuant to a reserve for bad debts is not allowed. Income of accrual basis partnerships should be adjusted for anticipated bad debts in order to derive a more accurate income analysis.

Cash basis partnerships do not report bad debts because sales are reported based on actual collections. As a result, there is usually no possibility of manipulation of income in this category of expense for cash basis partnerships.

Line 13: Rent In some cases, inquiry should be made concerning the identity of the lessor and the fair market value of the rental payment. If the lessor is a friend or relative of a partner, the probability of overstated rent that reduces profitability is enhanced. Examination of the facility lease is generally an integral part of the appraisal process. A bargain lease has the effect of overstating profitability; accordingly, an adjustment should be made to restate the annual rental to market.

A bargain lease suggests an asset with value that typically will not be disclosed in any discovery materials. Real estate experts are able to render opinions of value for leases whose stated rent is lower than market.

Line 14: Taxes and Licenses Real estate, personal property, and payroll taxes are reported here. Examination of tax bills and other supporting documentation may disclose unreported assets or misstated values.

Line 15: Interest The appearance of this expense evidence the existence of either secured or unsecured loans. Note that the Tax Cut and Jobs Act implemented a limitation to the amount of deductible interest to 30% of the businesses adjusted taxable income. As a result, the interest listed here may not reflect the interest the business actually paid.

Loan application files may be obtained from lenders. This documentation may help to confirm or uncover the existence of certain marital assets. Opinions of value are also found in these files. While the individual partners' opinion of the value of the real estate and/or the partnership may carry little weight at trial, it may be useful for settlement purposes. Personal financial statements from each of the partners may be found in the loan file. Opinions of value contained in the personal financial statement may also appear for other marital property. This information may promote settlement and save expert witness appraisal costs. In summary, loan files (frequently obtained from banks through subpoenas) may contain application forms and other informative documents that provide a cross-reference for checking the accuracy of marital asset values. The loan application usually includes a sworn statement of earning ability, an amount that can be compared with the income reported for the same period on the partnership tax return and on a partner's individual tax return. The spouse's credibility as a witness may be impaired by presenting evidence of major inconsistencies between the income shown on the loan application and the tax return income.

Line 16a and b: Depreciation Reported depreciation must be analyzed with a view to the impact of this expense on cash flow. Page 5 of the partnership tax return contains a balance sheet that includes a summary of the cost of depreciable property and the accumulated depreciation.

Analysis of depreciation and asset history may be provided either wholly or partially on Form 4562 and supporting schedules included in the return of a partnership claiming depreciation expense. The Dealmaker & Codehead partnership illustrates how a Form 4562 and its supporting schedule account for all of the partnership's depreciation. Probative information concerning the assets of the business, including date of acquisition and original cost, are shown on the supporting detail schedule. Additional asset information may be obtained from a partnership's internally prepared depreciation schedule or the workpapers maintained by its independent certified public accounting firm.

Depreciation schedules aid in identifying assets that have been written-off but still have value. Note the discrepancy between the total depreciation shown on the supporting schedules titled "2022 DEPRECIATION AND AMORTIZATION REPORT" and Line 16a of Page 1 of the Dealmaker & Codehead return. Of the total $72,964 depreciation, only $12,964 is shown on Page 1. The reason for this is Section 179 depreciation (explained further later), which is reported separately on Page 4 Line 12 of Form 1065. The effect of Section 179 may be to report certain assets still in use as fully depreciated. Although fully depreciation for tax purposes, recently acquired assets are not worthless, even though they may appear so on a financial statement or a tax return. Failure to make an adjustment to state these assets at fair market value will cause an understatement of the value of the partnership interest.

In addition to providing relevant data for determination of fair market value of fixed assets, the depreciation schedule is also useful for evaluating claimed cash flow needs of the business for investment in new equipment. Examination of yearly asset purchases can form part of the basis for an opinion concerning the annual outlay a partnership must make for capital asset acquisitions.

The first $1,080,000 (increasing to $1,160,000 in 2023 and subsequent years) of personal property additions in 2022 can generally be deducted as an expense under Internal Revenue Code (IRC) Section 179. In a partnership, this is a "pass-through" item, i.e., each partner is allocated his or her pro rata share of the $1,080,000 directly on their K-1 and reports the deduction as an offset to partnership income on Schedule E, Form 1040 of their personal return. That expense will be carried as a depreciation expense on Page 1, Line 12 of Form 4562 but will not appear as a reduction of partnership ordinary income.

Note that in Dealmaker & Codehead's Form 4562 Part 1 contains a summary of the Section 179 depreciation that totals $60,000. That is the amount passed through to the partners on their K-1s. The amount of $12,964 on Part IV, Line 22 represents the depreciation deduction reported on Page 1 of the return. That amount represents depreciation of prior years' purchases not subject to Section 179.

Depreciation amounts appearing on the tax return should be compared to financial statement depreciation. Difference between the tax return and financial depreciation are noted on Page 5, Schedule M-1, Lines 4a and 7a. Entries on this line warrant further analysis because rapid depreciation write-offs usually result in overstatement of annual operating costs and corresponding understatement of value for the business (especially when a capitalization of earnings method is used to value the business or its goodwill).

Examples of Form 4562 and supporting schedules are included only in the Dealmaker and Codehead hypothetical return included at the end of this section. Note the Hudson Grey Properties is not required to include the Form 4562 because is it a partnership with no current year asset additions, section 179 expense, vehicle depreciation, nor amortization expense. Section 179 depreciation has not been taken as it may not be used for real property. Compare the Dealmaker and Codehead return that does include the Section 179 depreciation. The pro rata amount of the depreciation is carried to each of the partners' K-1s so that the depreciation deduction can pass through the partnership to the individual tax return.

In both hypothetical returns, the supporting detail depreciation schedules, which are included here for your benefit, contain a description of the fixed assets, the date of acquisition and the cost. These facts often are of great import in determining fair market value of the fixed assets and are used by professional real and personal property appraisers as well as forensic accountants for this purpose.

Income analyses are also affected by the depreciation history of a partnership. Generally, depreciation is added back to arrive at true income because depreciation is a non-cash expense. Sometimes, however, depreciation expense approximates the amount of continual investment in equipment. In such fact situations, especially for permanent support, a better argument exists for the deduction of depreciation in arriving at true income. Another approach in this type of scenario is to deduct the average amounts spent over the last two to five years on asset acquisitions.

Line 17: Depletion Depletion is "depreciation" for natural resources. It represents a deduction for the capital investment that the partnership receives pro rata over the estimated productive life of the resource. Different tax methods, such as cost depletion and percentage depletion, are allowed for computation of the deduction.

Like depreciation, analysis of actual cash flow related to this expense is required to determine "true" income. Generally, the capital investment providing the basis for depreciation is not a recurring cost of the partnership; accordingly, depletion expense is usually added back to profit to arrive at representative income for the partnership.

For partnerships engaged in extracting natural resources, the partner/spouse's income may tie directly into the partnership income or may be quite different depending on his or her involvement in the day to day operations. The partner's position in the partnership should be evaluated to determine how much control that partner has over partnership procedures and policy because the more control a partner has the more probable it is that financial information may be manipulated. Determination of the degree of control may be accomplished more often through interview or deposition than document inspection. The partner's spouse or other partners may also be good sources of information in this regard.

"Oil and gas depletion" is not reported here because it is a "pass-through item" that is shown directly on the partners' K-1s.

Line 18: Retirement Plans Entries on this line denote the existence of a retirement plan. The amount shown represents payments made on behalf of employees, not the partners. Partners are treated in the same way as proprietors with respect to the retirement plan deductions. Retirement plan contributions made on behalf of a partner are presented as a separate line item on the partner's K-1. The partner takes this deduction on Line 16 of Schedule 1 attached to Form 1040. Determination of the value of the marital portion of the plan is essential for property division purposes.

Participant statements for the partner can usually be obtained from the plan administrator or from the participating spouse if the plan is self-directed.

The funding of nonqualified plans (nondeductible because they allow discrimination, i.e., non-inclusion of employees other than the business owner) will not be reported on the partnership income tax return. The existence of such a plan may be disclosed in the reconciliation of tax and book income shown on Schedule M-1 on Page 5 of the partnership tax return or as a partnership asset. If business records are properly maintained, the nonqualified plan balances should appear on the business balance sheet as an asset.

The contribution made to a partner's Keogh plan may in some cases be considered a proper reduction in arriving at income for support in temporary support hearings, the rationale being that in the short run, the partner is unable to alter the status quo. However, in permanent support circumstances, the amount of a partner's discretion and control over the continued existence of the plan will dictate whether it is appropriate to reduce the spouse's income for the annual contribution. Generally, the ability and control to terminate the plan without serious negative tax consequences suggests that contributions to the plan should not reduce income because it is not a reasonable and necessary business expense but only a personal choice on how to invest business profits.

Whether a partner can or will terminate a plan is a question of facts and circumstances. Minority partners may not have enough control over partnership decision making to do so. Partners who have the power to do so may be unwilling to terminate the plan because of their commitment to the employees of the partnership. Factors such as these must be considered when assessing whether contributions to the retirement plan should be considered as additional income available for support.

LINE 19: EMPLOYEE BENEFIT PROGRAMS Employee benefit programs are in addition to any retirement contributions reported on Line 18. Employee benefits include life and health insurance, dental insurance, and dependent care assistance programs. If employee benefits are claimed, a careful investigation should be made to determine whether the partnership is benefiting from these payments or if non-employee friends or relatives are in collusion to divert funds. In other words, this category of expense provides an opportunity to disguise personal expenditures as a business expense.

A partner's share of benefits, such as health insurance, is a "pass-through" item that appears directly on the partner's K-1 and is reported in appropriate places on the partner's individual income tax return.

LINE 20: OTHER DEDUCTIONS The total of all other deductible expenses for which no room has been allocated on Page 1 of Form 1065 is entered on this line. On the Dealmaker & Codehead return, there is a reference "See Statement 1." The statement contains a detailed listing of expenses by category.

The expense categories that may be included in other deductions are numerous and vary with the partnership's business activity *and often contain perquisites.* Examples of "Other Deductions" that frequently contain perquisites are presented in the following.

Analysis of partnership general ledgers can be very useful in spotting "perks" (perquisites or personal expense items). Some general ledgers contain complete details of all payees receiving partnership checks. Most businesses have computerizing their accounting. Computerization facilitates the inspection of account detail in a general ledger. If the payees listed in an account do not appear proper, investigation of underlying supporting documentation, such as canceled checks and vendor's invoices, merits consideration. Forensic accountants should be consulted to verify that the computerized financial records fairly reflect the transactional activity shown in the computerized accounting.

Automobile Expenses are frequently overstated both in terms of amount and degree of personal use involved. In either case, the actual business-related auto expenses should be investigated.

Overstated auto expenses or the cost of the personal use portion of the auto(s) are among the most common perquisites found on partnership tax returns. Inquiry of the partner/spouse, either through interview or deposition, is mandatory discovery for perquisite analysis where the amounts involved are material. The nature of the business activity should dovetail with the partner's explanations. Where such is not the case, forensic accountants frequently estimate a reasonable business use percentage based on discussions with a spouse or someone else who can testify as a percipient witness on this issue.

Insurance Expense is another account that frequently contains perquisites such as personal life insurance, in which one or more partners, or the partnership, is the beneficiary. Personal life insurance premium payments are not deductible; however, this expense is often found "buried" in the insurance expense. Another personal expense that may be included in insurance expense is automobile insurance on personal vehicles used only partially for business. To the extent that any insurance payments charged to the partnership personally benefit a partner, that "perk" should be included in the partner's income when determining earning capacity.

Inspection of insurance policies may reveal information regarding assets not otherwise disclosed. Liability riders on such items as artwork and special equipment may be uncovered through this process.

Legal or professional fees paid in connection with marital dissolution matters are not deductible by the partnership. If, through collusion of the partners, one partner's divorce-related professional fees and/or costs are paid and deducted by the partnership, the amount is considered a perk. Forensic accounting fees may also be treated in the same way. Comparing the current year's legal and professional fees expense with the amount shown in prior years' tax returns may disclose a significant variance. The larger the variance, the more probable the possibility of perquisites paid on behalf of the partner.

Office expenses or supplies are convenient slots to bury a multitude of personal expenses. The materiality of the amount should first be determined before undertaking a thorough investigation. Typically, a brief analysis of the company's general ledger and journals may indicate whether an in-depth investigation is warranted. Payments to "cash" are often found in this category.

Travel, meals, and entertainment are other deduction categories in which personal expenditures may be hidden. It is common practice for forensic accountants to investigate the charges to this account for the existence of perquisites. The process usually includes the examination of supporting documentation, such as credit card statements and expense reports, in conjunction with interviews with and/or deposition testimony of the partner/spouse. The relationship of the underlying business activity, or lack thereof, associated with the "Travel and Entertainment" expenditures is the pivotal element in determining personal versus business expenses. To the extent that these expenses are overstated, conclusions as to the value of the enterprise and income available for support are understated.

If a partner flies extensively for business reasons, significant frequent flyer mileage credits may have accumulated. Mileage summaries can be discovered and the mileage credits divided as a community asset.

Note that under current tax law, only 50% of meals and entertainment expense may be deducted. If the facts are that 100% of the expense is legitimately incurred for business purposes, a reduction in a partner's income for his or her pro rata share of the non-deductible 50% is in order.

Line 21: Total Deductions In a partnership, this summary line represents only a part of all the deductible expenses related to partnership activity. As cited above, many deductions are "flow-through" in nature and appear only on the K-1s. Other deductions may relate to rental or farm activity and appear only in supporting schedules.

In looking for perquisites, all schedules on the return containing deductions require inspection.

Line 22: Ordinary Income (Loss) The amount of income or loss is the starting point for the analysis of profitability. Reference should also be made to Page 4 when assessing income because that page generally contains additional income or expense items that do not appear on Page 1 because the tax law requires special treatment for those items.

Adjustments to income for perquisites and other items needed to restate income on a representative basis result in an opinion of "true profitability," the profit concept used for valuation and income analyses. Historical analysis of true profitability is mandatory for valuation purposes under IRS Revenue Ruling 59-60. Revenue Ruling 59-60 contains a thorough explanation of all factors and considerations necessary and appropriate for valuation of closely held businesses. Familiarity with the contents of this Revenue Ruling is essential for valuation experts.

Ordinary income or loss is shared by each of the partners on the basis of their contractual profit and loss percentages. If partners actively participate in the partnership business, their allocated amount of income is subject to "Self-Employment Tax." The "Self-Employment Tax" consists of a social security tax element and a "Medicare Tax" element and is reported on Schedule SE of the individual's income tax return. A ceiling exists on the amount of income subject to the self-employment social security tax of 12.4%, but there is no cap on the self-employment Medicare tax of 2.9%. In 2022, the cap on income subject to the self-employment social security tax of 12.4% is $147,000 ($160,200 in 2023). There is also an additional .9% assessed for higher income individuals ($250,000 for joint returns, $200,000 for single and head of household status and $125,000 for married filing separately). The end result for those partners earning in excess of the cap, is that once the cap is reached, the individual will have the portion previously earmarked for these taxes available for other expenditures. This should be taken into consideration when preparing budgets and setting support orders.

Income from self-employment can be reduced by a loss from another partnership, business, or farm owned and actively operated by the taxpayer. The amount of self-employment tax may be reduced if the partner is also receiving wages subject to FICA. Paying more social security tax than is required of such an individual is avoided in this manner. If the wages are in excess of the 2022 cap of $147,000 ($160,200 in 2023) for social security, no additional social security tax from business income is computed on Schedule SE of the individual income tax return.

SCHEDULE B: OTHER INFORMATION

Line 1: Type of Entity Three types of partnerships are the most common in family law matters: the general partnership, the limited partnership, and the limited liability company.

A general partnership is one in which all partners are personally liable for partnership debts.

In a limited partnership, only the general partner(s) are personally liable for partnership debts. The limited partners are not at risk beyond their investment.

The Limited Liability Company (LLC) is taxed like a partnership but, pursuant to the state statutes under which the LLC was formed, the partners or members may not be personally liable for the debts of the LLC.

Lines 2 and 3: Ownership and Subsidiary Ownership Obfuscation of ownership interests and complexity in business relationships result when multilevel partnership interests exist. To illustrate, an individual spouse may be a partner in a partnership that is the general partner for a limited partnership that invests in other partnerships. When such complexity exist, organization charts may be helpful to explain business structure to clients and judges.

Line 4: Requirements for Right to Omit Page 5 Information If a partnership has gross receipts of less than $250,000, has assets less than $1,000,000, and files its return on a timely basis, Page 5 of Form 1065 need not be submitted. Page 5 contains the balance sheets for the current and prior year-ends. It also contains a reconciliation of taxable income and financial statement income. Finally, it provides a schedule for the reconciliation of the partners' capital accounts the prior year's balance.

If the partnership is not required to file Page 4, valuable information for marital dissolution proceedings is omitted. The situation calls for greater examination of accounting records to determine the value of a spouse's partnership interest.

Line 5: Publicly Traded Partnerships Some partnerships are traded in the same way as publicly held corporations. Where such an interest is a marital asset, either a division in kind or the sale of the interest may constitute practical options for property division. Use of these alternatives will generally obviate the need for an appraisal of the interest by an expert because market value can be readily ascertained from recent sales data.

Line 6: Debt Forgiveness Cancellation or forgiveness of debt is considered taxable income. Whether such forgiveness affects a partner/spouse's income is a question of facts and circumstances. If the partnership was unable or unwilling to service the debt prior to the forgiveness or cancellation there should be no effect on income. An analysis of the actual debt service for the year may disclose what adjustments to income, if any, are required to arrive at representative income for the period.

Line 7: Material Advisor Disclosure Statement Abuses regarding deductibility of certain expenses in the 1980s led to tax reform laws that focused the IRS's attention on partnerships that come under the definition of tax shelters. Generally, a tax shelter is an investment in which individual partners obtain a write-off of their capital investment in a greater than two to one ratio. Tax liability stemming from IRS recalculation of tax due from partners who were involved in such investments in prior years has surfaced as a common marital liability in recent years. This liability is often referred to as "Phantom Income." Where a final determination of liability is pending, reservation of jurisdiction is generally maintained until final disposition of the matter.

Form 8918 was created in 2007 to enhance IRS oversight of tax shelter abuses and requires the partnership to disclose the names of persons who provided paid advice to partnerships in connection with certain tax reduction activities.

Line 8: Foreign Bank Accounts An answer of "Yes" here should alert lawyers to the possibility of diversion of funds. The transactional activity in the foreign bank account should be thoroughly analyzed to ascertain that funds have not been diverted for personal use or investment. See further explanation in comments for Line 16.

Line 9: Foreign Trust Discussion of related topics at Line 10 are relevant as well to foreign trusts. Greater scrutiny is usually a good strategy when foreign transactional activity exists.

Line 11: Distributions or Contributions of Like-Kind Exchange Property Property acquired in "like-kind" exchanges usually have a lower tax basis than other real property acquisitions. The lower tax basis gives rise to a higher taxable gain on the sale of such property. The IRS requires disclosure of the disposition of this type of property. Knowledge of tax basis is essential to property division between spouses. Seemingly equal divisions of property may be economically unequal if both spouses receive property that ostensibly have equal fair market values but where the tax bases are materially different.

Line 12: Distributions or a Tenancy-in-Common or Other Undivided Interest in Partnership Property An answer of "Yes" to this question means that the partnership distributed to its partners undivided interests in property owned by the partnership. Often, such a transaction is followed by a 1031 tax-free exchange of such property.

LINE 13: INFORMATION FOR U.S. PERSONS WITH RESPECT TO FOREIGN DISREGARDED ENTITIES An answer of "Yes" here should alert lawyers to the possibility of diversion of funds. The transactional activity in a foreign country should be thoroughly analyzed to ascertain that funds have not been diverted for personal use or investment. See further explanation in comments for Line 16.

LINE 14: FOREIGN PARTNERS An entry here should alert the reader to a possible diversion of funds outside the country. Partnership activity with the foreign partner may require extensive analysis. The inspection of that partner's personal records might be needed to ascertain that all income is properly stated on the partnership tax return.

Business activity abroad provides another possibility for hiding income. The impracticality and cost of performing discovery require creativity in dealing with this situation. Foreign forensic accountants may be used to help prepare appraisals of and income analyses for foreign branches of the partnership. If the matter proceeds to trial, the foreign accountant may have to appear to present his or her opinion. The payment of the foreign accountant's travel expenses may require a cost-benefit analysis in these circumstances.

LINE 15: INFORMATION FOR U.S. PERSONS WITH RESPECT TO CERTAIN FOREIGN PARTNERSHIPS An answer of "Yes" here should alert lawyers to the possibility of diversion of funds. The transactional activity in a foreign country should be thoroughly analyzed to ascertain that funds have not been diverted for personal use or investment. See further explanation in comments for Line 16.

LINE 16: FORM 1099 INFORMATION The most common Form 1099 issued by small business is the Form 1099-Misc. that is typically issued to independent contractors paid more than $600 during the tax year. A review of the persons to whom such payments are made can be obtained from a detailed general ledger. Scrutiny of the names shown and the purpose of the payment may result in discovery of personal expenditures listed as business expenses.

LINE 18: PARTNERS WHO ARE FOREIGN GOVERNMENTS Line 18 is a relatively new addition to the partnership questionnaire but generally has no relevance to family law.

DESIGNATED TAX MATTERS PARTNER

One partner, usually the general partner in a limited partnership, is designated as the "Tax Matters Partner." This partner represents all other partner with respect to judicial or administrative matters with the IRS.

Page 4: Schedule K: Partners' Distributive Shares Items

The primary purpose of this page is to disclose certain income and expense items that require special tax treatment by the partners. All line items on this page correlate to the same line items on each of the partners' individual K-1s. See the portion of this chapter dealing with K-1s for more explanatory comments on partners' distributive share items.

Page 5: Analysis of Net Income (Loss)

This section is purely informational for the IRS. The amount of income or loss allocated to the different types of legal entities that are partners is enumerated in this section.

Page 5: Schedule L: Balance Sheets Per Books

The opening and closing assets and liabilities of the partnership, and the related supporting schedules, are reflected in balance sheet section of the return. The partners' capital accounts, equal to the difference between assets and liabilities, is also shown on Schedule L.

The balance sheet is frequently the starting point for appraising a partnership interest. In most cases, the value of the partner/spouse's interest is based partially on the fair market value of assets and the stated amount of the liabilities shown on the balance sheet.

Because assets are stated at historical cost, which is frequently not the same as fair market value, forensic accountants and other business appraisers must adjust assets using marketplace factors. Unrealized appreciation in the value of assets is not recognized on the partnership return except when an asset is sold. At that point, the appreciation is transformed into recognizable gain. Such gains, whether capital or not, are passed through to the individual shareholders.

ASSETS

LINE 1: CASH Very little adjustment is generally required for this asset. Bank reconciliation worksheets are standard supporting documentation. The financial statements of the partnership, if any, may provide additional detail as to the location of the institutions at which funds are maintained.

Unusually high accumulations of cash may impact both income and valuation. From an income perspective, the accumulation may deprive the spouse of current disposable income from which to pay support. Whether or not the accumulation is a willful attempt to keep income at a minimum may be at issue.

When an unnecessarily high amount of cash is on hand, the appraiser must take this fact into consideration when preparing the business valuation. Under certain appraisal techniques, such as the "Excess Earnings Method," a return on the use of the net assets of the partnership is deducted from average earnings to arrive at the capitalizable excess earnings used to compute goodwill. Failure to adjust for excess cash will have the effect of reducing the intangible value (goodwill) of the partnership computed under the excess earnings method.

LINE 2A AND B: ACCOUNTS RECEIVABLE LESS ALLOWANCE FOR BAD DEBTS Accounts receivable is an important asset of many partnerships. If the partnership reports on an accrual basis, an entry will be found on these lines. The allowance for bad debt is deducted from the receivables. The fair market value of the accounts receivable is known as its "net realizable value." Analysis of the underlying accounts is essential for this determination. The net accounts receivable shown on partnership tax returns often do not represent net realizable value because of limitations imposed by tax law.

Cash basis partnerships may also have accounts receivable, even though no reference is made to them on the partnership return. Professional practice partnerships are the most common examples of cash basis partnerships with accounts receivable.

Determination of fair market value of accounts receivable requires a reasonable estimate of collectability. An estimate may be obtained by testing subsequent receipts in order to ascertain how much of the receivables were actually collected over time. In cases where insufficient time has elapsed to perform such testing, estimates based on past experience must be used. An "aging" of the receivables into 30-, 60-, 90-, 120-; and over 120-day groups provide guidance in repairing such estimates. Most businesses maintain aging analyses on a monthly basis.

Sometimes the accounts receivable valuation is not easily accomplished because of the unique nature of the underlying business. Examples include personal injury lawyers representing plaintiffs, criminal defense lawyers, and orthodontists.

Personal injury lawyers typically have no accounts receivable; however, a similar asset known as work in progress amounts to somewhat the same thing from a marital dissolution perspective. A detailed analysis of the disposition of cases begun during marriage must be undertaken to compute the marital interest in the funds received from those cases that result in the collection of contingent fees. The methods used to arrive at value are beyond the scope of this text but, needless to say, much creativity is required to make such an analysis persuasive.

The law partnership that specializes in criminal defense is an example of a practice that will typically contain accounts receivable at a negative value. The negative accounts receivable are liabilities that accountants refer to as "Unearned Revenue." Criminal defense practitioners generally require the fee for their services to be paid either wholly or partially in advance. The fee is then earned with future services. As in the case of work in progress of personal injury attorneys, calculation of unearned revenue requires creativity and a thorough understand of the underlying business activity.

Often associated with accounts receivable of cash basis partnerships is the calculation by a forensic CPA of a "Deferred Income Tax Liability." The partner receiving a share of these receivables post-separation will have to pay tax on them when received. Recognition of this fact requires the calculation of the deferred tax liability.

Because the partnership is a "pass-through" type entity, deferred income taxes must be calculated for cash basis partnerships as well in order not to overstate the value of the partner's interest. The pass-through nature of the entity eliminates the need for a partnership to provide for income taxes on earned revenue (unlike corporation who are required to do so under generally accepted accounting principles).

Line 3: Inventories Relevant documentation for intensive research and analysis of this account is usually readily available when the year-end for which ending inventory is determined is close to the date of the appraisal is performed. If an actual inventory count is taken, copies of the supporting detail should be obtained and reviewed. The procedures employed to make the count should be analyzed. Less analysis of procedures and valuation methodology is required if the taking of the inventory was observed by certified public accountants in conjunction with a certified audit.

Unreported sale of inventory ("Inventory going out the back door") during the post-separation period is a frequent allegation made by non-partner spouses. Testing of gross profit ratios with industry percentages and against prior years' percentages for the partnership may support such allegations. Testing mark-up percentages against gross profit is another tool available in some cases to spot irregularities in inventory value.

The method by which inventory is valued may significantly affect the partnership valuation. Inventories are frequently undervalued in order to report lower taxable profit. Greater motivation to manipulate inventory exists in divorce cases because lower profitability from lower inventory benefits the partner/spouse via a lower business valuation and less income available for support.

Inventory valuation methods are important factors in determining the appropriate amount of inventory. The method must conform to the best accounting practice in the particular trade or business. "Cost" means that the inventory is valued at the price paid. "Lower of cost or market" compares the cost of inventory, on an item by item basis, to the respective market value. The lower of the two values is used.

LIFO (last-in, first-out) and FIFO (first-in, first-out) are terms often used in connection with inventory valuation. If a LIFO method of costing inventory is used in an inflationary period, book value will tend to be understated. The FIFO method of costing inventory provides a more accurate representation of actual market value of the inventory because ending inventory is "costed" by reference to the most recent purchases of inventory.

Any changes in inventory accounting between prior years and the year of separation and subsequent period should be carefully investigated. Unusually large negative adjustments to inventory also warrant investigation.

Line 4: U.S. Government Obligations The IRS requires identification of assets held in this form. Investment interest income on U.S. government obligations should be accrued at the valuation date to insure that the full value of the partnership interest is calculated.

Line 5: Tax-Exempt Securities As in the case of U.S. government obligations, the IRS requires identification of assets held in this form. Interest from tax-exempt securities is reported on Line 19 of the K-1. While not taxable for federal income tax, the amount may represent additional income available to the partners.

Additional asset value may be uncovered through a calculation of interest and/or dividend income receivable for earnings that should have been accrued on these investments.

Line 6: Other Current Assets Other current assets are usually listed by type and amount on supporting schedules attached to the tax return. Typical examples of other current assets are loans to employees, prepaid expenses, and marketable securities.

Analysis of these assets may disclose that they are undervalued. Marketable securities that have appreciated will require an upward adjustment from historical to fair market value. The brokerage statement(s) at year-end should contain the appropriate fair market value information.

A review of the rent, taxes and insurance accounts in the general ledger may reveal that certain expenses have been paid for in advance. January rent for the following year paid in December of the current year is an example of an expense that causes an understatement of annual income and income unless consistently done for the last few years.

Line 7a: Loans to Partner (or Persons Related to Partnery) The line item is self-explanatory.

Line 7b: Mortgage and Real Estate Loans Secured loans frequently result from the sale of partnership real estate. Research concerning the origin of the loan may lead to useful discovery. It may be important for the forensic accountant to investigate the propriety of the disposition of prior assets owned by the partnership.

Interest income should be compared with the outstanding loan balance(s) to ascertain that all income has been reported and collections have been properly deposited to the partnership.

The collectability of the loans needs to be ascertained for valuation purposes. For example, a potential bad debt, not recognized for tax purposes until the asset is deemed completely or partially worthless, will nevertheless reduce the fair market value of the loan.

Another valuation adjustment is appropriate if the loan interest rate is either well below or above current market. Just as in the case of corporate bonds, the value of the loans will be a function of how the stated interest compares to market interest.

Line 8: Other Investments Investments in other partnerships or corporations are the most common types of assets in this category. The values indicated on the partnership balance sheet often do not reflect fair market value for these investments.

Where an investment in another enterprise is a significant partnership asset, a separate appraisal of the other entity may be required in order to arrive at fair market value of the partnership interest therein.

Line 9a and b: Building and Other Depreciable Assets Less Accumulated Depreciation As stated previously, historical cost is the basis for the amounts shown for assets. Consequently, capitalized real and personal property is presented at original cost. Annual depreciation expense taken is deducted from the cost to arrive at the "Book Value" of the fixed asset. Because depreciation expense is governed by tax guidelines, not actual asset deterioration and obsolescence, book value of fixed assets is usually not equal to fair market value.

Adjustment of fixed assets to fair market value is one of the most common appraisal procedures. Real estate is often restated to market based on an appraisal of the property performed by a real property expert. Automobiles are restated pursuant to "Blue Book" values. The value of other assets (equipment, machinery, furniture, and furnishings) may also be restated pursuant to appraisals prepared by experts.

The amount of cost and effort put into the restating of capital assets is a subjective determination depending on facts and circumstances. The materiality of the restatement involved is the primary factor considered. Like many other decisions made in marital dissolution proceedings, the cost and benefit of the additional appraisals need to be assessed by the lawyer, the client and forensic accountant.

General ledger expense accounts, such as "Repairs and Maintenance," "Computer Expense," and "Office Expense" may contain payments for assets that should have been capitalized. Failure to restate these items as capital expenditures will understate assets. Income will also be understated when capital expenditures are charged to expense.

Line 10a and b: Depletable Assets Less Accumulated Depletion Like depreciation, depletion deductions for natural resources are often not representative of the actual exhaustion of the resource. The fair market value of the remaining reserves should be determined where practical and meaningful to the spouses involved in the divorce. Thus, if the interest of the marital estate is relatively small, and the cost of determining value of the resource substantial, book value may be the most practical value to use. If the interest is material, an expert may be hired to provide an opinion of value.

Line 11: Land Land is not a depreciable asset; however, costs incurred to acquire land, such as prepaid interest ("Points"), are amortized (deducted over time) rather than entirely expensed in the year paid even if the partnership is on a cash basis.

Like other fixed assets, land is recorded at historical cost. Restating land to fair market value is a common appraisal adjustment that only affects valuation of the partnership interest. Adjustments to land value will not change income unless an installment sale of the land is imminent. Annual installment payments would ordinarily be treated as a continuing source of cash to the partnership.

Line 12a and b: Intangibles Assets Less Accumulated Amortization Amortization, like depreciation, refers to the deductibility of certain capital expenditures or organizational costs ratably over time. The primary difference between amortization and depreciation is the nature of the capital expenditures to which amortization applies. Examples of amortization have already been mentioned, i.e., depletion and capitalized interest. Other kinds of capital expenditures subject to amortization include "Leasehold Improvements," "Business Start-up Costs," "Pollution Control Facilities," and intangible assets.

The most well-known intangible asset in family law is "Goodwill." The calculation of goodwill in connection with the preparation of a business appraisal is common practice. For tax purposes and under generally accepted accounting principles, "Goodwill" appears on the balance sheet only when it is purchased. The difference between the price paid for a business and the fair market value of the tangible assets and other intangibles purchased is goodwill. Acquired goodwill may be amortized over a 15-year period under Internal Revenue Code Section 197.

If amortization of intangibles appears on the partnership balance sheet, the origin of the asset should be investigated. Understanding the nature and cost of the asset will determine how it should be handled in a marital dissolution appraisal. The purchase price paid for goodwill may also represent a comparable sale that may be relevant evidence of value of certain or all assets of the partnership.

Certain intangibles have no independent market value and are generally embodied in the calculation of goodwill. Examples included covenants not to compete, patents, copyrights, and licenses. Rights such as these are generally incorporated into the concept of appraised goodwill. Rarely will independent calculation of the value of intangibles other than goodwill appear in a business appraisal.

Line 13: Other Assets Non-current assets for which no line item has been provided on the balance sheet are generally listed on supporting schedules whose total is carried to this line. Examples of other assets include "Deposits," and "Notes Receivable."

Although improper for tax reporting, it is common practice for cash basis partnerships to deduct lease deposits and utility deposits. The value of a partnership will be understated unless these costs are listed as assets. Examination of relevant underlying documentation, such as facilities leases, will usually disclose the amount of the deposit.

Other assets often found listed in this section are secured and unsecured notes receivable. Secured and unsecured promissory notes are stated at historical cost for tax purposes. No reduction in value is permitted under tax law unless the note becomes worthless. These instruments need to be restated to fair market value for appraisal purposes. The most common factors evaluated by experts when determining fair market value of notes receivable are the implicit interest rates in comparison to market rates, the credit-worthiness of the borrower, and the underlying collateral. Use of these factors as a basis for comparison with notes traded in the marketplace may allow forensic accountants to estimate appraisal values.

Line 14: Total Assets Summation of all of the assets appears here for both the current and prior year-ends. This amount is also shown on Page 1, Box F. Total assets should equal total liabilities and capital.

LIABILITIES AND CAPITAL

Line 15: Accounts Payable Accrual basis partnerships enter the amounts due vendors at fiscal year-end here. No entry will usually appear on this line for cash basis partnerships.

Accounts payable for cash basis partnerships is determined by reviewing payments to vendors made after year-end. All payments for goods and services purchased during the tax year but not yet paid for represent the accounts payable of the partnership.

Failure to compute the accounts payable results in an overstatement of the value of the partnership interest.

Line 16: Mortgages, Notes, Bonds Payable in Less Than One Year The short-term portion of these liabilities is presented here. Further investigation of the books and records of the partnership is usually required in order to ascertain the nature and scope of these liabilities.

Please refer to the discussion of Line 19 for additional information about analyzing this liability.

Line 17: Other Current Liabilities Accrued expenses, payroll taxes payable, and unpaid retirement plan contributions are examples of other current liabilities. Accuracy of the accruals may be ascertained by examination of the pension plan contribution calculations and payroll tax returns.

Accrued expenses reflect the amount of overhead that has been incurred but is unpaid at year-end. Unpaid telephone and utility bills are common examples of expenses that may be accrued. Proper valuation procedures require inclusion of such liabilities. Cash basis income is generally unaffected by these expenses because the actual outflow of cash will occur in a future period.

Unearned income and deferred income taxes are current liabilities that do not appear on cash basis balance sheets but need to be considered in many business appraisals. Unearned income results from advances (e.g., retainers for lawyers) from clients or customers for which consideration has not yet been given.

Deferred income taxes exist when a tax is accrued in the current period that will have to be paid in later years. In divorce cases, the most common type of deferred income tax is associated with the addition of accounts receivable to the adjusted appraisal balance sheet of cash basis partnerships. Calculation of the amount of the deferred income tax is often at issue. To be persuasive, forensic accountants need to have reasonable support for the tax rates employed in their deferred income tax calculations. The effective individual income tax rate of the spouse for the same year is usually a reasonable basis for calculation.

Line 18: All Nonrecourse Loans Loans for which there is no personal liability are known as "Nonrecourse Indebtedness." Under the terms of such loans, the lender looks only to the secured property or collateral for repayment. Partners are not deemed "at risk" with respect to nonrecourse debt. Determination of liability under nonrecourse obligations should be made with reference to specific facts and circumstances.

Sometimes, a division in kind of the partnership interest appears most practical under the circumstances. Advising a client to agree to an equal division of the partnership without a complete knowledge of the client's exposure, both to third parties and the IRS, may be construed as negligence. Attorneys would be wise to obtain opinion letters from tax experts or others to provide more guidance on nonrecourse liability exposure in order to provide their clients with the assurance that such liability is not recourse liability.

The amount to which the partner is at risk limits the amount of deductible loss available. Generally, a partner's share of partnership loss is limited to the amount of cash contributed by the partner, the adjusted basis of property contributed, the amount of partnership borrowing for which the partner is personally liable, and a pro rata allocation of qualified non-recourse debt.

Line 19a: Loans from Partners The line item is self-explanatory.

Line 19b: Mortgages, Notes, Bonds Payable in More Than One Year The long-term portion of such liabilities is presented here. Further investigation of the books and records of the partnership is usually required in order to ascertain the nature and scope of these liabilities.

The accuracy and authenticity of long-term liabilities need to be analyzed in the appraisal process. Liabilities may be inaccurate if the interest and principal on loan payments have not been allocated properly. The authenticity of liabilities may be suspect in some instances, e.g., liabilities to relatives who do not demand payment and have never received payment.

Certain liabilities may not be included on partnership balance sheets for tax purposes. Examples include liabilities under lease obligations and legal liability that has not been adjudicated. Such liabilities may reduce the value of the partnership interest even if the amount of the ultimate liability cannot be ascertained.

If a partnership is liable on a lease even though it has moved out of a facility or no longer uses the original leased asset, the liability under the lease should be computed at present value for appraisal purposes. Failure to reduce value for such liability overstates the value of the partnership interest.

Line 20: Other Liabilities Long-term liabilities are presented in supporting schedules and the total is shown on this line. The amount presented reflects unsecured liabilities that may not have to be paid in the next fiscal year. Examples of other liabilities are the obligation to pay for goods or services under long-term contracts, and warranty liability for partnerships engaged in manufacturing.

Understanding the nature of the enterprise is essential to locating all possible liabilities. Exploration of this area with the managing partner through interview or deposition is advisable.

Line 21: Partners' Capital Accounts The sum of the individual partner's capital account balances at year-end appears on this line. The partners' capital is synonymous with net book value. The amount should conform to the balance shown on Schedule M-2, "Analysis of Partners' Capital Accounts." More on partners' capital is presented in the following.

Line 22: Total Liabilities and Capital The amount shown here should equal the total assets shown on Line 14 and Box F on Page 1.

Schedule M-1: Reconciliation of Income (Loss) per Books With Income (Loss) per Return (note that Schedule M-3 may be required for large partnerships)

LINE 1: NET INCOME (LOSS) PER BOOKS The profit or loss shown on a partnership's financial statements (books) is entered on this line. Financial statements of the partnership will usually show a different partnership profit or loss than the tax return because of timing differences in the recording of income and expense and the fact that certain book expense items are not deducted in arriving at partnership taxable income.

LINE 2: INCOME INCLUDED ON SCHEDULE K, LINES 1, 2, 3c, 6a, 7, 8, 9a, 10, AND 11 NOT RECORDED ON BOOKS THIS YEAR Entries in this category should be investigated to determine which presentation is more appropriate for valuation and income purposes. An example of an item that would appear here is the amount of advance payments received from customers for goods and services.

LINE 3: GUARANTEED PAYMENTS (OTHER THAN HEALTH INSURANCE) Partners who, under the terms of the partnership agreement or other written agreements, are guaranteed a certain amount of draw irrespective of their income or loss sharing percentages are said to receive guaranteed payments. Guaranteed payments are deducted in arriving at partnership taxable income. If they are not deducted on financial statements as an expense, the amount appears as a reconciliation item in this section.

The guaranteed payments made to a spouse/partner should be considered as income available in addition to any share of profits that are distributed. More discussion of this area is presented in the section on K-1s.

LINE 4: EXPENSES RECORDED ON BOOKS THIS YEAR NOT INCLUDED ON SCHEDULE K, LINES 1 THROUGH 13d AND 16l The two most common types of expenses of this kind are "Depreciation" and "Travel and Entertainment."

Accelerated depreciation taken in prior years' tax returns may result in more depreciation per books than for tax in the current year because assets may have been entirely depreciated for tax purposes and not fully depreciated for financial statement purposes. Amounts shown here may indicate that depreciation expense should be added back to income to arrive at true income for the partnership.

Under current tax rules, only 50% of business-related meals expenses are deductible for tax purposes (note that with the passage of the Tax Cut and Jobs Act in 2017 business entertainment is no longer deductible). Also note that for tax years 2021 and 2022, a special COVID provision allows a 100% deduction for meals purchased from a restaurant. However, 100% of these expenses are deducted for financial statement profit; accordingly, a reconciliation of this expense is always necessary when it exists. Travel expenses may also differ on financial statements because of a variety of statutory tax limitations. The type of limitation will depend on the nature of the expense. Generally, reasonable and necessary business-related travel expenses are deductible. Amounts shown here suggest the possibility of perquisites. Personal travel deducted by a partnership is common.

LINE 6: INCOME RECORDED ON BOOKS THIS YEAR NOT INCLUDED ON SCHEDULE K, LINES 1 THROUGH 11 Tax-exempt interest is the most common example of book income excluded from taxation. This income should be included in computing representative income. Existence of such income should alert the reader to tax-exempt investments owned by the partnership.

LINE 7: DEDUCTIONS INCLUDED ON SCHEDULE K, LINES 1 THROUGH 13d AND 16l, NOT CHARGED AGAINST BOOK INCOME THIS YEAR Depreciation is the most prominent example of this kind of expense. MACRS and other forms of accelerated depreciation allowed for tax purposes can result in tax depreciation being larger than depreciation on the books.

Depletion is another expense that can be higher for tax than on the financial statements.

LINE 9: INCOME (LOSS) The amount arrived at through the reconciliation should match line 1 of the Analysis of Net Income (Loss) Per Return at the top of Page 5 This is the total taxable income of the partnership from the various categories shown on Schedule K.

Schedule M-2: Analysis of Partners' Capital Accounts

The reconciliation of year-end partners' capital with beginning partners' capital is the primary purpose of this section. Capital contributions and distributions made by the partnership during the year are elements of this analysis. Any increases or decreases in capital other than capital contributions, distributions to partners, financial statement income may affect income and valuation. For example, the admission of new partners may affect profit and loss as well as equity percentage ownership of the partner/spouse. Such a change may be reflected in this section.

Schedule K-1: Partner's Share of Income, Credits, Deductions, Etc.

As stated previously, the partnership does not pay tax itself. The tax liability arising from partnership income flows through to the individual partners' tax returns. The K-1 is the vehicle through which this flow-through is accomplished.

The K-1 provides abundant information concerning an individual partner's interest in the partnership. It is generally the most important document for computing income from the partnership to the partner. The partners' K-1s for a few years should be examined to observe changes in percentages of profit sharing and equity. An analysis of prior years' capital and distributions may also affect reasonable estimates of future income and may impact upon an opinion of value for the partnership interest.

Each K-1 includes the name and identification number (social security number if the partner is an individual) of a partner and the partnership. A partner's pro rata share of the taxable income or loss generated by the partnership is disclosed on the K-1. The K-1 amounts are then reported on either a personal income tax return, corporate tax return or fiduciary tax return (for estates and trusts).

PART I: LINES A TO D Basic partnership information is entered in this section. The IRS center where the return is filed will vary with the location in which the partnership activity takes place. The designation "e-file" usually appears to denote the electronic filing of the tax return that may be the most common manner in which such returns are filed.

Publicly traded partnerships (PTP) are traded in the same way as publicly held corporations. As a result, market value can usually be readily ascertained from recent sales data. Special rules apply to losses from these entities. The delineation of the PTP on the K-1 exists because tax losses from a PTP may not be used to offset income from another PTP or another passive activity.

PART II: LINES E TO I Information about the type of partner is shown this section. A general partner is a partner who is personally liable for partnership debts.

A limited partner is not at risk for partnership debts beyond his or her investment.

A member of a Limited Liability Company (LLC) may not be personally liable for the debts of the partnership. This type of partnership is taxed like a partnership but treated like a corporation with respect to personal liability of the partners.

A partner may be an individual, a corporation, another partnership, an estate, or a trust. Knowledge of this fact assists in understanding complex business arrangements. Organization charts are often helpful for illustrating complex ownership schemes.

A foreign partnership interest creates a need for more scrutiny of partnership activity. Hidden assets in foreign accounts are more probable when one of the partners is a foreign national.

Part II: Line J Partner's share of profit, loss, and capital indicate percentages at the beginning and end of the year that denote changes that have occurred in the partner's partnership interest. Difference in beginning and ending percentages require investigation.

If profit and loss percentage has increased, there may have been a change in the number of partners or merely in the allocation between partners. Changes in the number of partners may or may not affect future income to the partner/spouse. Changes in percentage allocation usually have a material impact on a partner's income.

Partnership agreements generally control the percentages of profit and loss, and percentage of the partnership equity. Note that IRS rules generally do not allow for assignment of income such that allocations of profit and loss must generally follow any allocations of cash and property distributed. In other words, allocations of profit and loss must have economic substance. Instances frequently arise in family law matters in which no written agreements concerning these percentages exist. Under these circumstances, prior years' tax returns and other financial data need to be examined to determine how much of the profits and losses have been allocated to the partners. Correlation between diverse financial data may be the most persuasive evidence of a partner's interest. The entries in this portion of the K-1 are often the most important indicia of ownership percentages in cases where no written agreement has been created.

Line K: Partner's Share of Liabilities "Nonrecourse" loans are loans for which the partner has no personal liability. Under the terms of such loans, the lender looks only to the secured property or collateral of the partnership for repayment. Partners are not deemed "at risk" with respect to nonrecourse debt.

"Qualified nonrecourse financing" is nonrecourse debt that is borrowed from a financial institution for acquisition or improvement to real property. Such debt is permitted to be treated as an addition to basis thereby increasing the amount of loss to which a partner is entitled.

Recourse debt is debt for which the partner is personally liable. The partner's total exposure should be explored so there are all parties are informed of potential exposure.

Sometimes, a division in kind of the partnership interest appears most practical under the circumstances. Advising a client to agree to an equal division of the partnership without a complete knowledge of the client's exposure, both to third parties and the IRS, may be construed as negligence. Attorneys would be wise to obtain opinion letters from tax experts or others to provide the attorney and client with guidance in these matters.

The amount to which the partner is at risk limits the amount of deductible loss available. Generally, a partner's share of partnership loss is limited to the amount of cash contributed by the partner, the adjusted basis of property contributed, the amount of partnership borrowing for which the partner is personally liable, and a pro rata allocation of qualified nonrecourse financing.

Line L: The analysis of the partner's capital account is perhaps the most important line on the partnership tax return for family law purposes. At a glance, the reader can ascertain capital contributed during the year, allocated partnership income for the year, distributions to the partner made during the year, and the beginning and ending capital account balances.

Beginning Capital account should be the same amount as shown as ending capital on the previous year's K-1. If not, an irregularity exists that requires inquiry. The total beginning capital for all partners equals the ending capital balance shown on Page 5, Schedule L for the previous year.

Capital contributed during the year may take the form of cash or property. If property is contributed, the partner's carryover basis of the property is reported on this portion of the K-1. Complex tax rules govern gains and losses where the partner's adjusted basis (tax basis) in the property is different than fair market value.

Contributions of property should be investigated to determine character. In community property states, property may be separate, community or both. Determination of the value of the marital interest may depend on proper allocations of contributed property.

The source of cash contributions should also be identified to determine if the partner is entitled to reimbursement from the marital estate for separate property contributed to the partnership. Prior year returns should also be examined with this in mind.

Sometimes, capital contributions are made from current year's earnings. Under these circumstances, a partner's actual income may have to be adjusted to reflect the true amount of cash available from the partnership during the year. Whether the capital contribution is discretionary or not is an important element in deciding whether to consider the amount available for spousal and/or child support. Some lawyers argue that such an amount should always be considered available because the capital contribution is usually analogous to a forced savings account. Facts and circumstances in each case must be weighed to determine the propriety of deducting capital contributions from current income.

Current year increase (decrease) contains a net amount reflecting various items on the K-1 including the partner's share of income or loss items, deductions, and other non-deductible expenses or tax-free income. The components of the K-1 comprising this amount are usually more meaningful than the amount itself.

Note that on the K-1 for Mr. Herring in the Dealmaker & Codehead partnership, $173,686 appears on this line. This figure results from adding Lines 1 and then subtracting Line 12.

Withdrawals and distributions represent funds that the partner has received from the partnership during the year. Partners often refer to their distribution payments as "draws." The draw amount is often similar to the allocable partner income in service oriented partnership. It may be quite different in real estate partnerships.

What a partner receives in distributions during the year depends on the cash available during the year. Since cash may be generated from other sources than operations, (e.g., borrowing and sale of assets), instances occur when income and cash flow are not the same.

Forensic accountants preparing income analyses pay careful attention to the origin and nature of partnership distributions. In order to reflect representative income, a complete understanding of various aspect of partnership financial activity must be obtained.

Cash basis partnerships that are winding up their business activities may show more cash flow currently than in prior growth years. This anomaly occurs when a partnership is collecting accounts receivable earned in prior periods and has eliminated part or all of the cost of generating these accounts receivable, or has completely eliminated all overhead in contemplation of liquidation. In the alternative, it is not uncommon to find growth partnerships short of cash. Fixed and variable costs may be growing faster than collections. Borrowing to meet the needs of growth is often required in these situations.

Ending capital account is the change to beginning capital caused by capital contributions, current year increases or decreases, and withdrawals. The sum of all the individual K-1 capital accounts equals the partners' capital shown on the balance sheet on Page 5.

Beware of large negative capital accounts at the end of the tax year. Large negative capital accounts may signify the possibility of "phantom" gain when the partnership is liquidated. Hidden tax exposure should be researched so that a client can make prudent decisions concerning property settlement.

On the Hudson Grey Properties partnership income tax return (see Schedule L on Page 5), the ending negative capital account is $5,730. Any disposition of partnership assets, whether by foreclosure or sale of the property, will trigger a capital gain of at least $5,730 to the partners pro rata.

Line M: Did the partner contribute property with a built in gain or loss? If the answer is yes, the partner is required to attach a statement disclosing the details about the acquisition of the property and its tax basis.

PART III: PARTNER'S SHARE OF CURRENT YEAR INCOME, DEDUCTIONS, CREDITS, AND OTHER ITEMS

This section of the K-1 lists all of the pass-through items of income or loss, deductions, preference items, credits, and other pass-through tax amounts that are required for the preparation of the partner's individual tax return. Note that there are some items, like distributions, that do not flow through to the personal income tax return because there is no reporting requirement.

1. Ordinary Business Income (Loss) Ordinary business income (loss) is reported on Schedule E of the partner's individual tax return. Income from service partnerships usually reflects the partner's share of the partnership income shown on Page 1 of the return. Multiplying the partner's percentage of profit and loss by the partnership profit or loss should result in the same amount as shown on this line.

In those cases in which the partnership represents the spouse's primary work activity, a partner's share of income is a significant factor in determining income for support. The amount reflects the latest historical operating income of the business. Comparison with prior years may be helpful in establishing trends that might influence the court's decision concerning the amount of support.

Income may be passive or active depending on whether or not the partner materially participates in the business activity. If the partner does not materially participate in the production of income, losses will be considered passive. Limited partners who do not actively participate in the partnership will always report losses as passive. Passive losses may not be deductible in the current year and may have to be carried forward until some future time when either the partner is credited with a share of partnership income or the partnership interest is liquidated.

Responses to previous questions asked on the K-1 will assist the reader in determining the nature of the loss. Sometimes, passive losses do not impair income because they are generated from the use of initial capital contributions, depreciation, or borrowing. Where annual capital contributions of similar amount have consistently been made in prior years, inclusion of such an amount as a reduction of income may be appropriate.

2. Net Rental Real Estate Income (Loss) If the partnership has income or loss from rental real estate, each partner is allocated his or her share. The allocation is required because of limitations on deductibility of rental losses. Partners who actively participate in rental activity and report less than $150,000 in adjusted gross income on their personal return may be entitled to deduct up to $25,000 in losses for the year. Otherwise, rental activity is considered to be a passive activity subject to passive loss limitations.

Rental revenue and expenses are listed on supplemental schedules. Cash flow to the partnership from rental real estate is generally derived by adding depreciation back to rental income or loss and subtracting principal payments on mortgages. Depreciation information is usually provided either on the rental schedule or other supplemental schedules to the return. Whether this cash flow is relevant in calculating support paid by or to a specific partner may depend on the degree to which that partner controls his or her withdrawals from the partnership.

3. Other Net Rental Income (Loss) Rental losses generated from other than real estate rental activities are passive losses.

4. Guaranteed Payments Guaranteed payments represent separate remuneration to a partner for efforts extended on behalf of the partnership. In computing income from the partnership, the

guaranteed payments are added to the partner's other distributions from the partnership or his or her share of income or loss in some situations.

Guaranteed payments arise under various circumstances. Non-equity partners who work full time but do not have a percentage share of income often receive guaranteed payments as remuneration for services. Unlike their share of profit or loss, the guaranteed payments do not affect their capital account. Guaranteed payments may also arise as a fee for services provided in a capacity other than as a partner. In other words, guaranteed payments are special payments to a partner irrespective of that partner's share of profits and losses.

Lines 5 to 7: Interest Income, Ordinary Dividends, Qualified Dividends, and Royalties Interest, dividends, and royalties are the also known as "portfolio items." Portfolio income may not be netted against passive losses.

Portfolio income is not part of the partnership income shown on Page 1 because it is not generated from the income producing business activity of the partnership. Portfolio income should be matched with the size of investment type assets shown on the balance sheet on Page 5 of the return to see if a correlation exists. If not, examination of mid-year activity through inspection of bank statements, brokerage statements, or the general ledger of the partnership may be advisable.

Lines 8 and 9a, b, and c: Capital Gain Items: Ascertaining the nature and purpose of any dispositions of large amounts of liquid assets during the year may uncover diversions of capital made in contemplation of divorce.

Capital gains and losses are identified and explained in supporting schedules attached to the partnership return. Capital gain items usually reflect one-time sales of assets and will not represent a source of continuing income; however, certain recurring capital gains, such as those from installment sales, should be included in determining income available for support.

10. Net Section 1231 Gain (Loss) A section 1231 gain or loss generally results from the sale of business depreciable real property. Here again, the K-1 provides for splitting tax items to allow appropriate reporting in the individual returns. Section 1231 gains or losses need to be netted against other section 1231 gains and losses, not necessarily related to the partnership, on the partner's individual tax return.

11. Other Income (Loss) Other income (loss) is a designated area for pass through income not elsewhere described. Examples of income not subject to self-employment tax because the income was not generated from the business activity include insurance recovery, lawsuit settlements, and involuntary conversion proceeds.

12. Section 179 Expense Deduction Section 179 expense deduction is the election to write-off a maximum of $1,080,000 of depreciation for certain fixed assets acquired during the year (increasing to $1,160,000 in 2023 and subsequent years). Each partner may only take a pro rata share of the $1,080,000. If a partner purchases depreciable property used in other unincorporated businesses or rental activities, no more than $1,080,000 of aggregated Section 179 may be deducted on his or her personal return. Excess Section 179 deduction not allowed for the tax year may be carried forward an unlimited number of years. The partner's pro rata share of Section 179 depreciation is taken as an offset to partnership income on Schedule E of the individual income tax return.

As noted previously, depreciation must be analyzed with a view to the impact of this expense on income. Page 4 of the partnership tax return contains a balance sheet that includes a summary of the cost of depreciable property and the accumulated depreciation.

Analysis of depreciation and asset history may be provided either wholly or partially on Form 4562 and supporting schedules that are included in the return of a partnership claiming depreciation expense. Probative information concerning the assets of the business, including date of acquisition and original cost, are usually available on this form and supporting detail schedules. More asset information may be obtained from a partnership's internal depreciation schedules or the workpapers maintained by its independent certified public accounting firm.

Depreciation schedules aid in identifying assets that have been written-off but still have value. In addition to providing relevant data for determining the fair market value of the fixed assets, the depreciation schedule is also useful for evaluating claimed cash flow needs of the business for investment in new equipment.

13. Other Deductions Other deductions may relate to a number of different areas. One such area is "Deductions related to portfolio income," which are investment expenses. Margin interest and management fees related to securities portfolios are typical examples of this type of expense.

An analysis of whether the portfolio income will be the same from year to year is relevant to determining available income. An examination of the nature of and activity within the underlying portfolio should help in arriving at expected income from this source. Passive portfolios are more predictable than portfolios in which there is frequent trading activity. In most cases, the amount of passive income and related deductions are small enough to warrant assuming the same amount will recur annually; however, if amounts are material, thorough investigation may lead to other conclusions.

"Other deductions" represent other pass through items that are reported on the tax returns of the individual partners. The total amount of charitable contributions is a pass-through item that is listed separately because a partner can only deduct donations as an itemized deduction on his or her personal tax return. Each partner will generally receive a pro rata share of the amount based on the partner's share of profit and losses.

The nature of the contribution will determine whether it is a permissible deduction in arriving at income available for support. If the contribution does not relate to the production of income, it is probably a perquisite. Contribution made to organizations many of whose members are clients or customers of the partnership are likely to be considered appropriate reductions to income because those payments are in the nature of marketing expenses.

Other examples of "Other deductions" include partners' medical insurance premiums and contributions to retirement plans on behalf of partners (although note that some K-1s will report retirement plan contributions in a statement attached to Line 20). Because of limitations on deductibility, such expenses are passed through to the individual partner's personal tax return via this line item on the K-1.

Whether such fringe benefits paid by the partnerships are perquisites is often an issue in marital dissolution matters. The primary factor to consider is whether or not the expenses are discretionary. In temporary support situations, where maintaining the status quo is an important factor, the amount of control over certain expenditures is the pivotal question. If the fringe benefit payments must be made, whether the partner wants to or not, then the amounts should be deducted from income available for support. But if the partner is able to eliminate an expense, there may be a loss of a tax benefit but arguably the expense may be a perquisite that should be added back to income.

Even an item that is a legitimate tax deduction may be included in income available for support as a perquisite. Charitable contributions and retirement plan contributions are two examples of legitimate tax-deductible expenses that are frequently added back to income available as perquisites. Hence, the test of whether an expense is a legitimate reduction in income is whether the expense is reasonably related to the income producing activity of the partnership.

14. Self-Employment Earnings Self-employment earnings are aggregated and reported here. Ordinary income or loss is shared by each of the

partners on the basis of their contractual profit and loss percentages. If partners actively participate in the partnership business, their allocated amount of income is subject to "Self-Employment Tax." The "Self-Employment Tax" consists of a social security tax element and a "Medicare Tax" element and is reported on Schedule SE of the partner's individual income tax return. A ceiling exists on the amount of income subject to the self-employment social security tax of 12.4% but there is no cap on the self-employment Medicare tax of 2.9%. In 2022, the cap on income subject to the self-employment social security tax of 12.4% is $147,000 ($160,000 in 2023). There is also an additional .9% assessed for higher income individuals ($250,000 for joint returns, $200,000 for single and head of household status and $125,000 for married filing separately). The end result for those partners earning in excess of the cap, is that once the cap is reached, the individual will have the portion previously earmarked for social security tax available for other expenditures. This should be taken into consideration when preparing budgets and setting support orders.

Income from self-employment can be reduced by losses from other partnership(s), Schedule C businesses, or farms owned and actively operated by the partner. The amount of tax is also affected by wages earned by the partner from employment outside of the partnership. If the wages are in excess of the 2022 cap of $147,000 ($160,2000 in 2023) for social security, there is no additional social security tax from business income computed on Schedule SE of the individual income tax return.

15. Credits This portion of the K-1 is devoted to pass through credits. If credits relating to low income housing and real estate rehabilitation expenditures appear on the K-1, the amount of tax payable by the individual partner will be reduced. This factor should be considered in arriving at the amount of income available for support. Material credits affecting the calculation of the partner's personal income taxes are relevant to the calculation of spousal and child support. The tax effects of these credits should be explained in declarations or other forms of evidence presented to the court.

16. Foreign Transactions As of tax year 2022 this section has been replaced with separate Forms K-2 and/or K-3 and this line is used simply to note whether or not Schedule K-3 is included. The IRS provides certain exceptions eliminating the need for the partnership to prepare and include such forms. Because a working knowledge of these rules is generally not significant for family law purposes, a detailed explanation of the tax law in this regard is not presented here. Foreign transactions are flow through items reported on the partner's individual income tax. An entry on these forms if included should alert the reader to a possible diversion of funds outside the country. Partnership activity with the foreign partner may require extensive analysis. The inspection of that partner's personal records might be needed to ascertain that all income is properly stated on the partnership tax return.

Business activity abroad provides another possibility for hiding income. The impracticality and cost of performing discovery require creativity in dealing with this situation. Foreign forensic accountants may be employed to prepare appraisals of and income analyses for foreign branches of the partnership. If the matter proceeds to trial, the foreign accountant may have to appear to present his or her opinion. A cost-benefit analysis relative to the cost of paying the accountant's travel expenses to appear at trial is often warranted in these circumstances.

17. Alternative Minimum Tax (AMT) Items Tax preference items are reported in this area of the K-1. A tax preference is an addition to alternate minimum taxable income subject to alternative minimum tax on the personal return. The minimum tax is an attempt by the government to insure that certain deductions do not completely eliminate a taxpayer's tax liability. Examples are research and experimental expense and depreciation adjustments on property place in service after

1986. (AMT rules were introduced in 1986. This adjustment relates to depreciation for AMT purposes only.)

18. TAX-EXEMPT INCOME AND NONDEDUCTIBLE EXPENSE Tax exempt income is not taxable for federal income tax but may represent additional income available to the partner.

Additional asset value may be uncovered through a calculation of interest and/or dividend income receivable for earnings on non-taxable investments.

Certain costs of doing business are not deductible. The most common expense in this category is the nondeductible 50% portion of meals and 100% of entertainment expense. Though nondeductible, this expense may very well be an important aspect of the business activity of the partnership. When appropriate because it is truly business related, the nondeductible portion of meals and entertainment expense should be considered as a reduction in income. Conversely, if the expenses are truly personal, the deductible amount should be added back to income.

The nature and purpose of any entry here should be examined with regard to the effect on income. It may be an error to assume that because an expense is not deductible, it does not reduce income.

19. DISTRIBUTIONS Distributions are of primary importance in analyzing income. In some cases, the distributions are more relevant to a spouse's ability to pay support than are the partnership earnings. This general occurs when the partnership deducts large amounts of non-cash expenses such as depreciation on fixed assets and amortization from intangible assets such as purchased goodwill or leasehold improvements from a prior period. In other cases, the distributions may be atypical aberrations resulting from non-recurring borrowing or asset sales. Additional distributions may also result from a decrease in a partner's share of partnership liabilities. This type of adjustment affects valuation of the partner's interest and requires investigation.

Distributions may be in the form of property rather than money. Complex tax regulations are involved when property is distributed to a partner. The most important aspects of property distributions from a family law perspective include determining: (1) the fair market value of the property, (2) the reason for the distribution, and (3) the frequency of such distributions.

The basis of the property distributed will usually be the partnership's basis; however, if a partner purchased his or her interest from another partner, basis adjustments may be required. Basis and fair market value usually differ. Real or personal property appraisals may be required to determine fair market value.

20. OTHER INFORMATION Examples of flow through Items that are reported in this box are:

- Investment income and expense
- Fuel tax credits
- Recapture of low income housing credits, investment credits and other credits

Investment expense is a pass-through item that is reported on the tax returns of the individual partners. Interest expense deductions for individuals are generally limited to interest paid on personal residence mortgages and investment interest. Interest expense is deducted as investment interest if related to debts that are allocable to property held for investment. If, for example, the partnership invests in marketable securities on margin, the margin interest expense can be deducted against any passive interest and dividends earned by the partnership.

The existence of this line item indicates that investment property is owned by the partnership. Examination of other portions of the tax return, particularly the balance sheet on Page 5 and supporting schedules thereto, may reveal more information about the nature of the investment. If not, appropriate discovery should uncover supporting documentation, such as brokerage account statements, which might provide a basis for the determination of the fair market value of the investment.

SUMMARY

The K-1 represents the most informative schedule available to family law practitioners relative to cash flow from partnership interests. It is also provides the most informative data for computing a partner's taxable income from a partnership. But the K-1 by itself will usually not contain all of the information needed to prepare an appraisal of the partnership interest or determine income available for support from that source. It is always a good idea to request a copy of the complete partnership tax returns and all of the accountant's work papers used to prepare the returns.

12/31/22

2022 FEDERAL DEPRECIATION SCHEDULE

PAGE 1

DEALMAKER & CODEHEAD

95-0000001

NO.	DESCRIPTION	DATE ACQUIRED	DATE SOLD	COST/ BASIS	BUS. PCT.	CUR 179 BONUS	SPECIAL DEPR. ALLOW.	PRIOR 179/ BONUS/ SP. DEPR.	PRIOR DEC. BAL DEPR.	SALVAG /BASIS REDUCT	DEPR. BASIS	PRIOR DEPR.	METHOD	LIFE	RATE	CURRENT DEPR.
	FORM 1065															
	AUTO / TRANSPORT EQUIPMENT															
3	MERCEDES **	12/01/20		74,000				18,100			55,900	16,100	200DB HY	5	.19200	9,700
	TOTAL AUTO / TRANSPORT EQUIP			74,000		0	0	18,100	0	0	55,900	16,100				9,700
	FURNITURE AND FIXTURES															
2	FURNITURE & FIXTURES **	3/31/22		25,000		25,000					0		200DB HY	7		0
5	OFFICE FURNITURE **	6/15/17		85,000				85,000			0		200DB HY	5		0
	TOTAL FURNITURE AND FIXTURE			110,000		25,000	0	85,000	0	0	0	0				0
	MACHINERY AND EQUIPMENT															
1	COMPUTER **	6/30/22		15,000		15,000					0		200DB HY	5		0
4	PHONES SYSTEM **	9/30/22		20,000		20,000					0		200DB HY	5		0
6	COMPUTER EQUIPMENT **	2/01/18		15,000							15,000	12,408	200DB HY	5	.11520	1,728
7	COMPUTER EQUIPMENT **	3/01/20		3,000							3,000	1,560	200DB HY	5	.19200	576
8	COMPUTER EQUIPMENT **	6/15/20		5,000							5,000	2,600	200DB HY	5	.19200	960
	TOTAL MACHINERY AND EQUIPME			58,000		35,000	0	0	0	0	23,000	16,568				3,264
	TOTAL DEPRECIATION			242,000		60,000	0	103,100	0	0	78,900	32,668				12,964
	GRAND TOTAL DEPRECIATION			242,000		60,000	0	103,100	0	0	78,900	32,668				12,964

12/31/22 **2022 FEDERAL DEPRECIATION SCHEDULE** PAGE 2

DEALMAKER & CODEHEAD 95-0000001

NO.	DESCRIPTION	DATE ACQUIRED	DATE SOLD	COST/ BASIS	BUS. PCT.	CUR 179 BONUS	SPECIAL DEPR. ALLOW.	PRIOR 179/ BONUS/ SP. DEPR.	PRIOR DEC. BAL DEPR.	SALVAG /BASIS REDUCT	DEPR. BASIS	PRIOR DEPR.	METHOD	LIFE	RATE	CURRENT DEPR.

**ASSET INCLUDED IN UNADJUSTED BASIS IMMEDIATELY AFTER ACQUISITION FOR THE QBI CALCULATION.

Form **1065**

Department of the Treasury Internal Revenue Service

U.S. Return of Partnership Income

For calendar year 2022, or tax year beginning ____________, 2022, ending ____________, 20 ____.

Go to *www.irs.gov/Form1065* for instructions and the latest information.

OMB No. 1545-0123

2022

A Principal business activity: LEGAL	Type or Print: DEALMAKER & CODEHEAD 8462 GRAVEL DR., SUITE 711 TARZANA, CA 91357	**D** Employer identification no.: 95-0000001
B Principal product or service: SERVICES		**E** Date business started: 12/04/2002
C Business code number: 541190		**F** Total assets (see instructions): $ 243,898.

G Check applicable boxes: (1) ☐ Initial return (2) ☐ Final return (3) ☐ Name change (4) ☐ Address change (5) ☐ Amended return

H Check accounting method: (1) ☒ Cash (2) ☐ Accrual (3) ☐ Other (specify): ____________

I Number of Schedules K-1. Attach one for each person who was a partner at any time during the tax year: 3

J Check if Schedules C and M-3 are attached ☐

K Check if partnership: (1) ☐ Aggregated activities for section 465 at-risk purposes (2) ☐ Grouped activities for section 469 passive activity purposes

Caution: Include **only** trade or business income and expenses on lines 1a through 22 below. See the instructions for more information.

INCOME	1 a	Gross receipts or sales	1 a	3,405,694.		
	b	Returns and allowances	1 b			
	c	Balance. Subtract line 1b from line 1a			1 c	3,405,694.
	2	Cost of goods sold (attach Form 1125-A)			2	
	3	Gross profit. Subtract line 2 from line 1c			3	3,405,694.
	4	Ordinary income (loss) from other partnerships, estates, and trusts (attach statement)			4	
	5	Net farm profit (loss) (attach Schedule F (Form 1040))			5	
	6	Net gain (loss) from Form 4797, Part II, line 17 (attach Form 4797)			6	
	7	Other income (loss) (attach statement)			7	
	8	**Total income (loss).** Combine lines 3 through 7			8	3,405,694.
DEDUCTIONS (SEE INSTRS FOR LIMITATIONS)	9	Salaries and wages (other than to partners) (less employment credits)			9	1,363,144.
	10	Guaranteed payments to partners			10	
	11	Repairs and maintenance			11	11,110.
	12	Bad debts			12	
	13	Rent			13	237,187.
	14	Taxes and licenses			14	61,228.
	15	Interest (see instructions)			15	
	16a	Depreciation (if required, attach Form 4562)	16a	12,964.		
	b	Less depreciation reported on Form 1125-A and elsewhere on return	16b		16c	12,964.
	17	Depletion **(Do not deduct oil and gas depletion.)**			17	
	18	Retirement plans, etc.			18	
	19	Employee benefit programs			19	
	20	Other deductions (att stmt) SEE STATEMENT 1			20	1,149,221.
	21	**Total deductions.** Add the amounts shown in the far right column for lines 9 through 20			21	2,834,854.
	22	**Ordinary business income (loss).** Subtract line 21 from line 8			22	570,840.
TAX AND PAYMENT	23	Interest due under the look-back method — completed long-term contracts (attach Form 8697)			23	
	24	Interest due under the look-back method — income forecast method (attach Form 8866)			24	
	25	BBA AAR imputed underpayment (see instructions)			25	
	26	Other taxes (see instructions)			26	
	27	**Total balance due.** Add lines 23 through 26			27	
	28	Payment (see instructions)			28	
	29	**Amount owed.** If line 28 is smaller than line 27, enter amount owed			29	
	30	**Overpayment.** If line 28 is larger than line 27, enter overpayment			30	

Sign Here

Under penalties of perjury, I declare that I have examined this return, including accompanying schedules and statements, and to the best of my knowledge and belief, it is true, correct, and complete. Declaration of preparer (other than partner or limited liability company member) is based on all information of which preparer has any knowledge.

Signature of partner or limited liability company member ____________ Date ____________

May the IRS discuss this return with the preparer shown below? See instructions. ☒ Yes ☐ No

Paid Preparer Use Only

Print/Type preparer's name	Preparer's signature	Date	Check ☒ if self-employed	PTIN
RON E. THOMPSON	RON E. THOMPSON			P00166602
Firm's name	WHITE ZUCKERMAN WARSAVSKY LUNA HUNT LLP		Firm's EIN	95-4115549
Firm's address	15490 VENTURA BLVD 3RD FL SHERMAN OAKS, CA 91403		Phone no.	(818) 981-4226

BAA For Paperwork Reduction Act Notice, see separate instructions. PTPA0105 07/28/22 Form **1065** (2022)

Form 1065 (2022) DEALMAKER & CODEHEAD 95-0000001 Page **2**

Schedule B **Other Information**

	Yes	No
1 What type of entity is filing this return? Check the applicable box: **a** [X] Domestic general partnership **b** [ ] Domestic limited partnership **c** [ ] Domestic limited liability company **d** [ ] Domestic limited liability partnership **e** [ ] Foreign partnership **f** [ ] Other:		
2 At the end of the tax year: **a** Did any foreign or domestic corporation, partnership (including any entity treated as a partnership), trust, or tax-exempt organization, or any foreign government own, directly or indirectly, an interest of 50% or more in the profit, loss, or capital of the partnership? For rules of constructive ownership, see instructions. If "Yes," attach Schedule B-1, Information on Partners Owning 50% or More of the Partnership		X
b Did any individual or estate own, directly or indirectly, an interest of 50% or more in the profit, loss, or capital of the partnership? For rules of constructive ownership, see instructions. If "Yes," attach Schedule B-1, Information on Partners Owning 50% or More of the Partnership		X
3 At the end of the tax year, did the partnership: **a** Own directly 20% or more, or own, directly or indirectly, 50% or more of the total voting power of all classes of stock entitled to vote of any foreign or domestic corporation? For rules of constructive ownership, see instructions. If "Yes," complete (i) through (iv) below		X

(i) Name of Corporation	**(ii)** Employer Identification Number (if any)	**(iii)** Country of Incorporation	**(iv)** Percentage Owned in Voting Stock

b Own directly an interest of 20% or more, or own, directly or indirectly, an interest of 50% or more in the profit, loss, or capital in any foreign or domestic partnership (including an entity treated as a partnership) or in the beneficial interest of a trust? For rules of constructive ownership, see instructions. If "Yes," complete (i) through (v) below		X

(i) Name of Entity	**(ii)** Employer Identification Number (if any)	**(iii)** Type of Entity	**(iv)** Country of Organization	**(v)** Maximum Percentage Owned in Profit, Loss, or Capital

	Yes	No
4 Does the partnership satisfy **all four** of the following conditions? **a** The partnership's total receipts for the tax year were less than $250,000. **b** The partnership's total assets at the end of the tax year were less than $1 million. **c** Schedules K-1 are filed with the return and furnished to the partners on or before the due date (including extensions) for the partnership return. **d** The partnership is not filing and is not required to file Schedule M-3		X
If "Yes," the partnership is not required to complete Schedules L, M-1, and M-2; item F on page 1 of Form 1065; or item L on Schedule K-1.		
5 Is this partnership a publicly traded partnership, as defined in section 469(k)(2)?		X
6 During the tax year, did the partnership have any debt that was canceled, was forgiven, or had the terms modified so as to reduce the principal amount of the debt?		X
7 Has this partnership filed, or is it required to file, Form 8918, Material Advisor Disclosure Statement, to provide information on any reportable transaction?		X
8 At any time during calendar year 2022, did the partnership have an interest in or a signature or other authority over a financial account in a foreign country (such as a bank account, securities account, or other financial account)? See instructions for exceptions and filing requirements for FinCEN Form 114, Report of Foreign Bank and Financial Accounts (FBAR). If "Yes," enter the name of the foreign country.		X
9 At any time during the tax year, did the partnership receive a distribution from, or was it the grantor of, or transferor to, a foreign trust? If "Yes," the partnership may have to file Form 3520, Annual Return To Report Transactions With Foreign Trusts and Receipt of Certain Foreign Gifts. See instructions		X
10a Is the partnership making, or had it previously made (and not revoked), a section 754 election? See instructions for details regarding a section 754 election.		X
b Did the partnership make for this tax year an optional basis adjustment under section 743(b) or 734(b)? If "Yes," attach a statement showing the computation and allocation of the basis adjustment. See instructions		X
c Is the partnership required to adjust the basis of partnership assets under section 743(b) or 734(b) because of a substantial built-in loss (as defined under section 743(d)) or substantial basis reduction (as defined under section 734(d))? If "Yes," attach a statement showing the computation and allocation of the basis adjustment. See instructions		X

Form 1065 (2022) DEALMAKER & CODEHEAD 95-0000001 Page **3**

Schedule B **Other Information** *(continued)*

		Yes	No
11	Check this box if, during the current or prior tax year, the partnership distributed any property received in a like-kind exchange or contributed such property to another entity (other than disregarded entities wholly owned by the partnership throughout the tax year) . . . . ☐		
12	At any time during the tax year, did the partnership distribute to any partner a tenancy-in-common or other undivided interest in partnership property?		X
13	If the partnership is required to file Form 8858, Information Return of U.S. Persons With Respect to Foreign Disregarded Entities (FDEs) and Foreign Branches (FBs), enter the number of Forms 8858 attached. See instructions . . . . ______		
14	Does the partnership have any foreign partners? If "Yes," enter the number of Forms 8805, Foreign Partner's Information Statement of Section 1446 Withholding Tax, filed for this partnership . . . . ______		X
15	Enter the number of Forms 8865, Return of U.S. Persons With Respect to Certain Foreign Partnerships, attached to this return . . . . ______		
16a	Did you make any payments in 2022 that would require you to file Form(s) 1099? See instructions		X
b	If "Yes," did you or will you file required Form(s) 1099?		
17	Enter the number of Forms 5471, Information Return of U.S. Persons With Respect to Certain Foreign Corporations, attached to this return . . . . ______		
18	Enter the number of partners that are foreign governments under section 892. 0		
19	During the partnership's tax year, did the partnership make any payments that would require it to file Forms 1042 and 1042-S under chapter 3 (sections 1441 through 1464) or chapter 4 (sections 1471 through 1474)?		X
20	Was the partnership a specified domestic entity required to file Form 8938 for the tax year? See the Instructions for Form 8938		X
21	Is the partnership a section 721(c) partnership, as defined in Regulations section 1.721(c)-1(b)(14)?		X
22	During the tax year, did the partnership pay or accrue any interest or royalty for which one or more partners are not allowed a deduction under section 267A? See instructions . . . . If "Yes," enter the total amount of the disallowed deductions . . . . $ ______		X
23	Did the partnership have an election under section 163(j) for any real property trade or business or any farming business in effect during the tax year? See instructions		X
24	Does the partnership satisfy one or more of the following? See instructions . . . . **a** The partnership owns a pass-through entity with current, or prior year carryover, excess business interest expense. **b** The partnership's aggregate average annual gross receipts (determined under section 448(c)) for the 3 tax years preceding the current tax year are more than $27 million and the partnership has business interest expense. **c** The partnership is a tax shelter (see instructions) and the partnership has business interest expense. If "Yes" to any, complete and attach Form 8990.		X
25	Is the partnership attaching Form 8996 to certify as a Qualified Opportunity Fund? . . . . If "Yes," enter the amount from Form 8996, line 15 . . . . $ ______		X
26	Enter the number of foreign partners subject to section 864(c)(8) as a result of transferring all or a portion of an interest in the partnership or of receiving a distribution from the partnership . . . . ______ Complete Schedule K-3 (Form 1065), Part XIII, for each foreign partner subject to section 864(c)(8) on a transfer or distribution.		
27	At any time during the tax year, were there any transfers between the partnership and its partners subject to the disclosure requirements of Regulations section 1.707-8?		X
28	Since December 22, 2017, did a foreign corporation directly or indirectly acquire substantially all of the properties constituting a trade or business of your partnership, and was the ownership percentage (by vote or value) for purposes of section 7874 greater than 50% (for example, the partners held more than 50% of the stock of the foreign corporation)? If "Yes," list the ownership percentage by vote and by value. See instructions. Percentage: By vote: ______ By value: ______		X
29	Reserved for future use		
30	Is the partnership electing out of the centralized partnership audit regime under section 6221(b)? See instructions. If "Yes," the partnership must complete Schedule B-2 (Form 1065). Enter the total from Schedule B-2, Part III, line 3 . . . . ______ If "No," complete Designation of Partnership Representative below.		X

Designation of Partnership Representative (see instructions)

Enter below the information for the partnership representative (PR) for the tax year covered by this return.

Name of PR ALISHIA M. CODEHEAD

U.S. address of PR: 3358 CASE AVE.
LOS ANGELES, CA 91753

U.S. phone number of PR

If the PR is an entity, name of the designated individual for the PR

U.S. address of designated individual ______

U.S. phone number of designated individual

BAA Form **1065** (2022)

PTPA0112 12/13/22

Form 1065 (2022) DEALMAKER & CODEHEAD 95-0000001 Page **4**

Schedule K	**Partners' Distributive Share Items**		**Total amount**
Income (Loss)	1 Ordinary business income (loss) (page 1, line 22)	1	570,840.
	2 Net rental real estate income (loss) (attach Form 8825)	2	
	3 a Other gross rental income (loss) 3a		
	b Expenses from other rental activities (attach stmt) 3b		
	c Other net rental income (loss). Subtract line 3b from line 3a	3c	
	4 Guaranteed payments: a Services 4a b Capital 4b		
	c Total. Add lines 4a and 4b	4c	
	5 Interest income	5	
	6 Dividends and dividend equivalents: a Ordinary dividends	6a	
	b Qualified dividends 6b c Dividend equivalents 6c		
	7 Royalties	7	
	8 Net short-term capital gain (loss) (attach Schedule D (Form 1065))	8	
	9 a Net long-term capital gain (loss) (attach Schedule D (Form 1065))	9a	
	b Collectibles (28%) gain (loss) 9b		
	c Unrecaptured section 1250 gain (attach statement) 9c		
	10 Net section 1231 gain (loss) (attach Form 4797)	10	
	11 Other income (loss) (see instructions) Type:	11	
Deductions	12 Section 179 deduction (attach Form 4562)	12	60,000.
	13 a Contributions	13a	
	b Investment interest expense	13b	
	c Section 59(e)(2) expenditures: (1) Type: (2) Amount:	13c(2)	
	d Other deductions (see instructions) Type:	13d	
Self-Employment	14 a Net earnings (loss) from self-employment	14a	376,754.
	b Gross farming or fishing income	14b	
	c Gross nonfarm income	14c	
Credits	15 a Low-income housing credit (section 42(j)(5))	15a	
	b Low-income housing credit (other)	15b	
	c Qualified rehabilitation expenditures (rental real estate) (attach Form 3468, if applicable)	15c	
	d Other rental real estate credits (see instructions) Type:	15d	
	e Other rental credits (see instructions) Type:	15e	
	f Other credits (see instructions) Type:	15f	
International	16 Attach Schedule K-2 (Form 1065), Partners' Distributive Share Items—International, and check this box to indicate that you are reporting items of international tax relevance ☐		
Alternative Minimum Tax (AMT) Items	17 a Post-1986 depreciation adjustment	17a	-664.
	b Adjusted gain or loss	17b	
	c Depletion (other than oil and gas)	17c	
	d Oil, gas, and geothermal properties – gross income	17d	
	e Oil, gas, and geothermal properties – deductions	17e	
	f Other AMT items (attach stmt)	17f	
Other Information	18 a Tax-exempt interest income	18a	
	b Other tax-exempt income	18b	
	c Nondeductible expenses	18c	
	19 a Distributions of cash and marketable securities	19a	500,000.
	b Distributions of other property	19b	
	20 a Investment income	20a	
	b Investment expenses	20b	
	c Other items and amounts (attach stmt)		
	21 Total foreign taxes paid or accrued	21	

BAA PTPA0134 07/28/22 Form **1065** (2022)

Form 1065 (2022) DEALMAKER & CODEHEAD 95-0000001 Page **5**

Analysis of Net Income (Loss) per Return

1 Net income (loss). Combine Schedule K, lines 1 through 11. From the result, subtract the sum of Schedule K, lines 12 through 13d, and 21	1	510,840.

2 Analysis by partner type:	**(i)** Corporate	**(ii)** Individual (active)	**(iii)** Individual (passive)	**(iv)** Partnership	**(v)** Exempt Organization	**(vi)** Nominee/Other
a General partners	173,686.	337,154.				
b Limited partners						

Schedule L Balance Sheets per Books

Assets	Beginning of tax year (a)	(b)	End of tax year (c)	(d)
1 Cash		13,474.		148,612.
2a Trade notes and accounts receivable				
b Less allowance for bad debts				
3 Inventories				
4 U.S. Government obligations				
5 Tax-exempt securities				
6 Other current assets (attach stmt) SEE ST 2		166,602.		62,018.
7a Loans to partners (or persons related to partners)				
b Mortgage and real estate loans				
8 Other investments (attach stmt)				
9a Buildings and other depreciable assets	182,000.		242,000.	
b Less accumulated depreciation	135,768.	46,232.	208,732.	33,268.
10a Depletable assets				
b Less accumulated depletion				
11 Land (net of any amortization)				
12a Intangible assets (amortizable only)				
b Less accumulated amortization				
13 Other assets (attach stmt)				
14 Total assets		226,308.		243,898.
Liabilities and Capital				
15 Accounts payable				
16 Mortgages, notes, bonds payable in less than 1 year				
17 Other current liabilities (attach stmt) SEE ST 3		110,309.		110,309.
18 All nonrecourse loans				
19a Loans from partners (or persons related to partners)				
b Mortgages, notes, bonds payable in 1 year or more				
20 Other liabilities (attach stmt)				
21 Partners' capital accounts		115,999.		133,589.
22 Total liabilities and capital		226,308.		243,898.

Schedule M-1 Reconciliation of Income (Loss) per Books With Analysis of Net Income (Loss) per Return

Note: The partnership may be required to file Schedule M-3. See instructions.

1 Net income (loss) per books	510,840.	**6** Income recorded on books this year not included on Schedule K, lines 1 through 11 (itemize): **a** Tax-exempt interest $	
2 Income included on Schedule K, lines 1, 2, 3c, 5, 6a, 7, 8, 9a, 10, and 11, not recorded on books this year (itemize):			
3 Guaranteed payments (other than health insurance)		**7** Deductions included on Schedule K, lines 1 through 13d, and 21, not charged against book income this year (itemize): **a** Depreciation $	
4 Expenses recorded on books this year not included on Schedule K, lines 1 through 13d, and 21 (itemize): **a** Depreciation $ **b** Travel and entertainment $		**8** Add lines 6 and 7	
5 Add lines 1 through 4	510,840.	**9** Income (loss) (Analysis of Net Income (Loss), line 1). Subtract line 8 from line 5	510,840.

Schedule M-2 Analysis of Partners' Capital Accounts

1 Balance at beginning of year	115,999.	**6** Distributions: **a** Cash	500,000.
2 Capital contributed: **a** Cash		**b** Property	
b Property		**7** Other decreases (itemize):	
3 Net income (loss) (see instructions)	510,840.		
4 Other increases (itemize):		**8** Add lines 6 and 7	500,000.
5 Add lines 1 through 4	626,839.	**9** Balance at end of year. Subtract line 8 from line 5	133,589.

651121

☐ Final K-1 ☐ Amended K-1 OMB No. 1545-0123

Schedule K-1 (Form 1065) **2022**
Department of the Treasury
Internal Revenue Service

For calendar year 2022, or tax year beginning / / 2022 ending / /

Partner's Share of Income, Deductions, Credits, etc.
See separate instructions.

Part I Information About the Partnership

A Partnership's employer identification number
95-0000001

B Partnership's name, address, city, state, and ZIP code
DEALMAKER & CODEHEAD
8462 GRAVEL DR., SUITE 711
TARZANA, CA 91357

C IRS center where partnership filed return: E-FILE

D ☐ Check if this is a publicly traded partnership (PTP)

Part II Information About the Partner

E Partner's SSN or TIN (Do not use TIN of a disregarded entity. See instructions.)
95-1234567

F Name, address, city, state, and ZIP code for partner entered in E. See instructions.
GRANT A. HERRING
A PROFESSIONAL CORPORATION
8465 GAEL DR., SUITE 711
LOS ANGELES, CA 91357

G [X] General partner or LLC member-manager ☐ Limited partner or other LLC member

H1 [X] Domestic partner ☐ Foreign partner

H2 ☐ If the partner is a disregarded entity (DE), enter the partner's: TIN ____ Name ____

I1 What type of entity is this partner? CORPORATION

I2 If this partner is a retirement plan (IRA/SEP/Keogh/etc.), check here ☐

J Partner's share of profit, loss, and capital (see instructions):

	Beginning	Ending
Profit	34 %	34 %
Loss	34 %	34 %
Capital	34 %	34 %

Check if decrease is due to sale or exchange of partnership interest ☐

K Partner's share of liabilities:

	Beginning	Ending
Nonrecourse	$	$
Qualified nonrecourse financing	$	$
Recourse	$	$

Check this box if item K includes liability amounts from lower-tier partnerships ☐

L **Partner's Capital Account Analysis**

Beginning capital account	$ 39,439.
Capital contributed during the year	$
Current year net income (loss)	$ 173,686.
Other increase (decrease) (attach explanation)	$
Withdrawals and distributions	$(170,000.)
Ending capital account	$ 43,125.

M Did the partner contribute property with a built-in gain (loss)?
☐ **Yes** [X] **No** If "Yes," attach statement. See instructions.

N **Partner's Share of Net Unrecognized Section 704(c) Gain or (Loss)**
Beginning $
Ending $

Part III Partner's Share of Current Year Income, Deductions, Credits, and Other Items

1	Ordinary business income (loss)	194,086.
2	Net rental real estate income (loss)	
3	Other net rental income (loss)	
4a	Guaranteed payments for services	
4b	Guaranteed payments for capital	
4c	Total guaranteed payments	
5	Interest income	
6a	Ordinary dividends	
6b	Qualified dividends	
6c	Dividend equivalents	
7	Royalties	
8	Net short-term capital gain (loss)	
9a	Net long-term capital gain (loss)	
9b	Collectibles (28%) gain (loss)	
9c	Unrecaptured section 1250 gain	
10	Net section 1231 gain (loss)	
11	Other income (loss)	
12	Section 179 deduction	20,400.
13	Other deductions	
14	Self-employment earnings (loss)	
15	Credits	
16	Schedule K-3 is attached if checked ☐	
17	Alternative minimum tax (AMT) items	
18	Tax-exempt income and nondeductible expenses	
19	Distributions	A 170,000.
20	Other information	
21	Foreign taxes paid or accrued	

22 ☐ More than one activity for at-risk purposes*
23 ☐ More than one activity for passive activity purposes*
*See attached statement for additional information.

For IRS Use Only

651121

Schedule K-1 **2022**
(Form 1065)
Department of the Treasury
Internal Revenue Service

For calendar year 2022, or tax year

beginning / / 2022 ending / /

☐ Final K-1 ☐ Amended K-1

OMB No. 1545-0123

Partner's Share of Income, Deductions, Credits, etc.

See separate instructions.

Part I Information About the Partnership

A Partnership's employer identification number
95-0000001

B Partnership's name, address, city, state, and ZIP code

DEALMAKER & CODEHEAD
8462 GRAVEL DR., SUITE 711
TARZANA, CA 91357

C IRS center where partnership filed return: E-FILE

D ☐ Check if this is a publicly traded partnership (PTP)

Part II Information About the Partner

E Partner's SSN or TIN (Do not use TIN of a disregarded entity. See instructions.)
987-65-4321

F Name, address, city, state, and ZIP code for partner entered in E. See instructions.

MICHAEL H. DEALMAKER
793 BRUIEF ST.
LOS ANGELES, CA 91357

G ☒ General partner or LLC member-manager ☐ Limited partner or other LLC member

H1 ☒ Domestic partner ☐ Foreign partner

H2 ☐ If the partner is a disregarded entity (DE), enter the partner's: TIN ______ Name ______

I1 What type of entity is this partner? INDIVIDUAL

I2 If this partner is a retirement plan (IRA/SEP/Keogh/etc.), check here ☐

J Partner's share of profit, loss, and capital (see instructions):

	Beginning	Ending
Profit	33 %	33 %
Loss	33 %	33 %
Capital	33 %	33 %

Check if decrease is due to sale or exchange of partnership interest ☐

K Partner's share of liabilities:

	Beginning	Ending
Nonrecourse	$	$
Qualified nonrecourse financing	$	$
Recourse	$	$

Check this box if item K includes liability amounts from lower-tier partnerships ☐

L **Partner's Capital Account Analysis**

Beginning capital account	$ 38,280.
Capital contributed during the year	$
Current year net income (loss)	$ 168,577.
Other increase (decrease) (attach explanation)	$
Withdrawals and distributions	$(165,000.)
Ending capital account	$ 41,857.

M Did the partner contribute property with a built-in gain (loss)?
☐ **Yes** ☒ **No** If "Yes," attach statement. See instructions.

N **Partner's Share of Net Unrecognized Section 704(c) Gain or (Loss)**
Beginning $
Ending $

Part III Partner's Share of Current Year Income, Deductions, Credits, and Other Items

1	Ordinary business income (loss)	188,377.
2	Net rental real estate income (loss)	
3	Other net rental income (loss)	
4a	Guaranteed payments for services	
4b	Guaranteed payments for capital	
4c	Total guaranteed payments	
5	Interest income	
6a	Ordinary dividends	
6b	Qualified dividends	
6c	Dividend equivalents	
7	Royalties	
8	Net short-term capital gain (loss)	
9a	Net long-term capital gain (loss)	
9b	Collectibles (28%) gain (loss)	
9c	Unrecaptured section 1250 gain	
10	Net section 1231 gain (loss)	
11	Other income (loss)	
12	Section 179 deduction	19,800.
13	Other deductions	

Line	Item	Code	Amount
14	Self-employment earnings (loss)	A	188,377.
15	Credits		
16	Schedule K-3 is attached if checked ☐		
17	Alternative minimum tax (AMT) items	A	-219.
18	Tax-exempt income and nondeductible expenses		
19	Distributions	A	165,000.
20	Other information	Z*	STMT
21	Foreign taxes paid or accrued		

22 ☐ More than one activity for at-risk purposes*
23 ☐ More than one activity for passive activity purposes*
*See attached statement for additional information.

For IRS Use Only

BAA For Paperwork Reduction Act Notice, see the Instructions for Form 1065. www.irs.gov/Form1065 **Schedule K-1 (Form 1065) 2022**

PARTNER 2 PTPA0312L 07/28/22

Statement A—QBI Pass-through Entity Reporting (Schedule K-1, Box 20, Code Z)

Partnership's name: DEALMAKER & CODEHEAD	**Partnership's EIN:** 95-0000001
Partner's name: MICHAEL H. DEALMAKER	**Partner's identifying number:** 987-65-4321

	DEALMAKER & CODEHEAD		
Partner's share of:	☐ PTP ☐ Aggregated ☒ SSTB	☐ PTP ☐ Aggregated ☐ SSTB	☐ PTP ☐ Aggregated ☐ SSTB
QBI or qualified PTP items subject to partner-specific determinations:			
Ordinary business income (loss)	188,377.		
Rental income (loss)			
Royalty income (loss)			
Section 1231 gain (loss)			
Other income (loss)			
Section 179 deduction	19,800.		
Other deductions			
W-2 wages	449,838.		
UBIA of qualified property	79,860.		
Qualified REIT dividends			

Partner's share of:	☐ PTP ☐ Aggregated ☐ SSTB	☐ PTP ☐ Aggregated ☐ SSTB	☐ PTP ☐ Aggregated ☐ SSTB
QBI or qualified PTP items subject to partner-specific determinations:			
Ordinary business income (loss)			
Rental income (loss)			
Royalty income (loss)			
Section 1231 gain (loss)			
Other income (loss)			
Section 179 deduction			
Other deductions			
W-2 wages			
UBIA of qualified property			

PARTNER 2

BAA For Paperwork Reduction Act Notice, see the Instructions for Form 1065. PTPA1515 12/15/22 **Statement A (Form 1065) (2022)**

651121

Schedule K-1 (Form 1065) **2022**
Department of the Treasury
Internal Revenue Service
For calendar year 2022, or tax year
beginning / / 2022 ending / /

☐ Final K-1 ☐ Amended K-1 OMB No. 1545-0123

Partner's Share of Income, Deductions, Credits, etc.
See separate instructions.

Part I Information About the Partnership

A Partnership's employer identification number
95-0000001

B Partnership's name, address, city, state, and ZIP code
DEALMAKER & CODEHEAD
8462 GRAVEL DR., SUITE 711
TARZANA, CA 91357

C IRS center where partnership filed return: E-FILE

D ☐ Check if this is a publicly traded partnership (PTP)

Part II Information About the Partner

E Partner's SSN or TIN (Do not use TIN of a disregarded entity. See instructions.)
123-45-6789

F Name, address, city, state, and ZIP code for partner entered in E. See instructions.
ALISHIA M. CODEHEAD
3358 CASE AVE.
LOS ANGELES, CA 91753

G [X] General partner or LLC member-manager ☐ Limited partner or other LLC member

H1 [X] Domestic partner ☐ Foreign partner

H2 ☐ If the partner is a disregarded entity (DE), enter the partner's: TIN ______ Name ______

I1 What type of entity is this partner? INDIVIDUAL

I2 If this partner is a retirement plan (IRA/SEP/Keogh/etc.), check here ☐

J Partner's share of profit, loss, and capital (see instructions):

	Beginning	Ending
Profit	33 %	33 %
Loss	33 %	33 %
Capital	33 %	33 %

Check if decrease is due to sale or exchange of partnership interest ☐

K Partner's share of liabilities:

	Beginning	Ending
Nonrecourse	$	$
Qualified nonrecourse financing	$	$
Recourse	$	$

Check this box if item K includes liability amounts from lower-tier partnerships ☐

L **Partner's Capital Account Analysis**

Beginning capital account	$ 38,280.
Capital contributed during the year	$
Current year net income (loss)	$ 168,577.
Other increase (decrease) (attach explanation)	$
Withdrawals and distributions	$(165,000.)
Ending capital account	$ 41,857.

M Did the partner contribute property with a built-in gain (loss)?
☐ **Yes** [X] **No** If "Yes," attach statement. See instructions.

N **Partner's Share of Net Unrecognized Section 704(c) Gain or (Loss)**
Beginning $
Ending $

Part III Partner's Share of Current Year Income, Deductions, Credits, and Other Items

1	Ordinary business income (loss)	188,377.
2	Net rental real estate income (loss)	
3	Other net rental income (loss)	
4a	Guaranteed payments for services	
4b	Guaranteed payments for capital	
4c	Total guaranteed payments	
5	Interest income	
6a	Ordinary dividends	
6b	Qualified dividends	
6c	Dividend equivalents	
7	Royalties	
8	Net short-term capital gain (loss)	
9a	Net long-term capital gain (loss)	
9b	Collectibles (28%) gain (loss)	
9c	Unrecaptured section 1250 gain	
10	Net section 1231 gain (loss)	
11	Other income (loss)	
12	Section 179 deduction	19,800.
13	Other deductions	
14	Self-employment earnings (loss)	A 188,377.
15	Credits	
16	Schedule K-3 is attached if checked ☐	
17	Alternative minimum tax (AMT) items	A -219.
18	Tax-exempt income and nondeductible expenses	
19	Distributions	A 165,000.
20	Other information	Z* STMT
21	Foreign taxes paid or accrued	

22 ☐ More than one activity for at-risk purposes*
23 ☐ More than one activity for passive activity purposes*

*See attached statement for additional information.

For IRS Use Only

BAA For Paperwork Reduction Act Notice, see the Instructions for Form 1065. www.irs.gov/Form1065 **Schedule K-1 (Form 1065) 2022**
PARTNER 3 PTPA0312L 07/28/22

Statement A—QBI Pass-through Entity Reporting (Schedule K-1, Box 20, Code Z)

Partnership's name: DEALMAKER & CODEHEAD	**Partnership's EIN:** 95-0000001
Partner's name: ALISHIA M. CODEHEAD	**Partner's identifying number:** 123-45-6789

Partner's share of:	DEALMAKER & CODEHEAD ☐ PTP ☐ Aggregated ☒ SSTB	☐ PTP ☐ Aggregated ☐ SSTB	☐ PTP ☐ Aggregated ☐ SSTB
QBI or qualified PTP items subject to partner-specific determinations:			
Ordinary business income (loss)	188,377.		
Rental income (loss)			
Royalty income (loss)			
Section 1231 gain (loss)			
Other income (loss)			
Section 179 deduction	19,800.		
Other deductions			
W-2 wages	449,838.		
UBIA of qualified property	79,860.		
Qualified REIT dividends			

Partner's share of:	☐ PTP ☐ Aggregated ☐ SSTB	☐ PTP ☐ Aggregated ☐ SSTB	☐ PTP ☐ Aggregated ☐ SSTB
QBI or qualified PTP items subject to partner-specific determinations:			
Ordinary business income (loss)			
Rental income (loss)			
Royalty income (loss)			
Section 1231 gain (loss)			
Other income (loss)			
Section 179 deduction			
Other deductions			
W-2 wages			
UBIA of qualified property			

PARTNER 3

Form **4562**

Department of the Treasury Internal Revenue Service

Depreciation and Amortization
(Including Information on Listed Property)
Attach to your tax return.
Go to *www.irs.gov/Form4562* for instructions and the latest information.

OMB No. 1545-0172

2022

Attachment Sequence No. **179**

Name(s) shown on return: DEALMAKER & CODEHEAD

Identifying number: 95-0000001

Business or activity to which this form relates: FORM 1065

Part I — Election To Expense Certain Property Under Section 179
Note: If you have any listed property, complete Part V before you complete Part I.

1	Maximum amount (see instructions)		1	1,080,000.
2	Total cost of section 179 property placed in service (see instructions)		2	60,000.
3	Threshold cost of section 179 property before reduction in limitation (see instructions)		3	2,700,000.
4	Reduction in limitation. Subtract line 3 from line 2. If zero or less, enter -0-		4	0.
5	Dollar limitation for tax year. Subtract line 4 from line 1. If zero or less, enter -0-. If married filing separately, see instructions		5	1,080,000.

6 (a) Description of property	(b) Cost (business use only)	(c) Elected cost
5-YEAR COMPUTER	15,000.	15,000.
7-YEAR FURNITURE & FIXTURES	25,000.	25,000.
7 Listed property. Enter the amount from line 29	7	20,000.

8	Total elected cost of section 179 property. Add amounts in column (c), lines 6 and 7		8	60,000.
9	Tentative deduction. Enter the **smaller** of line 5 or line 8		9	60,000.
10	Carryover of disallowed deduction from line 13 of your 2021 Form 4562		10	0.
11	Business income limitation. Enter the smaller of business income (not less than zero) or line 5. See instrs		11	570,840.
12	Section 179 expense deduction. Add lines 9 and 10, but don't enter more than line 11		12	60,000.
13	Carryover of disallowed deduction to 2023. Add lines 9 and 10, less line 12	13	0.	

Note: Don't use Part II or Part III below for listed property. Instead, use Part V.

Part II — Special Depreciation Allowance and Other Depreciation (**Don't** include listed property. See instructions.)

14	Special depreciation allowance for qualified property (other than listed property) placed in service during the tax year. See instructions	14	
15	Property subject to section 168(f)(1) election	15	
16	Other depreciation (including ACRS)	16	

Part III — MACRS Depreciation (**Don't** include listed property. See instructions.)

Section A

17	MACRS deductions for assets placed in service in tax years beginning before 2022	17	3,264.
18	If you are electing to group any assets placed in service during the tax year into one or more general asset accounts, check here ☐		

Section B — Assets Placed in Service During 2022 Tax Year Using the General Depreciation System

(a) Classification of property	(b) Month and year placed in service	(c) Basis for depreciation (business/investment use only — see instructions)	(d) Recovery period	(e) Convention	(f) Method	(g) Depreciation deduction
19a 3-year property						
b 5-year property						
c 7-year property						
d 10-year property						
e 15-year property						
f 20-year property						
g 25-year property			25 yrs		S/L	
h Residential rental property			27.5 yrs	MM	S/L	
			27.5 yrs	MM	S/L	
i Nonresidential real property			39 yrs	MM	S/L	
				MM	S/L	

Section C — Assets Placed in Service During 2022 Tax Year Using the Alternative Depreciation System

(a) Classification of property	(b) Month and year placed in service	(c) Basis for depreciation	(d) Recovery period	(e) Convention	(f) Method	(g) Depreciation deduction
20a Class life					S/L	
b 12-year			12 yrs		S/L	
c 30-year			30 yrs	MM	S/L	
d 40-year			40 yrs	MM	S/L	

Part IV — Summary (See instructions.)

21	Listed property. Enter amount from line 28	21	9,700.
22	**Total.** Add amounts from line 12, lines 14 through 17, lines 19 and 20 in column (g), and line 21. Enter here and on the appropriate lines of your return. Partnerships and S corporations — see instructions	22	12,964.
23	For assets shown above and placed in service during the current year, enter the portion of the basis attributable to section 263A costs	23	

BAA For Paperwork Reduction Act Notice, see separate instructions. FDIZ0812L 06/28/22 Form **4562** (2022)

Form 4562 (2022) DEALMAKER & CODEHEAD 95-0000001 Page **2**

Part V Listed Property (Include automobiles, certain other vehicles, certain aircraft, and property used for entertainment, recreation, or amusement.)

Note: For any vehicle for which you are using the standard mileage rate or deducting lease expense, complete **only** 24a, 24b, columns (a) through (c) of Section A, all of Section B, and Section C if applicable.

Section A – Depreciation and Other Information (Caution: See the instructions for limits for passenger automobiles.**)**

24a Do you have evidence to support the business/investment use claimed? [X] **Yes** [ ] **No** **24b** If 'Yes,' is the evidence written? [X] **Yes** [ ] **No**

(a) Type of property (list vehicles first)	**(b)** Date placed in service	**(c)** Business/investment use percentage	**(d)** Cost or other basis	**(e)** Basis for depreciation (business/investment use only)	**(f)** Recovery period	**(g)** Method/Convention	**(h)** Depreciation deduction	**(i)** Elected section 179 cost
25 Special depreciation allowance for qualified listed property placed in service during the tax year and used more than 50% in a qualified business use. See instructions . . . **25**								
26 Property used more than 50% in a qualified business use:								
MERCEDES	12/01/20	100.0	74,000.	55,900.	5.0	200DB HY	9,700.	
PHONES SYSTE	9/30/22	100.0	20,000.		5.0	200DB HY		20,000.
27 Property used 50% or less in a qualified business use:								
28 Add amounts in column (h), lines 25 through 27. Enter here and on line 21, page 1 . . . **28**							9,700.	
29 Add amounts in column (i), line 26. Enter here and on line 7, page 1 . . . **29**								20,000.

Section B – Information on Use of Vehicles

Complete this section for vehicles used by a sole proprietor, partner, or other 'more than 5% owner,' or related person. If you provided vehicles to your employees, first answer the questions in Section C to see if you meet an exception to completing this section for those vehicles.

	(a) Vehicle 1		**(b)** Vehicle 2		**(c)** Vehicle 3		**(d)** Vehicle 4		**(e)** Vehicle 5		**(f)** Vehicle 6	
30 Total business/investment miles driven during the year (**don't** include commuting miles)												
31 Total commuting miles driven during the year												
32 Total other personal (noncommuting) miles driven												
33 Total miles driven during the year. Add lines 30 through 32												
	Yes	No	Yes	No	Yes	No	Yes	No	Yes	No	Yes	No
34 Was the vehicle available for personal use during off-duty hours?												
35 Was the vehicle used primarily by a more than 5% owner or related person?												
36 Is another vehicle available for personal use?												

Section C – Questions for Employers Who Provide Vehicles for Use by Their Employees

Answer these questions to determine if you meet an exception to completing Section B for vehicles used by employees who **aren't** more than 5% owners or related persons. See instructions.

	Yes	No
37 Do you maintain a written policy statement that prohibits all personal use of vehicles, including commuting, by your employees?		
38 Do you maintain a written policy statement that prohibits personal use of vehicles, except commuting, by your employees? See the instructions for vehicles used by corporate officers, directors, or 1% or more owners		
39 Do you treat all use of vehicles by employees as personal use?		
40 Do you provide more than five vehicles to your employees, obtain information from your employees about the use of the vehicles, and retain the information received?		
41 Do you meet the requirements concerning qualified automobile demonstration use? See instructions. **Note:** If your answer to 37, 38, 39, 40, or 41 is 'Yes,' don't complete Section B for the covered vehicles.		

Part VI Amortization

(a) Description of costs	**(b)** Date amortization begins	**(c)** Amortizable amount	**(d)** Code section	**(e)** Amortization period or percentage	**(f)** Amortization for this year
42 Amortization of costs that begins during your 2022 tax year (see instructions):					
43 Amortization of costs that began before your 2022 tax year . . . **43**					
44 **Total.** Add amounts in column (f). See the instructions for where to report . . . **44**					

2022 | **FEDERAL STATEMENTS** | **PAGE 1**

DEALMAKER & CODEHEAD | **95-0000001**

STATEMENT 1
FORM 1065, LINE 20
OTHER DEDUCTIONS

ADVERTISING	$	853.
APPRAISAL SERVICES		67,990.
AUTO AND TRUCK EXPENSE		2,099.
BANK CHARGES		10.
BUSINESS DEVELOPMENT		3,112.
CLIENT DEVELOPMENT		21,485.
CONSULTANTS		128,702.
COURT REPORTERS		64,193.
DESPOSITION		2,296.
EXPERT WITNESS		12,183.
FILING AND RECORDING FEES		22,746.
INSURANCE		114,156.
LEGAL AND PROFESSIONAL		46,784.
LEGAL LIBRARY RESEARCH SERVICES		2,777.
LIBRARY AND SUBSCRIPTIONS		51,106.
MEALS		13,093.
MESSENGER AND DELIVERY		29,482.
MISCELLANEOUS		59,548.
OFFICE EXPENSE		99,668.
PARALEGAL		2,501.
PARKING AND TOLLS		14,800.
PAYROLL SERVICES		1,454.
POSTAGE		9,014.
PRINTING		82,459.
PROFESSIONAL FEES		45,155.
RECRUITING		158,575.
SEMINARS		1,350.
SO CAL ATTORNEY SERVICE		13,916.
STORAGE		7,040.
TELEPHONE		31,925.
TRAVEL		38,531.
UTILITIES		218.
TOTAL	$	1,149,221.

STATEMENT 2
FORM 1065, SCHEDULE L, LINE 6
OTHER CURRENT ASSETS

		BEGINNING		ENDING
NOTE RECEIVABLE	$	54,584.	$	50,000.
PREPAID RENT		1,709.		1,709.
TRUST ACCOUNT		110,309.		10,309.
TOTAL	$	166,602.	$	62,018.

2022	FEDERAL STATEMENTS	PAGE 2
	DEALMAKER & CODEHEAD	95-0000001

STATEMENT 3
FORM 1065, SCHEDULE L, LINE 17
OTHER CURRENT LIABILITIES

	BEGINNING	ENDING
OTHER CURENT LIABILITIES	$ 110,309.	$ 110,309.
TOTAL	$ 110,309.	$ 110,309.

12/31/22

2022 FEDERAL DEPRECIATION SCHEDULE

PAGE 1

HUDSON GREY PROPERTIES

95-0000002

NO.	DESCRIPTION	DATE ACQUIRED	DATE SOLD	COST/ BASIS	BUS. PCT.	CUR 179 BONUS	SPECIAL DEPR. ALLOW.	PRIOR 179/ BONUS/ SP. DEPR.	PRIOR DEC. BAL DEPR.	SALVAG /BASIS REDUCT	DEPR. BASIS	PRIOR DEPR.	METHOD	LIFE	RATE	CURRENT DEPR.
	RENTAL REAL ESTATE - RESIDENTIAL RENRAL REAL ESTATE															
	BUILDINGS															
1	BUILDING **	2/01/04		1,050,607							1,050,607	682,895	S/L MM	27.5	.03636	38,200
	TOTAL BUILDINGS			1,050,607		0	0	0	0	0	1,050,607	682,895				38,200
	FURNITURE AND FIXTURES															
2	FURNITURE AND FIXTURES	2/01/04		20,029							20,029	20,029	200DB HY	7		0
3	FURNITURE AND FIXTURES **	6/15/19		6,500							6,500	3,658	200DB HY	7	.12490	812
	TOTAL FURNITURE AND FIXTURE			26,529		0	0	0	0	0	26,529	23,687				812
	IMPROVEMENTS															
4	IMPROVEMENTS **	6/15/19		113,214							113,214	10,464	S/L MM	27.5	.03636	4,116
	TOTAL IMPROVEMENTS			113,214		0	0	0	0	0	113,214	10,464				4,116
	LAND															
5	LAND	2/01/04		142,578							142,578					0
	TOTAL LAND			142,578		0	0	0	0	0	142,578	0				0
	TOTAL DEPRECIATION			1,332,928		0	0	0	0	0	1,332,928	717,046				43,128
	GRAND TOTAL DEPRECIATION			1,332,928		0	0	0	0	0	1,332,928	717,046				43,128

12/31/22 **2022 FEDERAL DEPRECIATION SCHEDULE** PAGE 2

HUDSON GREY PROPERTIES 95-0000002

NO.	DESCRIPTION	DATE ACQUIRED	DATE SOLD	COST/ BASIS	BUS. PCT.	CUR 179 BONUS	SPECIAL DEPR. ALLOW.	PRIOR 179/ BONUS/ SP. DEPR.	PRIOR DEC. BAL DEPR.	SALVAG /BASIS REDUCT	DEPR. BASIS	PRIOR DEPR.	METHOD	LIFE	RATE	CURRENT DEPR.

**ASSET INCLUDED IN UNADJUSTED BASIS IMMEDIATELY AFTER ACQUISITION FOR THE QBI CALCULATION.

Form **1065** — Department of the Treasury, Internal Revenue Service

U.S. Return of Partnership Income

For calendar year 2022, or tax year beginning ____________, 2022, ending ____________, 20 ____.

Go to *www.irs.gov/Form1065* for instructions and the latest information.

OMB No. 1545-0123

2022

A Principal business activity: RENTALS	Type or Print: HUDSON GREY PROPERTIES 2558 LINCOLN ST., SUITE 456 LOS ANGELES, CA 91234	D Employer identification no.: 95-0000002
B Principal product or service: RESIDENTIAL		E Date business started: 2/01/2003
C Business code number: 531110		F Total assets (see instructions): $ 660,511.

G Check applicable boxes: (1) ☐ Initial return (2) ☐ Final return (3) ☐ Name change (4) ☐ Address change (5) ☐ Amended return

H Check accounting method: (1) ☒ Cash (2) ☐ Accrual (3) ☐ Other (specify):

I Number of Schedules K-1. Attach one for each person who was a partner at any time during the tax year: 2

J Check if Schedules C and M-3 are attached ☐

K Check if partnership: (1) ☐ Aggregated activities for section 465 at-risk purposes (2) ☐ Grouped activities for section 469 passive activity purposes

Caution: Include **only** trade or business income and expenses on lines 1a through 22 below. See the instructions for more information.

INCOME	1 a	Gross receipts or sales	1a		
	b	Returns and allowances	1b		
	c	Balance. Subtract line 1b from line 1a		1c	
	2	Cost of goods sold (attach Form 1125-A)		2	
	3	Gross profit. Subtract line 2 from line 1c		3	
	4	Ordinary income (loss) from other partnerships, estates, and trusts (attach statement)		4	
	5	Net farm profit (loss) (attach Schedule F (Form 1040))		5	
	6	Net gain (loss) from Form 4797, Part II, line 17 (attach Form 4797)		6	
	7	Other income (loss) (attach statement)		7	
	8	**Total income (loss).** Combine lines 3 through 7		8	
DEDUCTIONS (SEE INSTRS FOR LIMITATIONS)	9	Salaries and wages (other than to partners) (less employment credits)		9	
	10	Guaranteed payments to partners		10	
	11	Repairs and maintenance		11	
	12	Bad debts		12	
	13	Rent		13	
	14	Taxes and licenses		14	
	15	Interest (see instructions)		15	
	16 a	Depreciation (if required, attach Form 4562)	16a		
	b	Less depreciation reported on Form 1125-A and elsewhere on return	16b	16c	
	17	Depletion **(Do not deduct oil and gas depletion.)**		17	
	18	Retirement plans, etc.		18	
	19	Employee benefit programs		19	
	20	Other deductions (att stmt)		20	
	21	**Total deductions.** Add the amounts shown in the far right column for lines 9 through 20		21	
	22	**Ordinary business income (loss).** Subtract line 21 from line 8		22	
TAX AND PAYMENT	23	Interest due under the look-back method — completed long-term contracts (attach Form 8697)		23	
	24	Interest due under the look-back method — income forecast method (attach Form 8866)		24	
	25	BBA AAR imputed underpayment (see instructions)		25	
	26	Other taxes (see instructions)		26	
	27	**Total balance due.** Add lines 23 through 26		27	
	28	Payment (see instructions)		28	
	29	**Amount owed.** If line 28 is smaller than line 27, enter amount owed		29	
	30	**Overpayment.** If line 28 is larger than line 27, enter overpayment		30	

Sign Here

Under penalties of perjury, I declare that I have examined this return, including accompanying schedules and statements, and to the best of my knowledge and belief, it is true, correct, and complete. Declaration of preparer (other than partner or limited liability company member) is based on all information of which preparer has any knowledge.

Signature of partner or limited liability company member — Date

May the IRS discuss this return with the preparer shown below? See instructions. ☒ Yes ☐ No

Paid Preparer Use Only

Print/Type preparer's name	Preparer's signature	Date	Check ☒ if self-employed	PTIN
RON E. THOMPSON	RON E. THOMPSON			P00166602

Firm's name: WHITE ZUCKERMAN WARSAVSKY LUNA HUNT LLP — Firm's EIN: 95-4115549

Firm's address: 15490 VENTURA BLVD 3RD FL, SHERMAN OAKS, CA 91403 — Phone no. (818) 981-4226

BAA For Paperwork Reduction Act Notice, see separate instructions. PTPA0105 07/28/22 Form **1065** (2022)

Form 1065 (2022) HUDSON GREY PROPERTIES 95-0000002 Page 2

Schedule B Other Information

		Yes	No
1	What type of entity is filing this return? Check the applicable box: a ☐ Domestic general partnership b ☒ Domestic limited partnership c ☐ Domestic limited liability company d ☐ Domestic limited liability partnership e ☐ Foreign partnership f ☐ Other:		
2	At the end of the tax year: a Did any foreign or domestic corporation, partnership (including any entity treated as a partnership), trust, or tax-exempt organization, or any foreign government own, directly or indirectly, an interest of 50% or more in the profit, loss, or capital of the partnership? For rules of constructive ownership, see instructions. If "Yes," attach Schedule B-1, Information on Partners Owning 50% or More of the Partnership		X
	b Did any individual or estate own, directly or indirectly, an interest of 50% or more in the profit, loss, or capital of the partnership? For rules of constructive ownership, see instructions. If "Yes," attach Schedule B-1, Information on Partners Owning 50% or More of the Partnership	X	
3	At the end of the tax year, did the partnership: a Own directly 20% or more, or own, directly or indirectly, 50% or more of the total voting power of all classes of stock entitled to vote of any foreign or domestic corporation? For rules of constructive ownership, see instructions. If "Yes," complete (i) through (iv) below		X

(i) Name of Corporation	(ii) Employer Identification Number (if any)	(iii) Country of Incorporation	(iv) Percentage Owned in Voting Stock

	Yes	No
b Own directly an interest of 20% or more, or own, directly or indirectly, an interest of 50% or more in the profit, loss, or capital in any foreign or domestic partnership (including an entity treated as a partnership) or in the beneficial interest of a trust? For rules of constructive ownership, see instructions. If "Yes," complete (i) through (v) below		X

(i) Name of Entity	(ii) Employer Identification Number (if any)	(iii) Type of Entity	(iv) Country of Organization	(v) Maximum Percentage Owned in Profit, Loss, or Capital

		Yes	No
4	Does the partnership satisfy **all four** of the following conditions? a The partnership's total receipts for the tax year were less than $250,000. b The partnership's total assets at the end of the tax year were less than $1 million. c Schedules K-1 are filed with the return and furnished to the partners on or before the due date (including extensions) for the partnership return. d The partnership is not filing and is not required to file Schedule M-3		X
	If "Yes," the partnership is not required to complete Schedules L, M-1, and M-2; item F on page 1 of Form 1065; or item L on Schedule K-1.		
5	Is this partnership a publicly traded partnership, as defined in section 469(k)(2)?		X
6	During the tax year, did the partnership have any debt that was canceled, was forgiven, or had the terms modified so as to reduce the principal amount of the debt?		X
7	Has this partnership filed, or is it required to file, Form 8918, Material Advisor Disclosure Statement, to provide information on any reportable transaction?		X
8	At any time during calendar year 2022, did the partnership have an interest in or a signature or other authority over a financial account in a foreign country (such as a bank account, securities account, or other financial account)? See instructions for exceptions and filing requirements for FinCEN Form 114, Report of Foreign Bank and Financial Accounts (FBAR). If "Yes," enter the name of the foreign country.		X
9	At any time during the tax year, did the partnership receive a distribution from, or was it the grantor of, or transferor to, a foreign trust? If "Yes," the partnership may have to file Form 3520, Annual Return To Report Transactions With Foreign Trusts and Receipt of Certain Foreign Gifts. See instructions		X
10a	Is the partnership making, or had it previously made (and not revoked), a section 754 election? See instructions for details regarding a section 754 election.		X
b	Did the partnership make for this tax year an optional basis adjustment under section 743(b) or 734(b)? If "Yes," attach a statement showing the computation and allocation of the basis adjustment. See instructions		X
c	Is the partnership required to adjust the basis of partnership assets under section 743(b) or 734(b) because of a substantial built-in loss (as defined under section 743(d)) or substantial basis reduction (as defined under section 734(d))? If "Yes," attach a statement showing the computation and allocation of the basis adjustment. See instructions		X

BAA PTPA0112 07/28/22 Form **1065** (2022)

Form 1065 (2022) HUDSON GREY PROPERTIES 95-0000002 Page **3**

Schedule B **Other Information** *(continued)*

		Yes	No
11	Check this box if, during the current or prior tax year, the partnership distributed any property received in a like-kind exchange or contributed such property to another entity (other than disregarded entities wholly owned by the partnership throughout the tax year) ☐		
12	At any time during the tax year, did the partnership distribute to any partner a tenancy-in-common or other undivided interest in partnership property?		X
13	If the partnership is required to file Form 8858, Information Return of U.S. Persons With Respect to Foreign Disregarded Entities (FDEs) and Foreign Branches (FBs), enter the number of Forms 8858 attached. See instructions ____		
14	Does the partnership have any foreign partners? If "Yes," enter the number of Forms 8805, Foreign Partner's Information Statement of Section 1446 Withholding Tax, filed for this partnership ____		X
15	Enter the number of Forms 8865, Return of U.S. Persons With Respect to Certain Foreign Partnerships, attached to this return ____		
16a	Did you make any payments in 2022 that would require you to file Form(s) 1099? See instructions		X
b	If "Yes," did you or will you file required Form(s) 1099?		
17	Enter the number of Forms 5471, Information Return of U.S. Persons With Respect to Certain Foreign Corporations, attached to this return ____		
18	Enter the number of partners that are foreign governments under section 892. 0		
19	During the partnership's tax year, did the partnership make any payments that would require it to file Forms 1042 and 1042-S under chapter 3 (sections 1441 through 1464) or chapter 4 (sections 1471 through 1474)?		X
20	Was the partnership a specified domestic entity required to file Form 8938 for the tax year? See the Instructions for Form 8938		X
21	Is the partnership a section 721(c) partnership, as defined in Regulations section 1.721(c)-1(b)(14)?		X
22	During the tax year, did the partnership pay or accrue any interest or royalty for which one or more partners are not allowed a deduction under section 267A? See instructions If "Yes," enter the total amount of the disallowed deductions $____		X
23	Did the partnership have an election under section 163(j) for any real property trade or business or any farming business in effect during the tax year? See instructions		X
24	Does the partnership satisfy one or more of the following? See instructions **a** The partnership owns a pass-through entity with current, or prior year carryover, excess business interest expense. **b** The partnership's aggregate average annual gross receipts (determined under section 448(c)) for the 3 tax years preceding the current tax year are more than $27 million and the partnership has business interest expense. **c** The partnership is a tax shelter (see instructions) and the partnership has business interest expense. If "Yes" to any, complete and attach Form 8990.		X
25	Is the partnership attaching Form 8996 to certify as a Qualified Opportunity Fund? If "Yes," enter the amount from Form 8996, line 15 $____		X
26	Enter the number of foreign partners subject to section 864(c)(8) as a result of transferring all or a portion of an interest in the partnership or of receiving a distribution from the partnership ____ Complete Schedule K-3 (Form 1065), Part XIII, for each foreign partner subject to section 864(c)(8) on a transfer or distribution.		
27	At any time during the tax year, were there any transfers between the partnership and its partners subject to the disclosure requirements of Regulations section 1.707-8?		X
28	Since December 22, 2017, did a foreign corporation directly or indirectly acquire substantially all of the properties constituting a trade or business of your partnership, and was the ownership percentage (by vote or value) for purposes of section 7874 greater than 50% (for example, the partners held more than 50% of the stock of the foreign corporation)? If "Yes," list the ownership percentage by vote and by value. See instructions. Percentage: By vote: ____ By value: ____		X
29	Reserved for future use		
30	Is the partnership electing out of the centralized partnership audit regime under section 6221(b)? See instructions. If "Yes," the partnership must complete Schedule B-2 (Form 1065). Enter the total from Schedule B-2, Part III, line 3 ____ If "No," complete Designation of Partnership Representative below.		X

Designation of Partnership Representative (see instructions)

Enter below the information for the partnership representative (PR) for the tax year covered by this return.

Name of PR JEREMY R. HUDSON

U.S. address of PR	2873 PRAIRE ST. LOS ANGELES, CA 93456	U.S. phone number of PR	

If the PR is an entity, name of the designated individual for the PR

U.S. address of designated individual		U.S. phone number of designated individual	

BAA Form **1065** (2022)

PTPA0112 12/13/22

Form 1065 (2022) HUDSON GREY PROPERTIES 95-0000002 Page 4

Schedule K — Partners' Distributive Share Items

			Total amount
Income (Loss)	1 Ordinary business income (loss) (page 1, line 22)	1	
	2 Net rental real estate income (loss) (attach Form 8825)	2	147,434.
	3a Other gross rental income (loss) — 3a		
	b Expenses from other rental activities (attach stmt) — 3b		
	c Other net rental income (loss). Subtract line 3b from line 3a	3c	
	4 Guaranteed payments: a Services 4a — b Capital 4b		
	c Total. Add lines 4a and 4b	4c	
	5 Interest income	5	
	6 Dividends and dividend equivalents: a Ordinary dividends	6a	
	b Qualified dividends 6b — c Dividend equivalents 6c		
	7 Royalties	7	
	8 Net short-term capital gain (loss) (attach Schedule D (Form 1065))	8	
	9a Net long-term capital gain (loss) (attach Schedule D (Form 1065))	9a	
	b Collectibles (28%) gain (loss) — 9b		
	c Unrecaptured section 1250 gain (attach statement) — 9c		
	10 Net section 1231 gain (loss) (attach Form 4797)	10	
	11 Other income (loss) (see instructions) Type:	11	
Deductions	12 Section 179 deduction (attach Form 4562)	12	
	13a Contributions	13a	
	b Investment interest expense	13b	
	c Section 59(e)(2) expenditures: (1) Type: (2) Amount:	13c(2)	
	d Other deductions (see instructions) Type:	13d	
Self-Employment	14a Net earnings (loss) from self-employment	14a	
	b Gross farming or fishing income	14b	
	c Gross nonfarm income	14c	
Credits	15a Low-income housing credit (section 42(j)(5))	15a	
	b Low-income housing credit (other)	15b	
	c Qualified rehabilitation expenditures (rental real estate) (attach Form 3468, if applicable)	15c	
	d Other rental real estate credits (see instructions) Type:	15d	
	e Other rental credits (see instructions) Type:	15e	
	f Other credits (see instructions) Type:	15f	
International	16 Attach Schedule K-2 (Form 1065), Partners' Distributive Share Items—International, and check this box to indicate that you are reporting items of international tax relevance ☐		
Alternative Minimum Tax (AMT) Items	17a Post-1986 depreciation adjustment	17a	16.
	b Adjusted gain or loss	17b	
	c Depletion (other than oil and gas)	17c	
	d Oil, gas, and geothermal properties — gross income	17d	
	e Oil, gas, and geothermal properties — deductions	17e	
	f Other AMT items (attach stmt)	17f	
Other Information	18a Tax-exempt interest income	18a	
	b Other tax-exempt income	18b	
	c Nondeductible expenses	18c	
	19a Distributions of cash and marketable securities	19a	100,000.
	b Distributions of other property	19b	
	20a Investment income	20a	
	b Investment expenses	20b	
	c Other items and amounts (attach stmt) SEE STATEMENT 1		
	21 Total foreign taxes paid or accrued	21	

BAA PTPA0134 07/28/22 Form 1065 (2022)

Form 1065 (2022) HUDSON GREY PROPERTIES 95-0000002 Page **5**

Analysis of Net Income (Loss) per Return

1 Net income (loss). Combine Schedule K, lines 1 through 11. From the result, subtract the sum of Schedule K, lines 12 through 13d, and 21	1	147,434.

2 Analysis by partner type:	**(i)** Corporate	**(ii)** Individual (active)	**(iii)** Individual (passive)	**(iv)** Partnership	**(v)** Exempt Organization	**(vi)** Nominee/Other
a General partners		73,717.				
b Limited partners		73,717.				

Schedule L Balance Sheets per Books

	Beginning of tax year		End of tax year	
Assets	**(a)**	**(b)**	**(c)**	**(d)**
1 Cash		85,579.		136,971.
2a Trade notes and accounts receivable				
b Less allowance for bad debts				
3 Inventories				
4 U.S. Government obligations				
5 Tax-exempt securities				
6 Other current assets (attach stmt)				
7a Loans to partners (or persons related to partners)				
b Mortgage and real estate loans				
8 Other investments (attach stmt)				
9a Buildings and other depreciable assets	1,132,928.		1,132,928.	
b Less accumulated depreciation	717,046.	415,882.	760,174.	372,754.
10a Depletable assets				
b Less accumulated depletion				
11 Land (net of any amortization)		142,578.		142,578.
12a Intangible assets (amortizable only)	15,000.		15,000.	
b Less accumulated amortization	6,292.	8,708.	6,792.	8,208.
13 Other assets (attach stmt)				
14 Total assets		652,747.		660,511.
Liabilities and Capital				
15 Accounts payable				
16 Mortgages, notes, bonds payable in less than 1 year		245,550.		220,880.
17 Other current liabilities (attach stmt) SEE ST 2		20,361.		20,361.
18 All nonrecourse loans				
19a Loans from partners (or persons related to partners)		440,000.		425,000.
b Mortgages, notes, bonds payable in 1 year or more				
20 Other liabilities (attach stmt)				
21 Partners' capital accounts		-53,164.		-5,730.
22 Total liabilities and capital		652,747.		660,511.

Schedule M-1 Reconciliation of Income (Loss) per Books With Analysis of Net Income (Loss) per Return

Note: The partnership may be required to file Schedule M-3. See instructions.

1 Net income (loss) per books	147,434.	**6** Income recorded on books this year not included on Schedule K, lines 1 through 11 (itemize): **a** Tax-exempt interest $	
2 Income included on Schedule K, lines 1, 2, 3c, 5, 6a, 7, 8, 9a, 10, and 11, not recorded on books this year (itemize):			
3 Guaranteed payments (other than health insurance)		**7** Deductions included on Schedule K, lines 1 through 13d, and 21, not charged against book income this year (itemize): **a** Depreciation $	
4 Expenses recorded on books this year not included on Schedule K, lines 1 through 13d, and 21 (itemize): **a** Depreciation $ **b** Travel and entertainment $			
		8 Add lines 6 and 7	
5 Add lines 1 through 4	147,434.	**9** Income (loss) (Analysis of Net Income (Loss), line 1). Subtract line 8 from line 5	147,434.

Schedule M-2 Analysis of Partners' Capital Accounts

1 Balance at beginning of year	-53,164.	**6** Distributions: **a** Cash	100,000.
2 Capital contributed: **a** Cash		**b** Property	
b Property		**7** Other decreases (itemize):	
3 Net income (loss) (see instructions)	147,434.		
4 Other increases (itemize):			
		8 Add lines 6 and 7	100,000.
5 Add lines 1 through 4	94,270.	**9** Balance at end of year. Subtract line 8 from line 5	-5,730.

Form **8825** (Rev. November 2018) Department of the Treasury Internal Revenue Service

Rental Real Estate Income and Expenses of a Partnership or an S Corporation

► Attach to Form 1065 or Form 1120S.
► Go to *www.irs.gov/Form8825* for the latest information.

OMB No. 1545-0123

Name: HUDSON GREY PROPERTIES

Employer identification number: 95-0000002

1 Show the type and address of each property. For each rental real estate property listed, report the number of days rented at fair rental value and days with personal use. See instructions. See page 2 to list additional properties.

	Physical address of each property – street, city, state, ZIP code	Type – Enter code 1–8; see page 2 for list	Fair Rental Days	Personal Use Days
A	9 MAIN STREET LOS ANGELES, CA 90069	2	365	
B				
C				
D				

Rental Real Estate Income		Properties A	B	C	D
2 Gross rents	2	510,272.			
Rental Real Estate Expenses					
3 Advertising	3	7,270.			
4 Auto and travel	4	274.			
5 Cleaning and maintenance	5	21,996.			
6 Commissions	6				
7 Insurance	7	11,476.			
8 Legal and other professional fees	8	4,636.			
9 Interest (see instructions)	9	32,000.			
10 Repairs	10	85,292.			
11 Taxes	11	42,670.			
12 Utilities	12	45,556.			
13 Wages and salaries	13	47,755.			
14 Depreciation (see instructions)	14	43,128.			
15 Other (list) ► SEE STATEMENT 3	15	20,785.			
16 Total expenses for each property. Add lines 3 through 15	16	362,838.			
17 Income or (loss) from each property. Subtract line 16 from line 2	17	147,434.			

18a Total gross rents. Add gross rents from line 2, columns A through H	18a	510,272.
b Total expenses. Add total expenses from line 16, columns A through H	18b	-362,838.
19 Net gain (loss) from Form 4797, Part II, line 17, from the disposition of property from rental real estate activities	19	
20a Net income (loss) from rental real estate activities from partnerships, estates, and trusts in which this partnership or S corporation is a partner or beneficiary (from Schedule K-1)	20a	
b Identify below the partnerships, estates, or trusts from which net income (loss) is shown on line 20a. Attach a schedule if more space is needed. (1) Name (2) Employer identification number		
21 Net rental real estate income (loss). Combine lines 18a through 20a. Enter the result here and on: • **Form 1065 or 1120S:** Schedule K, line 2	21	147,434.

Form 8825 (Rev. 11-2018) HUDSON GREY PROPERTIES 95-0000002 Page 2

1 Show the type and address of each property. For each rental real estate property listed, report the number of days at fair rental value and days with personal use. See instructions.

	Physical address of each property – street, city, state, ZIP code	Type – Enter code 1–8; see below for list	Fair Rental Days	Personal Use Days
E				
F				
G				
H				

		Properties			
Rental Real Estate Income		E	F	G	H
2 Gross rents	2				
Rental Real Estate Expenses					
3 Advertising	3				
4 Auto and travel	4				
5 Cleaning and maintenance	5				
6 Commissions	6				
7 Insurance	7				
8 Legal and other professional fees	8				
9 Interest (see instructions)	9				
10 Repairs	10				
11 Taxes	11				
12 Utilities	12				
13 Wages and salaries	13				
14 Depreciation (see instructions)	14				
15 Other (list) ►	15				
16 Total expenses for each property. Add lines 3 through 15	16				
17 Income or (loss) from each property. Subtract line 16 from line 2	17				

Allowable Codes for Type of Property

1 – Single Family Residence
2 – Multi-Family Residence
3 – Vacation or Short-Term Rental
4 – Commercial
5 – Land
6 – Royalties
7 – Self-Rental
8 – Other (include description with the code on Form 8825 or on a separate statement)

SCHEDULE B-1
(Form 1065)
(Rev. August 2019)
Department of the Treasury
Internal Revenue Service

Information on Partners Owning 50% or More of the Partnership

► **Attach to Form 1065.**
► **Go to *www.irs.gov/Form1065* for the latest information.**

OMB No. 1545-0123

Name of partnership	Employer identification number (EIN)
HUDSON GREY PROPERTIES	95-0000002

Part I **Entities Owning 50% or More of the Partnership** (Form 1065, Schedule B, Question 2a (Question 3a for 2009 through 2017))

Complete columns (i) through (v) below for any foreign or domestic corporation, partnership (including any entity treated as a partnership), trust, tax-exempt organization, or any foreign government that owns, directly or indirectly, an interest of 50% or more in the profit, loss, or capital of the partnership (see instructions).

(i) Name of Entity	(ii) Employer Identification Number (if any)	(iii) Type of Entity	(iv) Country of Organization	(v) Maximum Percentage Owned in Profit, Loss, or Capital

Part II **Individuals or Estates Owning 50% or More of the Partnership** (Form 1065, Schedule B, Question 2b (Question 3b for 2009 through 2017))

Complete columns (i) through (iv) below for any individual or estate that owns, directly or indirectly, an interest of 50% or more in the profit, loss, or capital of the partnership (see instructions).

(i) Name of Individual or Estate	(ii) Identifying Number (if any)	(iii) Country of Citizenship (see instructions)	(iv) Maximum Percentage Owned in Profit, Loss, or Capital
JEREMY R. HUDSON	987-65-4321	UNITED STATES	50.000
THOMAS L. GREY	123-45-6789	UNITED STATES	50.000

BAA For Paperwork Reduction Act Notice, see the Instructions for Form 1065. Schedule **B-1** (Form 1065) (Rev. 8-2019)

PTPA1301L 07/18/19

651121

Schedule K-1 (Form 1065) **2022**
Department of the Treasury
Internal Revenue Service
For calendar year 2022, or tax year
beginning / / 2022 ending / /

☐ Final K-1 ☐ Amended K-1 OMB No. 1545-0123

Partner's Share of Income, Deductions, Credits, etc.
See separate instructions.

Part I Information About the Partnership

A Partnership's employer identification number
95-0000002

B Partnership's name, address, city, state, and ZIP code
HUDSON GREY PROPERTIES
2558 LINCOLN ST., SUITE 456
LOS ANGELES, CA 91234

C IRS center where partnership filed return: E-FILE

D ☐ Check if this is a publicly traded partnership (PTP)

Part II Information About the Partner

E Partner's SSN or TIN (Do not use TIN of a disregarded entity. See instructions.)
123-45-6789

F Name, address, city, state, and ZIP code for partner entered in E. See instructions.
THOMAS L. GREY
513 VISTA DRIVE
LOS ANGELES, CA 92345

G ☐ General partner or LLC member-manager ☒ Limited partner or other LLC member

H1 ☒ Domestic partner ☐ Foreign partner

H2 ☐ If the partner is a disregarded entity (DE), enter the partner's: TIN ______ Name ______

I1 What type of entity is this partner? INDIVIDUAL

I2 If this partner is a retirement plan (IRA/SEP/Keogh/etc.), check here ☐

J Partner's share of profit, loss, and capital (see instructions):

	Beginning	Ending
Profit	50 %	50 %
Loss	50 %	50 %
Capital	50 %	50 %

Check if decrease is due to sale or exchange of partnership interest ☐

K Partner's share of liabilities:

	Beginning	Ending
Nonrecourse	$	$
Qualified nonrecourse financing	$ 227,500.	$ 212,500.
Recourse	$	$

Check this box if item K includes liability amounts from lower-tier partnerships ☐

L **Partner's Capital Account Analysis**

Beginning capital account	$ -26,582.
Capital contributed during the year	$
Current year net income (loss)	$ 73,717.
Other increase (decrease) (attach explanation)	$
Withdrawals and distributions	$(50,000.)
Ending capital account	$ -2,865.

M Did the partner contribute property with a built-in gain (loss)?
☐ Yes ☒ No If "Yes," attach statement. See instructions.

N **Partner's Share of Net Unrecognized Section 704(c) Gain or (Loss)**
Beginning $
Ending $

Part III Partner's Share of Current Year Income, Deductions, Credits, and Other Items

1	Ordinary business income (loss)	
2	Net rental real estate income (loss)	* 73,717.
3	Other net rental income (loss)	
4a	Guaranteed payments for services	
4b	Guaranteed payments for capital	
4c	Total guaranteed payments	
5	Interest income	
6a	Ordinary dividends	
6b	Qualified dividends	
6c	Dividend equivalents	
7	Royalties	
8	Net short-term capital gain (loss)	
9a	Net long-term capital gain (loss)	
9b	Collectibles (28%) gain (loss)	
9c	Unrecaptured section 1250 gain	
10	Net section 1231 gain (loss)	
11	Other income (loss)	
12	Section 179 deduction	
13	Other deductions	
14	Self-employment earnings (loss)	
15	Credits	
16	Schedule K-3 is attached if checked ☐	
17	Alternative minimum tax (AMT) items	A 8.
18	Tax-exempt income and nondeductible expenses	
19	Distributions	A 50,000.
20	Other information	N* STMT; Z* STMT
21	Foreign taxes paid or accrued	

22 ☐ More than one activity for at-risk purposes*
23 ☐ More than one activity for passive activity purposes*
*See attached statement for additional information.

For IRS Use Only

BAA For Paperwork Reduction Act Notice, see the Instructions for Form 1065. www.irs.gov/Form1065 **Schedule K-1 (Form 1065) 2022**
PARTNER 1 PTPA0312L 07/28/22

HUDSON GREY PROPERTIES 95-0000002

SCHEDULE K-1 (FORM 1065) 2022 **SUPPLEMENTAL INFORMATION** PAGE 2

BOX 2
RENTAL REAL ESTATE ACTIVITIES

PROPERTY TYPE AND ADDRESS	GROSS INCOME	NET EXPENSES	NET INCOME	PASSIVE NONPASS	SEC. 1231 TOTAL
TYPE: 2 - MULTI-FAMILY RESIDENCE 9 MAIN STREET LOS ANGELES, CA 90069	255,136.	181,419.	$ 73,717.	PASSIVE	
		TOTAL	$ 73,717.		

BOX 20, CODE N
BUSINESS INTEREST EXPENSE
INCLUDED AS A DEDUCTION ON THE FOLLOWING LINE(S)

BELOW IS DEDUCTIBLE BUSINESS INTEREST EXPENSE FOR INCLUSION IN THE SEPARATE LOSS CLASS FOR COMPUTING ANY BASIS LIMITATION (DEFINED IN SECTION 704(D), REGULATION SECTION 1.163(J)-6(H)).

SCHEDULE K-1, LINE 2 .... $ 16,000.

PARTNER 1: THOMAS L. GREY 123-45-6789

SPSL1201L 07/06/22

Statement A—QBI Pass-through Entity Reporting (Schedule K-1, Box 20, Code Z)

Partnership's name: HUDSON GREY PROPERTIES	**Partnership's EIN:** 95-0000002
Partner's name: THOMAS L. GREY	**Partner's identifying number:** 123-45-6789

	HUDSON GREY PROPERTIES		
Partner's share of:	☐ PTP ☐ Aggregated ☐ SSTB	☐ PTP ☐ Aggregated ☐ SSTB	☐ PTP ☐ Aggregated ☐ SSTB
QBI or qualified PTP items subject to partner-specific determinations:			
Ordinary business income (loss)			
Rental income (loss)	73,717.		
Royalty income (loss)			
Section 1231 gain (loss)			
Other income (loss)			
Section 179 deduction			
Other deductions			
W-2 wages	23,877.		
UBIA of qualified property	585,160.		
Qualified REIT dividends			

Partner's share of:	☐ PTP ☐ Aggregated ☐ SSTB	☐ PTP ☐ Aggregated ☐ SSTB	☐ PTP ☐ Aggregated ☐ SSTB
QBI or qualified PTP items subject to partner-specific determinations:			
Ordinary business income (loss)			
Rental income (loss)			
Royalty income (loss)			
Section 1231 gain (loss)			
Other income (loss)			
Section 179 deduction			
Other deductions			
W-2 wages			
UBIA of qualified property			

PARTNER 1

BAA For Paperwork Reduction Act Notice, see the Instructions for Form 1065. PTPA1515 12/15/22 **Statement A (Form 1065) (2022)**

651121

Schedule K-1 (Form 1065) **2022**
Department of the Treasury
Internal Revenue Service

For calendar year 2022, or tax year
beginning / / 2022 ending / /

☐ Final K-1 ☐ Amended K-1

OMB No. 1545-0123

Partner's Share of Income, Deductions, Credits, etc.

See separate instructions.

Part I Information About the Partnership

A Partnership's employer identification number
95-0000002

B Partnership's name, address, city, state, and ZIP code

HUDSON GREY PROPERTIES
2558 LINCOLN ST., SUITE 456
LOS ANGELES, CA 91234

C IRS center where partnership filed return: E-FILE

D ☐ Check if this is a publicly traded partnership (PTP)

Part II Information About the Partner

E Partner's SSN or TIN (Do not use TIN of a disregarded entity. See instructions.)
987-65-4321

F Name, address, city, state, and ZIP code for partner entered in E. See instructions.

JEREMY R. HUDSON
2873 PRAIRE ST.
LOS ANGELES, CA 93456

G [X] General partner or LLC member-manager ☐ Limited partner or other LLC member

H1 [X] Domestic partner ☐ Foreign partner

H2 ☐ If the partner is a disregarded entity (DE), enter the partner's: TIN ____ Name ____

I1 What type of entity is this partner? INDIVIDUAL

I2 If this partner is a retirement plan (IRA/SEP/Keogh/etc.), check here ☐

J Partner's share of profit, loss, and capital (see instructions):

	Beginning	Ending
Profit	50 %	50 %
Loss	50 %	50 %
Capital	50 %	50 %

Check if decrease is due to sale or exchange of partnership interest ☐

K Partner's share of liabilities:

	Beginning	Ending
Nonrecourse	$	$
Qualified nonrecourse financing	$ 212,500.	$ 212,500.
Recourse	$	$

Check this box if item K includes liability amounts from lower-tier partnerships ☐

L **Partner's Capital Account Analysis**

Beginning capital account	$ -26,582.
Capital contributed during the year	$
Current year net income (loss)	$ 73,717.
Other increase (decrease) (attach explanation)	$
Withdrawals and distributions	$(50,000.)
Ending capital account	$ -2,865.

M Did the partner contribute property with a built-in gain (loss)?
☐ **Yes** [X] **No** If "Yes," attach statement. See instructions.

N **Partner's Share of Net Unrecognized Section 704(c) Gain or (Loss)**
Beginning $
Ending $

Part III Partner's Share of Current Year Income, Deductions, Credits, and Other Items

1	Ordinary business income (loss)		14	Self-employment earnings (loss)	
2	Net rental real estate income (loss)	* 73,717.			
3	Other net rental income (loss)		15	Credits	
4a	Guaranteed payments for services				
4b	Guaranteed payments for capital		16	Schedule K-3 is attached if checked ☐	
4c	Total guaranteed payments		17	Alternative minimum tax (AMT) items	A 8.
5	Interest income				
6a	Ordinary dividends				
6b	Qualified dividends		18	Tax-exempt income and nondeductible expenses	
6c	Dividend equivalents				
7	Royalties				
8	Net short-term capital gain (loss)		19	Distributions	
9a	Net long-term capital gain (loss)				A 50,000.
9b	Collectibles (28%) gain (loss)				
9c	Unrecaptured section 1250 gain		20	Other information	N* STMT
10	Net section 1231 gain (loss)				Z* STMT
11	Other income (loss)				
12	Section 179 deduction		21	Foreign taxes paid or accrued	
13	Other deductions				

22 ☐ More than one activity for at-risk purposes*
23 ☐ More than one activity for passive activity purposes*
*See attached statement for additional information.

For IRS Use Only

BAA For Paperwork Reduction Act Notice, see the Instructions for Form 1065. www.irs.gov/Form1065 **Schedule K-1 (Form 1065) 2022**

PARTNER 2

PTPA0312L 07/28/22

HUDSON GREY PROPERTIES 95-0000002

SCHEDULE K-1 (FORM 1065) 2022 **SUPPLEMENTAL INFORMATION** PAGE 2

BOX 2
RENTAL REAL ESTATE ACTIVITIES

PROPERTY TYPE AND ADDRESS	GROSS INCOME	NET EXPENSES	NET INCOME	PASSIVE NONPASS	SEC. 1231 TOTAL
TYPE: 2 - MULTI-FAMILY RESIDENCE 9 MAIN STREET LOS ANGELES, CA 90069	255,136.	181,419.	$ 73,717.	PASSIVE	
		TOTAL	$ 73,717.		

BOX 20, CODE N
BUSINESS INTEREST EXPENSE
INCLUDED AS A DEDUCTION ON THE FOLLOWING LINE(S)

BELOW IS DEDUCTIBLE BUSINESS INTEREST EXPENSE FOR INCLUSION IN THE SEPARATE LOSS CLASS FOR COMPUTING ANY BASIS LIMITATION (DEFINED IN SECTION 704(D), REGULATION SECTION 1.163(J)-6(H)).

SCHEDULE K-1, LINE 2 .... $ 16,000.

PARTNER 2: JEREMY R. HUDSON 987-65-4321

SPSL1201L 07/06/22

Statement A—QBI Pass-through Entity Reporting (Schedule K-1, Box 20, Code Z)

Partnership's name: HUDSON GREY PROPERTIES	**Partnership's EIN:** 95-0000002
Partner's name: JEREMY R. HUDSON	**Partner's identifying number:** 987-65-4321

	HUDSON GREY PROPERTIES		
Partner's share of:	☐ PTP ☐ Aggregated ☐ SSTB	☐ PTP ☐ Aggregated ☐ SSTB	☐ PTP ☐ Aggregated ☐ SSTB
QBI or qualified PTP items subject to partner-specific determinations:			
Ordinary business income (loss)			
Rental income (loss)	73,717.		
Royalty income (loss)			
Section 1231 gain (loss)			
Other income (loss)			
Section 179 deduction			
Other deductions			
W-2 wages	23,878.		
UBIA of qualified property	585,161.		
Qualified REIT dividends			

Partner's share of:	☐ PTP ☐ Aggregated ☐ SSTB	☐ PTP ☐ Aggregated ☐ SSTB	☐ PTP ☐ Aggregated ☐ SSTB
QBI or qualified PTP items subject to partner-specific determinations:			
Ordinary business income (loss)			
Rental income (loss)			
Royalty income (loss)			
Section 1231 gain (loss)			
Other income (loss)			
Section 179 deduction			
Other deductions			
W-2 wages			
UBIA of qualified property			

PARTNER 2

2022 **FEDERAL STATEMENTS** **PAGE 1**

HUDSON GREY PROPERTIES **95-0000002**

STATEMENT 1
FORM 1065, SCHEDULE K, LINE 20C
OTHER REPORTABLE ITEMS

BUSINESS INTEREST EXPENSE (INFORMATIONAL ONLY FOR BASIS LIMITATIONS)
INCLUDED AS A DEDUCTION ON THE FOLLOWING LINES(S)

SCHEDULE K, LINE 2	$ 32,000.

STATEMENT 2
FORM 1065, SCHEDULE L, LINE 17
OTHER CURRENT LIABILITIES

	BEGINNING	ENDING
SECURITY DEPOSIT	$ 20,361.	$ 20,361.
TOTAL	$ 20,361.	$ 20,361.

STATEMENT 3
FORM 8825, LINE 15
OTHER EXPENSES

PROPERTY A: 9 MAIN STREET LOS ANGELES, CA 90069
PROPERTY B:
PROPERTY C:
PROPERTY D:

	PROPERTY A	PROPERTY B	PROPERTY C	PROPERTY D
AMORTIZATION	$ 500.			
EMPLOYEE BENEFITS	2,804.			
MANAGEMENT	14,679.			
MISCELLANEOUS	1,379.			
OFFICE EXPENSE	1,423.			
TOTAL	$ 20,785.			

PART THREE: CORPORATIONS

Form 1120: U.S. Corporation Income Tax Return

➢ FACT PATTERN FOR PROFESSIONAL CORPORATION

Ledger & Post, An Accountancy Corporation, consists of two shareholders. It is a C Corporation that pays a salary to its officer/shareholders. The salary is usually determined such that no taxable income is reported by the corporation.

➢ FACT PATTERN FOR A CORPORATION INVOLVED IN WHOLESALE DISTRIBUTION OF PRODUCTS

Fashion Apparel, Inc. is a C Corporation owned by Catherine P. Anderson. She draws a minimal salary. Though profitable in 2022, the corporation has had a history of losses.

➢ FACT PATTERN FOR S CORPORATION INVOLVED IN PROVIDING IMPORT SALES

Straight Edge, Inc. is an S Corporation owned by Mr. Collins. He draws a modest amount of salary but enjoys a sizable annual distribution of profits from the corporation.

➢ OVERVIEW OF "C" CORPORATE TAXATION

With the exception of the S Corporation, which is treated like a partnership, corporations generally pay income tax on earnings and are often referred to as "C" Corporations. (The overview of the "S" Corporation appears in the following section.) Unlike the other predominant types of business tax returns, the C Corporation's owners may be subject to double taxation. Earnings are taxed at the corporate level, and if these same earnings are distributed as dividends, they are taxed again at the individual level.

The corporation tax return consists of an income statement, balance sheet, and information statement for the corporation. A reconciliation format within the return is used to denote differences between taxable income and financial statement income (also known as "Book Income").

As a result, a very thorough financial overview of a business or practice is usually available from the tax return itself.

All Forms 1120 contain Pages 1 through 5 plus as many supporting schedules as required to supplement and explain entries on the first four pages. Unlike the S Corporation tax return, the C Corporation does not include K-1s for each of the shareholders because it is not a flow through entity, i.e., income taxes are paid at the corporate level.

Income from all sources is reported on the first page. Page 2 is comprised of questions regarding dividends received from other corporations. Page 3 contains three sections. The first section reflects the calculation of the corporate income tax. The second section is reserved for future use and the third section reflects the income tax payments the corporation has made. Schedule K begins on Page 4 and is used to describe the nature of the business and its accounting method, i.e., cash, accrual or otherwise the next part of Page 2. Schedule K continues on Page 5 with questions regarding the stock ownership of the corporation and various other questions that provide the IRS with important information about the corporation's activities. Page 6 contains comparative balance sheets for the current and prior year-ends. Also reported on Page 6 are the reconciliation of taxable income to book income, and the reconciliation of the beginning and ending retained earnings.

Additional supporting schedules are required to report other corporation activity. The most common of these schedules is Form 4562, the depreciation detail summary. Examples of Form 4562 and other supporting corporation tax forms are included in the hypothetical tax returns at the end of this section.

➢ OVERVIEW OF "S" CORPORATE TAXATION

An S Corporation is a corporation in which taxable income and losses are passed through to the individual shareholders. In effect, it is a corporation that is treated like a partnership for tax purposes. The ability to recognize business losses on the individual tax returns of shareholder is one of the major considerations in deciding to elect S Corporation status. The avoidance of double taxation at the corporate level is another consideration for the S Corporation election.

The election is only available under specific circumstances. In general, to qualify as an S Corporation, the corporation must consist of 100 or fewer individual shareholders (none of whom are non-resident aliens) and have only one class of stock issued and outstanding. Partnerships, corporations, and certain trusts cannot be shareholders.

The S Corporation is a flow through entity. This means that taxable income, deductions, and credits are passed through to the individual shareholders for reporting on their individual income tax returns. In other words, shareholders of the corporation are treated like partners for tax purposes only. In all other respects, the corporation retains the same legal status as a C Corporation.

The S Corporation tax return, like the C Corporation, is a combination income statement, balance sheet, and information report for the corporation. A reconciliation format within the return is used to denote differences between taxable income and financial statement income (also known as "Book Income"). As a result, a very thorough financial overview of a business or practice is usually available from the tax return itself.

All Forms 1120S contain pages one through five plus as many supporting schedules as required to supplement and to explain entries on the first five pages. In addition, K-1s for each of the shareholders are included to inform shareholders of their allocation of income, deductions, and credits.

Income from a trade or business is reported on the first page. Page 2 is used to report information concerning the nature of the corporate activity and its ownership characteristics. Page 3 contains information very much like a partnership tax return Page 3. The total of all K-1 items that flow through to the shareholders is summarized on this page. Page 4 contains comparative balance sheets for the current and prior year-ends. The reconciliation of taxable income to book income, and the reconciliation of the beginning and ending "Accumulated Adjustment Account," the S Corporation's equivalent of retained earnings is reported on Page 5. The "Accumulated Adjustment Account" is used to calculate the taxability of distributions to shareholders. A more detailed explanation of this concept is presented in the analysis of Page 5.

Additional supporting schedules are required to report other corporation activity. The most common of these schedules are Schedule D for Form 1120S, where capital gains and losses are reported, and Form 4562, the depreciation detail summary. Examples of Schedule D and Form 4562 are included in the hypothetical tax returns at the end of this section.

S Corporations, like partnerships, contain K-1s for each of the shareholders that reflect the taxable income and deductible expenses allocable to each shareholder. Complete discussion and explanation is presented later in this section after the section on C Corporations.

FORM 1120: C CORPORATION TAX RETURNS

Page 1: U.S. Corporation Return of Income C Corporation

Most corporations may report on a calendar or fiscal year or otherwise depending on the nature of the underlying business activity. Generally, professional practices and other personal service corporations must report on a calendar year basis unless the corporation can establish a business purpose for adopting another fiscal year. Non-service type corporations may elect a fiscal year-end other than a December 31 when the alternative year-end coincides with the corporation's business cycle.

Greater complexity in the preparation of income analyses for support is more likely to exist where substantial income, loss or cash flow is derived from activities of a corporation that reports on a fiscal year other than December 31. This complexity arises because salary or dividends from a corporation is reflected on the personal income tax return on a calendar year basis.

Note that a corporation return for a fiscal year ending November 30, 2023 is considered a 2022 corporation tax return because the fiscal year began in 2022. To illustrate, let us assume a corporation with a November 30, 2023 year-end that is 100% owned by the officer/spouse. The corporate income tax return will reflect income for eleven months of 2023 and one month of 2022. Further, assume that 100% of the officer's fiscal year salary is paid in the form of a $100,000 bonus paid in November 2023. Under these circumstances, the officer receives a 2022 W-2 that does not contain this $100,000 bonus because it was received in 2023. If one were to look only at the personal return for 2022, it would appear to indicate that cash flow from wages for 2022 would not be the same as the salary shown on the corporation's tax return unless the officer/spouse received the same exact $100,000 bonus in November of 2022 (that was reported on the 2021 corporate tax return). Careful review of monthly activity within the corporation is required in order to ascertain the accurate amount of income to the officer for the calendar year in question. Errors resulting from overlooking the timing problems associated with non-calendar fiscal year corporations perceived earning ability.

Line A: Corporate tax returns for consolidated entities and corporations that are personal holding companies need to check the boxes in this area. Box 3 requires disclosure if the business is a personal service corporation. A personal service corporation is one in which the major source of revenue is not the sale or manufacture or a product.

Corporations that own interests in other corporations or that are part of a group of corporations with common shareholder ownership may file on a consolidated basis.

Generally, a "Personal Holding Company" is a corporation that receives most of its revenue from investment income sources. An additional tax of 20% is imposed on the undistributed income from such corporations. The rules governing these tax entities are intricately defined in the Internal

Revenue Code. Because of the high rate of tax imposed on such corporations, the appearance of this type of return in family law matters is rare.

Schedule M-3 is a form required of larger corporations that rarely appear in family law cases.

Line B: Corporation may obtain an "Employer ID Number" by filing Form SS-4. The ID number is reflected on all payroll tax forms the corporation is required to file.

Line D: "Total Assets" shown here should be exactly the same as the total assets on Page 5, Schedule L, Line 15. A quick idea of the size of the business can be gleaned from this number.

INCOME

Line 1a: Gross Receipts or Sales Gross receipts or sales, commonly referred to as the business's "Gross," is usually a very significant statistics for valuation purposes. Non-accountants frequently use the terms "Income," "Revenue," and "Gross Income" interchangeably. This is a common area of confusion that lawyers should avoid. The gross receipts are synonymous with revenue for a corporation that operates on a cash basis. If the corporation operates on an accrual basis, gross cash receipts may not be the same amount as corporate revenue even though they are placed on the same line on the tax return. In the case of accrual basis corporations, the revenue represents what the business has billed or sold while the cash receipts are the collections of its accounts receivable. "Income" is the difference between revenue and expenses. It is synonymous with "Profit" or the "Bottom Line."

Fashion Apparel, Inc.'s tax return, shown at the end of this section, is an example of a corporation that reports on an accrual basis. The $1,147,545 shown on Line 1 represents corporate sales that have been billed to customers. The amount is obtained from a summary of yearly sales contained in the company's general ledger and sales journal. The amount of sales does not equate to the amount collected on its accounts receivable.

The "Gross" is an important element of tax return analysis. Often, a business or practice is sold on the basis of multiples of gross receipts. Comparison with prior years "Gross" will provide information for a historical trend analysis of sales or fees. If a decrease in revenue in the current period has occurred, the cause for the reduction should be ascertained through interview, deposition, or document inspection. The concern generally focuses on whether the decrease was the result of lower productivity engendered by the divorce or just market conditions. Whether this decrease was caused by the psychological effects of the divorce or by a willful slowdown are possibilities requiring investigation.

A trend analysis is also appropriate for corporate income analysis. Revenue and income trends are important factors to consider in appraising a commercial business. Divorce effects may be highlighted by reference to such analyses.

Many closely held cash basis corporations commit tax evasion by depositing checks received in December into the business bank account in January of the following year. Under the law, any checks received in December are considered constructively received and must be reported in the fiscal year that the month of December falls. If a corporation has just begun this practice of holding checks in December of 2022, the "Gross" of the business is understated by the amount of the held checks. This results in a lower amount of corporation taxable income allocable to the officer/shareholder and a lower apparent income for that spouse. If this practice of holding checks has been consistently followed for years, an analysis of the amounts involved for the prior versus the current year will provide the most accurate representation of annual gross receipts.

Unusually low amounts of reported gross in corporations that handle cash, particularly retail businesses such as restaurants, may indicate unreported income. Analysis of cash register tapes and other business records may be helpful in determining the amount of unreported income in some circumstances. When information required for such an analysis is unavailable, other procedures are employed by forensic accountants to assist in quantifying the unreported income.

One such procedure relies upon statistical gross profit information for the industry to suggest appropriate levels of gross receipts. The quantification of what the "Gross" should be is achieved by dividing the actual "Cost of Goods Sold" of the subject business by the industry percentage for "Cost of Goods Sold." Comparing the gross profit ("Revenue" less "Cost of Goods Sold"—also known as "Gross Margin") of the subject business to industry statistical information provides a quick method for determining the probability of unreported income.

An analysis of the mark-up on the company's merchandise may also be revealing. If the typical mark-up is 25% (let's say $1.25 on goods that cost $1.00), then the gross profit to be expected is 20% ($.25 divided by $1.25). If the corporation tax return reflects a materially lower "Gross Profit" enhanced scrutiny is advisable. The value of this type of approach is substantially reduced in corporations that have a large product mix or in cases where merchandise is frequently discounted.

Another way of proving unreported income exists, albeit more time-consuming and costly than those mentioned, is the lifestyle analysis. A disparity between the parties' lifestyle and their adjusted gross income for the period reported on the individual income tax return (this would include salary from and dividends paid by the closely held corporation) may provide a reasonable estimate of unreported income under certain circumstances. If the unreported income is stored in a safe deposit box and not exhausted on living expenses, the lifestyle analysis will not prove very useful. The lifestyle approach requires an accounting for all sources and uses of cash for a particular period. The accounting should include deposits to the parties' personal accounts that may have emanated from gifts, inheritance, borrowing, or prior year loan repayments. Cash balances at both the beginning and the end of the period need to be ascertained in order to calculate the amount of cash flow funded by savings on hand at the beginning of the period. Classification of recorded expenditures by the parties during the particular period under scrutiny may reveal expenditures well in excess of reported income. Additionally, such classification may disclose either small or nonexistent expenditures for known costs of living such as housekeeper costs and grocery expenses. An estimate of the reasonable monthly cost of such expenditures may then be added to the reported cost of living to arrive at the total lifestyle of the parties.

Line 1b: Returns and Allowances This represents sold merchandise that has been returned or, in the case of a personal service corporations, a refund of an overpayment. While seemingly similar, "Returns and Allowances" should not be confused with "Bad Debts" discussed in the following.

Line 2: Cost of Goods Sold Professional practice and service corporations typically report nothing on this line. Commercial businesses with inventories report the cost relating to the products sold on this line. Form 1125-A is the area of the corporation tax return in which additional information relative to "Cost of Goods Sold" is reported. A more detailed explanation of this area is included in the discussion of Form 1125-A presented later.

Line 3: Gross Profit The gross profit is the difference between "Gross receipts or sales" ("Revenue") and the cost of merchandise sold. Reference to the percentage of "Gross Profit" to "Revenue" is an important indicator of corporation economic trends. A decline in the gross profit percentage may indicate greater price competition in the industry or higher raw material costs. Variances in the year of divorce warrant concern and scrutiny. Both "Revenue" and "Cost of Goods Sold" may impact this percentage. As mentioned previously, a divergence from industry norms may signify that the subject corporation is not reporting revenue. More on "Gross Profit" (also known as "Gross Margin") is presented below in the discussion of Schedule A.

Line 4: Dividends Corporations that own stock in other corporations may receive dividends. A special deduction is allowed for dividends received. This is discussed under Page 2, Schedule C.

Line 5: Interest Interest received from corporate investments is reported here. The C Corporation is not a flow through entity. Thus, it pays tax on all sources of income.

Line 6: Gross Rents A corporation with income or loss from rentals reports its gross rent collected here. Unlike flow through entities, the C Corporation includes rental income as taxable corporate income. Passive loss limitations associated with individual income tax generally do not apply to corporations.

Line 7: Gross Royalties Royalties from mineral rights, theatrical rights, and other various and sundry sources are totaled on this line. The nature and source of the royalties must be obtained in order to prepare meaningful cash flow analysis. Usually, the amount received over the last 12 months is the best indicator of cash flow from this source. But if information exists that suggests otherwise, the representative anticipated future cash flow may well be different than the historical cash flow.

Line 8: Capital Gain Net Income Corporation income tax returns have their own Schedule D on which to report capital gains and losses. The same definition of a capital asset applies to corporations as to individuals; however, corporate capital gains are taxed at regular corporate rates like other corporate income. Generally, corporate investments and other assets not directly used in the business activity are capital assets.

Capital gains and losses should not be considered in computing representative income available for support if the transaction(s) giving rise to the gains or losses are not recurring.

Line 9: Net Gain or (Loss) from Form 4797 The gain from disposition of real or personal property used in the business activity is reflected here. An entry on this line indicates that a sale of assets has taken place during the year. For cash flow purposes, a sale of business assets generally is not a recurring business activity. Consequently, a representative cash flow analysis for the year should exclude these proceeds. Form 4797 is used to determine the capital gain versus ordinary income portion of gain from sale of business-related capital assets.

Casualty and theft losses can be deducted from ordinary income. The deductible losses include losses from fire, storm, shipwreck, or other casualty or theft. If the property was covered by insurance, the insurance claim for reimbursement of loss has to be filed timely. The corporate return of Fashion Apparel, Inc. contains a $5,834 casualty loss. Section B of Form 4684 is included in the tax return and indicates that the casualty loss was based on the theft of inventory. Note that the casualty loss is then generally carried to Form 4797.

Line 10: Other Income Miscellaneous sources of income not specifically delineated in Lines 1 through 9 are reported here. Typically, income that does not recur annually is inserted on this line. Examples of other income are proceeds from successfully litigated lawsuits and insurance proceeds. Non-recurring sources of income are usually not considered cash available for support because it is speculative to suggest that such items will continually be earned by a spouse. But large amounts of cash generated by such income that remain within the corporation will result in an increase in investment income that should be taken into consideration as a source of additional cash flow to the officer/shareholder.

Line 11: Total Income (Loss) The summation of the preceding is not as significant from an analytical perspective as its components, but it is a point of reference.

DEDUCTIONS

Expenses are often converted into percentages and compared with prior years. Anomalies and deviations can be more easily identified through use of analysis of comparative percentages (also known as "Common Size" comparative income statements).

Line 12: Compensation of Officers Entries on this line are tied to Schedule 1125-E of the return. Schedule 1125-E will list all officers receiving compensation during the year. Although corporations with total receipts of less than $500,000 do not have to enter this information, officer compensation information is nevertheless frequently reported on the form.

The amount of compensation received by the spouse is one of the most important factors in both income and valuation analyses. Historical compensation summaries are useful in the determination of representative and reasonable compensation. Representative compensation is a key factor in income analyses. Compensation of comparably situated individuals may be a critical component of a goodwill analysis prepared for the appraisal of a business.

Line 13: Salary and Wages Are friends and relatives on payroll who do not really perform full services for compensation received? Inspection of payroll tax returns and, where available, payroll journals will identify those persons on payroll. To the extent that "Salary and Wages" are overstated, conclusions as to the value of the enterprise and cash flow available for support are understated.

Closely related, but usually not included in "Salary and Wages," are payments to independent contractors. Corporations are required to file IRS Form 1099 to report all payments to independent contractors in excess of $600 per year. Reviewing the payees listed on the 1099 forms may disclose payments to friends or relatives.

Line 14: Repairs and Maintenance In closely held corporations where the officer/shareholder has unfettered control of all expenditures, closer scrutiny of this expense item is advised. Frequently, personal residence repairs and improvements are run through this account. Vendors who provide goods or services to the corporation may also provide additional *personal* goods or services. The "out-spouse" may be helpful in identifying companies or individuals who have provided good or services for the parties personally that have been paid for out of the corporation.

Capital expenditures that are written off as an expense of the period are often classified as repair expense. The effect of improper recording of capital assets is the understatement of business income. If the asset was purchased outright, actual cash flow for the period may be properly reflected; however, income reports prepared for support hearings should contain an adjustment for this item. Appropriate adjustment to income requires that the amount of capital expenditures charged to expense be added back. By this means, projected future income does not include the non-recurring costs of asset acquisitions. If, on the other hand, it is common practice for the corporation to regularly upgrade and replace assets, no adjustment, or only a partial adjustment, may be necessary.

Line 15: Bad Debts Cash basis corporations are allowed to deduct bad debts only to the extent that they have been previously reported as income to the enterprise or as a loan to a customer. This is a rare occurrence. Corporations seeking to suppress income may report bad debts from friends and relatives that are not true business debts, or they may write off debts in the year of a pending divorce suit and then report them as income in a later tax year if the debts are collected. In either event, the profitability of the business is understated. The understatement affects both the appraisal of the corporation and the calculation of a spouse's cash flow from the corporation.

Accrual basis corporations must use the specific charge-off method to deduct business bad debts. Only direct write-offs are allowed. In terms of income or business value, this means that receivables reported on the corporate tax return may be overvalued and income overstated because the tax law does not allow a deduction using a reserve for bad debts. Income of accrual basis corporations should be adjusted for anticipated bad debts in order to derive a more accurate income conclusion.

Line 16: Rents In some cases, inquiry should be made concerning the identity of the lessor and the fair market value of the rental payment. If the lessor is a friend or relative of the officer/shareholder of a closely held corporation, the probability of overstated rent that reduces profitability is enhanced. Examination of the facility lease is generally an integral part of the appraisal process. A bargain lease has the effect of overstating profitability; accordingly, an adjustment should be made to restate the annual rental to market.

A bargain lease suggests an asset with value that typically will not be disclosed in any discovery materials. Real estate experts are able to render opinions of value for leases whose stated rent is lower than market.

Line 17: Taxes and Licenses Real estate, personal property, and payroll taxes are reported here. Examination of tax bills and other supporting documentation may disclose unreported assets or misstated values.

Line 18: Interest An amount shown here evidences the existence of either secured or unsecured loans. Note that the Tax Cut and Jobs Act implemented a limitation to the amount of deductible interest to 30% of the businesses adjusted taxable income. As a result, the interest listed here may not reflect the interest the business actually paid. Loan application files may be obtained from lenders. This documentation may help to confirm or uncover the existence of certain marital assets. Opinions of value are also found in these files. While the individual officer/shareholder's opinion of the value of the real estate and/or the corporation may carry little weight at trial, it may be useful for settlement purposes. Personal financial statements from the officer/shareholder spouse may be found in the loan file. The officer's opinions of value of other marital assets may also appear in the loan file. This information may promote settlement and save expert witness appraisal costs. In summary, loan files may contain application forms and other informative documents that provide a cross-reference for checking the accuracy of marital asset values. The loan application usually includes a sworn statement of earning ability, an amount that can be compared with the income reported for the same period on the corporation tax return and on the officer/shareholder's individual tax return. The spouse's credibility as a witness may be impaired by presenting evidence of major inconsistencies between the income shown on the loan application and the tax return income.

Line 19: Charitable Contributions Corporate contributions are limited to 10% of reported corporate taxable income. The nature of the contribution will determine whether it is a permissible deduction in arriving at cash flow available for support. If the contribution is not relevant to the production of income, it is probably a perquisite. Contribution made to organizations many of whose members are clients or customers of the partnership are likely to be considered appropriate reductions to cash flow.

Line 20: Depreciation Reported depreciation must be analyzed with a view to the impact of this expense on cash flow. Page 6 of the corporation tax return contains a balance sheet that includes a summary of the cost of depreciable property and the accumulated depreciation.

Analysis of depreciation and asset history may be provided either wholly or partially on Form 4562 and supporting schedules included in the return of a corporation claiming depreciation expense. Note, however, that detail depreciation schedules are generally not required to be attached to the return. Probative information concerning the assets of the business, including date of acquisition and original cost, are usually available on this form and supporting detail schedules that may be included in the return. More asset information may be obtained from a corporation's internally prepared depreciation schedule or the work papers maintained by its independent certified public accounting firm.

Depreciation schedules aid in identifying assets that have been written off but still have value. This is particularly true when Section 179 depreciation has been taken (see next paragraph).

The net book value of an asset, the difference between what it cost and the amount of accumulated depreciation, is usually not indicative of fair market value.

In addition to providing relevant data for determining the fair market value of the fixed assets, the depreciation schedule is also useful for evaluating the probability of claimed cash flow needs of the business for investment in new equipment.

The first $1,080,000 of personal property additions in 2022 may be deducted under Internal Revenue Code (IRC) Section 179. The immediate deduction of all or a substantial part of the cost of an asset requires an adjustment to income to arrive at representative cash flow. In other words, Section 179 depreciation is typically added back to income to arrive at cash flow.

Depreciation amounts appearing on the tax return should be compared to financial statement depreciation. Differences between the tax return and financial depreciation are noted on Page 6, Schedule M-1, Lines 5a and 8a. Entries on these lines warrant further analysis because rapid depreciation write-offs usually result in overstatement of annual operating costs and corresponding understatement of value for the business (especially when a capitalization of earnings method is used to value the business or its goodwill).

Examples of Form 4562 and supporting schedules are available in the hypothetical returns included at the end of this section.

Depreciation does not always parallel asset deterioration. If an asset is depreciated rapidly or if Section 179 depreciation is used to write off the entire asset in the year of acquisition, the fair market value of the asset may be greater than its depreciated value (also known as book value). Where one suspects the fixed assets of a business to be worth materially more than book value, it is wise to suggest the engagement of a personal property appraiser to determine the fair market value of the fixed assets.

Line 21: Depletion Depletion is "depreciation" for natural resources. It represents a deduction for the capital investment that the corporation receives pro rata over the estimated productive life of the resource. Different tax methods, such as cost depletion and percentage depletion, are allowed for computation of the deduction.

Like depreciation, analysis of actual cash flow related to this expense is required to determine "true" cash flow. Generally, the capital investment providing the basis for depreciation is not a recurring cost of the corporation; accordingly, depletion expense is considered a non-cash expense that is usually added back to profit to arrive at representative cash flow for the corporation.

Line 22: Advertising Amounts shown here should be evaluated for perquisite possibility. Misclassification of personal travel and entertainment may sometimes be erroneously included in advertising expense. Examination of supporting accounting records such as general ledgers and journals will reveal whether perks are included in advertising expense.

Line 23: Pension, Profit-Sharing, Etc., Plans Entries on this line denote the existence of one or more corporate retirement plans. The amount shown represents payments made on behalf of both the officer/shareholder and other employees. Determination of the value of the marital portion of the officer/shareholder's interest in retirement plans is essential for property division purposes.

Qualified plans (those that meet IRS standards for deductibility) require the annual filing of IRS

Forms in the 5500 series. The qualified plan tax returns generally reveal substantial probative information of trust value. Participant statements for the officer/shareholder may usually be obtained from the retirement plan administrators.

The funding of nonqualified plans (non-deductible because they allow discrimination, i.e., non-inclusion of employees other than the business owners) will not be reported on the corporation income tax return. The existence of such a plan may be disclosed in the reconciliation of tax and book income shown on Schedule M-1 on Page 6 of the corporation tax return. If business records are properly maintained, the nonqualified plan balances should appear on the business balance sheet as an asset.

The amount contributed to the retirement plan on behalf of the officer/shareholder may be added back to arrive at income available for support if the contribution is discretionary and/or controllable by the spouse. Frequently, in the case of temporary support orders, the shareholder spouse does not have the discretion and control to avoid making the contribution. Under the circumstances, the retirement plan contribution on the spouse's behalf should not be added back to arrive at income available for support. In all other circumstances, contributions to retirement plans represent non-taxable compensation that may be considered perquisites because they are discretionary.

LINE 24: EMPLOYEE BENEFIT PROGRAMS Employee benefit programs are in addition to any retirement contributions reported on Line 24. Employee benefits may include life and health insurance, dental insurance, and dependent care assistance programs. If employee benefits are claimed, a careful investigation should be made to determine whether the officer/shareholder is benefiting from these payments or if non-employee friends or relatives are in collusion to divert funds. In other words, this category of expense provides an opportunity to disguise personal expenditures as a business expense.

LINE 25: RESERVED FOR FUTURE USE

LINE 26: OTHER DEDUCTIONS The total of all other deductible expenses for which no room has been allocated on Page 1 of Form 1120 is entered on this line. The expense categories that may be included here are numerous and vary with the corporation's business activity. "Other deductions" may contain perquisites. Examples of "Other deductions" that frequently contain perquisites are presented in the following. Each of the hypothetical returns contains supporting detail summaries that include other deductions.

Analysis of corporation general ledgers and journals may be very useful in spotting "perks" (perquisites or personal expense items). Some general ledgers contain complete details of all payees receiving corporation checks. Most, businesses computerize their accounting. Computerization facilitates the inspection of account detail in a general ledger. If the payees listed in an account do not appear proper, investigation of underlying supporting documentation, such as canceled checks and vendor's invoices, merits consideration.

Automobile Expenses are frequently overstated both in terms of amount and degree of personal use involved. In either case, the actual business-related auto expenses should be investigated. Overstated auto expenses or the cost of the personal use portion of the auto(s) are among the most common perquisites found on corporation tax returns. Inquiry of the shareholder/spouse, either through interview or deposition, is mandatory discovery for perquisite analysis where the amounts involved are material. The nature of the business activity should dovetail with the spouse's explanations. Where such is not the case, forensic accountants frequently estimate a reasonable business use percentage based on the nature of the business.

Insurance Expense is another account that frequently contains perquisites such as personal life insurance, in which the officer/shareholder, or the corporation, is the beneficiary. Personal life insurance premium payments are not deductible; however, this expense is often found "buried" in insurance expense. Another personal expense that may be included in insurance expense is automobile insurance on the officer/shareholder's personal vehicle(s) used only partially for business. To the extent that any insurance payments paid by the corporation personally benefit either spouse, that "perk" should be included in the officer/shareholder's income when determining earning capacity.

Inspection of insurance policies may reveal information regarding assets not otherwise disclosed. Liability riders on such items as artwork and special equipment may be uncovered through this process.

Legal or professional fees paid in connection with marital dissolution matters are not deductible by the corporation. If divorce-related professional fees are paid and deducted by the corporation, the amount is considered a perk. Forensic accounting fees may also be treated in the same way. Comparing the current year's legal and professional expense with the amount shown in prior years' tax returns may disclose a significant variance. As the variance grows larger so does the probability that a perk exists.

Office expenses or supplies are convenient slots to bury a multitude of personal expenses. The materiality of the amount should first be determined before undertaking a thorough investigation. Typically, a brief analysis of the company's general ledger and journals may indicate whether an in-depth investigation is warranted. Payments to "cash" are often found in this category.

Travel, meals, and entertainment are other deduction categories in which personal expenditures may be hidden. It is common practice for forensic accountants to investigate the charges to this account for the existence of perquisites. The process usually includes the examination of supporting documentation, such as credit card statements and expense reports, in conjunction with interviews with and/or deposition testimony of the shareholder/spouse. The relationship of the underlying business activity, or lack thereof, associated with the "Travel and Entertainment" expenditures is the pivotal element in determining personal versus a business expense.

Note the $91,779 travel expense indicated on Statement 2 attached to the Fashion Apparel, Inc. tax return. If travel is a common industry expense, the probability that personal travel is being deducted is greater. The cost of an extra ticket for a family member or friend who does not participate in the business activity of the corporation is a common perk.

If the shareholder/spouse flies extensively for business reasons, significant frequent flyer mileage credits may have accumulated. Mileage summaries can be discovered, and the mileage credits divided as a community asset.

LINE 27: TOTAL DEDUCTIONS The sum total of all of the deductions listed above it is entered here.

LINE 28: TAXABLE INCOME BEFORE NET OPERATING LOSS DEDUCTION The income or loss shown here is the starting point for the analysis of profitability. Correct adjustments to income for perquisites and other items needed to restate income on a representative basis will result in "true profitability," the profit concept used for valuation and income analyses. Historical analysis of true profitability is mandatory for valuation purposes under IRS Revenue Ruling 59-60. Revenue Ruling 59-60 contains a thorough explanation of all factors and considerations necessary and appropriate for valuation of closely held businesses. Familiarity with the contents of this Revenue Ruling is essential for forensic accountants and other business appraisers.

The issue of whether or not to include the corporation's taxable income in income available for support is often a contentious area in those cases in which one spouse controls the corporation. Consideration should be given to the availability of cash generated by earnings that have not been distributed to shareholders. The amount of discretion and control over this item may be construed differently based on whether the issue is permanent or temporary alimony and/or child support. In temporary support situations, the undistributed earnings should not be considered if the corporation's ability to make additional distributions is impaired by legitimate business cash flow requirements. A California Appellate Court held that the legitimate need to use current year's profit to maintain the viability and/or profitability of a business warranted the exclusion from income available for support of that portion of the corporate profits reinvested in the business. As a general rule in all other cases, the undistributed income should be attributable to the officer/shareholder as income available for support.

Line 29a: Net Operating Loss Deduction Net operating losses are generally corporate losses from prior years that may be carried forward to offset current period income. Net operating loss carryovers reduce the amount of corporate income tax payable in the current period. The tax ramifications of the net operating loss should not be overlooked when advising the court of the after tax income available.

Note the $17,664 net operating loss (NOL) shown on Page 1 of Fashion Apparel, Inc.'s tax return. Since that reduction in income really relates to a prior period, the current cash flow of the corporation should not be reduced for the NOL. In fact, the NOL is a hidden asset (not shown on the corporate balance sheet for the prior year-end) because it results in the elimination of the corporate tax liability for the year.

Line 30: Taxable Income Taxable income represents the difference between the corporate income, deductions and NOLs. This is the amount included in the computation of tax paid by the corporation. As previously mentioned, the C Corporation is not a flow through entity. The tax paid by the corporation on its earnings reduces the amount available for distribution to a spouse/shareholder. Federal income tax payments are reductions to income only if undistributed corporate income is included as income available to the spouse/shareholder.

FORM 1125-A: COST OF GOODS SOLD

Line 1: Inventory at Beginning of Year This is the starting point for analyzing the cost of goods sold. The amount should match the ending inventory reported in the prior year's tax return. If it does not, the discrepancy should be questioned.

Reporting a higher than actual opening inventory will understate profit. As a result, analysis of last year's return and accompanying supporting documentation to verify the reliability of the opening inventory is recommended.

Line 2: Purchases The cost of inventory items purchased for sale by retailers and wholesalers appears on this line. If a corporation manufactures goods, the amount shown will represent raw material purchases.

Timing of expense is an important element in determining the reliability of the amount shown. Typically, businesses with inventories report on the accrual basis; accordingly, the date of purchase or delivery of the goods, not the date of payment for the goods, is the point at which the expense is recorded. Criteria for determining the date of purchase follow legal guidelines reflected in the Uniform Commercial Code. The contractual time at which goods change hands determines when goods are considered purchased under the accrual basis of accounting.

Consistency in reporting transactional activity with regular vendors is indicative of reliability in the timing of the expense. Inconsistency merits further analysis.

Accountants preparing audited or reviewed financial statements will test year-end transactions to determine appropriate reporting of purchases at the cut-off date, December 31 for all calendar year corporations. This accounting technique provides enhanced reliability of the amount reported.

The corporation's "Accounts Payable" is a balance sheet item that is closely associated with the recordation of purchases. In many businesses an accounts payable or purchases journal is maintained. Monthly summations of additions to accounts payable for purchases of goods or raw materials constitute the "Purchases" account reflected on the general ledger and, ultimately, the tax return.

Inspection of the purchases journal and the cash disbursement journal is recommended when suspicion exists that personal items have been paid for by the business. Examples of corporations that warrant analysis for inventory used personally are restaurants, electronics retailers, computer stores, and clothing outlets.

Line 3: Cost of Labor Generally, this line is used by businesses that manufacture goods. Only direct labor costs of manufacturing are included.

Administrative salaries should not be included in this area of the return. As pointed out in the discussion of Line 13 of Page 1, "Salaries and Wages," obtaining the names of all employees is advisable to ascertain whether friends and relatives who do not actually perform real services for compensation received are on payroll. Inspection of payroll tax returns and, where available, payroll journals will identify those persons on payroll. To the extent that there is an overstatement of "Wages," conclusions as to the value of the enterprise and income available for support are understated.

Line 4: Additional Section 263A Costs Corporations that manufacture or resell a product are subject to "Uniform Capitalization Rules." (Resellers with gross receipts of less than $27 million are exempt from this rule.) Under these IRS regulations, indirect costs attributable to the cost of inventory are added to inventory. This type of cost is rarely an issue in marital dissolution matters because it generally does not arise in those corporations where manipulation of income is an issue.

Line 5: Other Costs Generally, "Other Costs" refers to overhead, also known as indirect costs of manufacturing. An entire branch of accounting, known as "Cost Accounting," is devoted to the study of allocating overhead expenses not directly related to the manufacture of the product. Portions of the rent, utilities, administrative labor, and property taxes are examples of types of indirect manufacturing expenses that are allocated to the cost of manufactured goods.

Line 7: Inventory at End of Year Because the year-end for which ending inventory is determined is often close to the time at which the appraisal is performed, the relevant documentation for intensive research and analysis of this account is usually readily available. If an actual inventory count is taken, copies of the supporting detail should be obtained and reviewed. The procedures employed to make the count should be analyzed. Less scrutiny of procedures and valuation methodology is required if the inventory was observed by certified public accountants in conjunction with a certified audit.

Unreported sale of inventory during the post-separation period is a common allegation made by the "out-spouse." Testing of gross profit ratios with industry percentages and against prior years' percentages for the corporation may support such allegations. Testing mark-up percentages against gross profit is another tool available in some cases to spot irregularities in inventory value.

Line 8: Cost of Goods Sold Cost of goods is carried forward to Page 1, Line 2.

Line 9a to f: Methods Used to Value Closing Inventory The method by which inventory is valued may significantly affect the corporation valuation. Inventories are frequently undervalued in order to report lower taxable profit. Greater motivation to manipulate inventory exists in divorce cases because lower profitability from lower inventory benefits the officer/shareholder spouse via a lower business valuation and less cash flow available for support.

Inventory valuation methods are important factors in determining the appropriate amount of inventory. The method must conform to the best accounting practice in the particular trade or business. "Cost" means that the inventory is valued at the price paid. "Lower of cost or market" means that the cost of inventory, on an item by item basis, is compared to the industry market value. The lower of the two values is then applied.

LIFO (last-in, first-out) and FIFO (first-in, first-out) are terms often used in connection with inventory valuation. If a LIFO method of costing inventory is used in an inflationary period, book value will tend to be understated. The FIFO method of costing inventory provides a more accurate representation of actual market value of the inventory because ending inventory is "costed" by reference to the most recent purchases.

Any changes in inventory accounting between prior years and the year of separation and the subsequent period should be carefully investigated. Unusually large negative adjustments to inventory also warrant research.

Page 2: Schedule C: Dividend and Special Deductions

C Corporations may be entitled to a dividends received deduction related to dividends received from other corporations depending on the type of corporation paying the dividend and the ownership interest of the corporation receiving the dividend.

Entries in this section of the tax return indicate that the corporation has or had an investment in another corporation during the year. The size and nature of the investment may affect valuation and cash flow. Stock market investments should be restated to market value for appraisal purposes. Investments in subsidiaries may require consolidation of corporate interests in order to determine the value of the marital asset. The consolidation for valuation purposes may be appropriate even if financial statements and tax returns are not prepared on a consolidated basis. The facts and circumstances of each case should dictate what is reasonable and prudent.

FORM 1125-E: COMPENSATION OF OFFICERS

Form 1125-E of the corporate tax return is usually of primary importance in the determination of officer/shareholder cash flow and earnings. For calendar year corporations, the amount of officer salary should match the amount reported on the officer's W-2 as Medicare Wages. If it does not, an irregularity exists. Medicare wages are not always reported as income on a personal tax return. A lower amount is reported for tax purposes if a spouse contributes to a 401K plan or has other employee deductions that reduce taxable income.

Wages paid to officers of corporations with fiscal years other than December 31 present a greater challenge for determination of cash flow because the amount reported on the corporation may not match the amount reported on the W-2 (prepared on a calendar year basis).

To illustrate, let us assume a corporation with a January 31, 2023 year-end that is 100% owned by the officer. The corporate income tax return will reflect salary for eleven months of 2022 and one month of 2023. Further, assume that 100% of the officer's fiscal year salary is paid in the form of a $100,000 bonus in January 2023. Under the circumstances, and assuming no further salary in 2022, the officer will receive a 2023 W-2 for $100,000, and no W-2 for 2022, assuming no salary was paid to the officer in January 2022. If one were to look only at the personal return for 2022, it would appear to indicate that there were no wages. But this is not the case. The salary was earned primarily in 2022. Careful review of monthly activity within the corporation is required in order to ascertain accurate income available to the officer for the calendar year under the circumstances. Errors resulting from overlooking the timing problems associated with non-calendar fiscal year corporations may distort perceived earning ability.

Wages paid to officers must meet IRS guidelines for reasonable compensation. If the IRS determines that compensation was unreasonably high, the excess will be deemed a dividend (resulting in double taxation).

Officer compensation shown on the tax return, while deductible, may not be reasonable for valuation purposes. Forensic accountants and other business appraisers are required to determine reasonable compensation for the officer/shareholder when preparing goodwill calculations using income approaches such as the capitalization of earnings approach.

In most closely held corporations, the amount of officer's compensation is not the same as reasonable or market compensation. This results from the desire to avoid double taxation and is usually achieved by increasing officer's salary to the point needed to reduce corporate profits to the desired level. Manipulation of profits by use of the year-end bonus is a common phenomenon in closely held corporations.

The amount of time devoted to the business is also shown in this section. This is an important factor in determination of reasonable or market compensation. Other factors to be considered are:

1. The nature and size of the business.
2. The qualifications of the officer.
3. The extent and scope of the officer's responsibilities.
4. The ratio of compensation to the gross and net income of the business.
5. What comparable businesses are paying to similarly situated individuals.
6. The historical salary paid to the officer.

Stock ownership is also entered in this section. Comparison of the percentage with the stock register of the corporation is important when the spouse owns less than 100% of the corporation. Ownership interest from time to time may affect the value of the marital interest in the corporation.

In community property jurisdictions, the ownership of stock in a corporation prior to marriage is presumptively separate property. Acquisition of stock during marriage is presumptively community. Forensic accountants trace ownership changes in these cases to provide guidance to attorneys on issues such as community interest and relevant valuation dates.

FORM 1125- E: LINE 3

A portion of the officer's compensation may be allocated to cost of goods sold where the corporation is involved in manufacturing. If this is the case, it may be prudent to check the officer/shareholder's payroll records to determine that all compensation is being reported in this section. Sometimes, as a result of tax preparation error, only the administrative compensation may be shown in this section.

Page 3: Schedule J: Tax Computation

Corporations including personal service corporations pay income taxes at a flat rate of 21%.

Personal service corporations are those in which employees who own 10% or more of the outstanding stock are the same people performing more than 20% of the personal services.

An analysis of true corporate profitability must consider the income tax liability of the C Corporation. In most closely held corporations, the amount of profit is eliminated through the payment of officer compensation in order to avoid double taxation of corporate profits, i.e., once at the corporate level and again at the individual level if and when corporate profits are distributed as dividends.

Page 4: Schedule K: Other Information

LINE 1: METHOD OF ACCOUNTING The two most common accounting methods are the "cash basis" and "accrual basis." When a corporation is on a cash basis, revenue is reported in the year in which it is actually or constructively received in the form of cash. Deductions are taken only for expenses actually paid during the year. In contrast, accrual basis corporations report revenue when it is earned (when the right to receive it is created). Thus, if a customer was billed for an item received on December 31, 2022, but the customer did not pay for until February 1, 2023, the business reporting on an accrual basis would still record the income in 2022 even though the merchandise was paid for in the subsequent year. On the accrual basis, expenses may be deducted when incurred, whether paid or not in the tax year.

If the accounting method changes from cash to accrual or vice versa between two tax years, adjustments to taxable income resulting from the change should have no effect on income. The accounting transition is merely a change in form that does not change the underlying economic reality.

Corporations whose business activity includes the sale of inventory must use the accrual basis of accounting unless their average annual gross receipts do not exceed $27 million. Service corporations, such as professional practices, generally are on a cash basis. A cash basis corporation does not report accounts receivables on its Schedule L (Page 6). As a result, for purposes of valuation, forensic accountants must obtain this information from the corporation's non-tax accounting records. Discovery of the net realizable value of accounts receivable is important for valuation purposes as it is often one of the largest assets of a business or practice.

Receivables present an interesting problem when cash basis corporations are valued in family law matters if the spouse charged with the accounts receivables will also be required to pay support from the collection of the same receivables. The perceived "double-dip" may appear particularly inequitable in property divisions where one party is awarded the corporation and is paying support while assets of equal stated value are awarded to the other spouse. Nevertheless, California courts have consistently upheld the opinion that it is proper to include earnings as income available for support from those same receivables the spouse received in the property division.

The "double-dip" effect, while appearing inequitable, can be better understood in terms of accrual basis accounting. On an accrual basis, the paying spouse is actually providing support from current accrual basis earnings. This can be illustrated by a hypothetical in which it is assumed that the business or practice is terminated at date of separation and the shareholder/spouse finds a job as an employee. In this situation, no apparent inequity exists if the spousal support is based on wages that are received currently because the corporate accounts receivable in this situation would be allocated to both parties based on their equal ownership interest in the corporation.

In cases where the corporation will be valued at date of separation, the "double-dip" effect may be eliminated through a segregation of collections of pre- and post-separation accounts receivable. The payer spouse may accomplish this result by creating a new corporation for all post-separation activity. As a result, both parties will report their share of income emanating from pre-separation activity. The tax advantages and disadvantages of this procedure must be evaluated on a case by case basis. If economically feasible, the segregation facilitates the presentation of "true" income from current operations because collection of prior period receivables will not affect cash basis income. Despite the frequency of the "double-dip" scenario, such segregation of accounts receivable is rare.

Another manner of reporting revenue and expense is known as "Percentage of Completion." Used primarily in the construction industries. Motion picture projects generally utilize a similar method of accounting known as the "Income Forecast Method. These methods dictate that revenue and expenses be recognized in conjunction with the progress of the construction project(s). Under the Percentage of Completion method, advance payments in anticipation of completion of certain percentages of a project are recorded as liabilities rather than as revenue. When each phase of construction is completed, the revenue associated with that phase is considered earned. At that point, the liability is extinguished and the revenue earned in connection with the phase is recognized.

The completed contract method is another accounting method for reporting income and expenses in the construction industry. Under this method, income and expenses of a project are reported in the year that a contract is completed.

LINE 2A: BUSINESS ACTIVITY CODE NO. Business code numbers are used by the government to compile statistical economic information. A listing of such codes can be accessed through the IRS website, www.IRS.gov.

LINE 2B AND C: BUSINESS ACTIVITY AND PRODUCT OR SERVICES The box provided for "Business Activity" and the other box for "Product or Service" are self-explanatory. The hypothetical tax returns shown at the end of the narrative contain examples of how these questions are answered.

Line 3: Subsidiaries and Affiliates If a corporation owned more than a 50% interest in another corporation, information concerning the other corporation must be provided to the IRS. Similarly, corporations owned by other corporations or part of a group of corporations under common ownership must submit, information concerning the other corporation(s) to the IRS.

Understanding of relationships between affiliated corporations is important for the preparation of appraisal reports and income analyses in family law matters. In cases of 100% owned subsidiaries, consolidation for appraisal purposes is usual and customary. A more difficult appraisal problem exists when the parent owns less than a 100% interest in the subsidiary. A separate appraisal of the subsidiary is usually required under these circumstances. The appraised value of the subsidiary may then be included as an asset of the parent corporation.

Common ownership of a number of corporations by the shareholder spouse creates another complexity for forensic accountants in marital dissolution matters. Investigation of the ownership and control of each of the corporations is a fundamental requirement in these cases. An analysis of the business's ownership interests and attributes should be undertaken to determine if the businesses should be consolidated into one appraisal.

Evaluation of income for shareholders of corporations with subsidiaries and/or affiliates also poses a challenging task for forensic accountants. The degree of control a parent corporation exercises over the subsidiary may ultimately dictate how the subsidiary's earnings will be construed for income available for support purposes. Even if the subsidiary has never paid dividends, income to the parent may be imputed if it is anticipated that such earnings will be distributed during the alimony and/or child support period.

Line 4: Corporate Ownership The information provided here advises the reader of the percentage ownership interests of controlling shareholders and if there is foreign ownership. Discovery should be undertaken to ascertain that the information shown is correct. Changes in ownership interest during the year are sometimes not communicated to the accountant who prepares the corporate tax return.

Where minority interests exist, discounts and premiums for the marital interest may have to be considered. If the shareholder spouse is a minority owner, the marital interest may be less than the pro rata percentage ownership applied to the total value of the corporation. The lower value may result from minority and marketability discounts. A minority discount is appropriate in instances where a shareholder lacks significant control in making corporate decisions that impact upon his or her ability to draw compensation from the corporation. This generally occurs when another shareholder, or another group of shareholders, runs the company.

In the alternative, if a shareholder spouse owns less than 100% of the stock in a corporation but is in total control of all important corporate decisions, the value of the interest will be enhanced. A premium for control is usually added to the pro rata ownership value in such cases.

The ownership of a material interest in a corporation by a foreign shareholder may cause additional difficulties if the ownership interest is material and the foreign shareholder is unavailable for deposition or subpoena. The possibility of diversion of funds to foreign bank accounts may exist and should be thoroughly investigated.

Corporate activity of a foreign subsidiary may require extensive analysis. The inspection of that subsidiary's records might be needed to ascertain that the investment in the foreign subsidiary and cash flow generated by it are properly accounted for on the U.S. corporation tax return.

Business activity abroad provides another possibility for hiding income. The impracticality and cost of performing discovery abroad requires creativity in dealing with this situation. Foreign forensic accountants may be used to help prepare appraisals of and cash flow analyses for foreign subsidiary corporations. If the matter proceeds to trial, the foreign accountant may have to appear to present his or her opinion. The payment of the foreign accountant's travel expenses requires a cost-benefit analysis in these circumstances.

The names of the shareholders shown here should correspond to other discovery information reflecting the ownership of the corporation. Discrepancies should be investigated.

LINE 5: Line 5 contains a set of questions designed to inform the IRS of any interests the corporation may have in foreign corporations.

LINES 6 TO 18: Lines 6 to 18 consist of questions regarding corporate activities and corporate adherence to IRS regulation.

LINE 9: On **Line 9** the IRS seeks information regarding tax-exempt interest. An amount shown may be relevant for the determination of income available for support.

An entry on Line 16 may be relevant for the appraisal of the business. A change in ownership may denote a sale corporate stock. The terms of the sale may be a factor an appraiser may consider in arriving at a conclusion of the value of the corporation or the corporation's stock.

Line 18 contains a question about Section 351 transfers. The general rule of Section 351 is that no gain or loss shall be recognized if property is transferred to a corporation by one or more persons solely in exchange for stock in such corporation and immediately after the exchange such person or persons are in control of the corporation. Section 351 allows the tax free change in status from a partnership or a proprietorship to a corporation.

In California, the change in the form of a business does not constitute a new business. Accordingly, the appraiser may consider prior years' income of the unincorporated business as a factor in determining value.

Page 6: Schedule L: Balance Sheets Per Books

The opening and closing assets and liabilities of the corporation, and the related supporting schedules, are reflected in this section of the corporate tax return. The balance sheet is frequently the starting point for appraising a corporate interest. The value of the shareholder/spouse's interest is generally a function of the fair market value of assets and the stated amount of the liabilities shown on the balance sheet.

Because assets are stated at historical cost, which is frequently not the same as fair market value, forensic accountant and other business appraisers must adjust assets using marketplace factors. Unrealized appreciation in the value of assets is not recognized on the corporate return except when an asset is sold. At that point, the appreciation is transformed into recognizable gain. Such gains, whether capital or not, are recognized as taxable events by the C Corporation.

ASSETS

LINE 1: CASH Very little adjustment is generally required for this asset. Bank reconciliation worksheets are standard supporting documentation. The financial statements of the corporation, if available, may provide additional details concerning the location of the institutions at which funds are maintained.

Unusually high accumulations of cash may impact both cash flow and valuation. From a cash flow perspective, the accumulation may deprive the spouse of current disposable cash flow from which to pay support. Whether or not the accumulation is a willful attempt to keep cash flow at a minimum may be at issue.

When an unnecessarily high amount of cash is on hand, the appraiser must take this fact into consideration when preparing the business valuation. Under certain appraisal techniques, such as the "Excess Earnings Method," a return on the use of the net assets of the corporation is deducted from average earnings to arrive at the capitalizable excess earnings used to compute goodwill. Failure to adjust for excess cash not required for business operations will have the effect of reducing the intangible value (goodwill) of the corporation computed under the excess earnings method.

Line 2a and b: Accounts Receivable Less Allowance for Bad Debts Accounts receivable is a material asset of many corporations. If the corporation reports on an accrual basis, an entry will be found on these lines. The allowance for bad debt is deducted from the receivables. The fair market value of the accounts receivable is known as its "net realizable value." Analysis of the underlying accounts is essential for this determination. The net accounts receivable shown on corporate tax returns often do not represent net realizable value because of limitations imposed by tax law.

Cash basis corporations may also have accounts receivable, even though no reference is made to them on the corporate return. Personal service corporations are the most common examples of cash basis corporations with accounts receivable.

Determination of fair market value of accounts receivable requires a reasonable estimate of collectability. An estimate may be obtained by testing subsequent cash receipts in order to ascertain how much of the receivables were actually collected over time. In cases where insufficient time has elapsed to perform such testing, estimates based on past experience must be used. An "aging" of the receivables into 30-, 60-, 90-, 120-, and over 120-day groups provide guidance in repairing such estimates. Most businesses maintain aging analyses on a monthly basis.

Sometimes the accounts receivable valuation is not easily accomplished because of the unique nature of the underlying business. Examples include personal injury lawyers representing plaintiffs, criminal defense lawyers, and orthodontists.

An incorporated personal injury lawyer typically has no accounts receivable; however, a similar asset known as work in progress amounts to somewhat the same thing from a marital dissolution perspective. A detailed analysis of the disposition of cases begun during marriage must be undertaken to compute the marital interest in the funds received from those cases that result in the collection of contingent fees. The methods used to arrive at value are beyond the scope of this text but, needless to say, much creativity is required to make such an analysis persuasive.

The incorporated law firm that specializes in criminal defense is an example of a practice that will typically contain accounts receivable at a negative value. The negative accounts receivable are liabilities that accountants refer to as "Unearned Revenue." Criminal defense practitioners generally require the fee for their services to be paid either wholly or partially in advance. The fee is then earned with future services. As in the case of work in progress of personal injury attorneys, calculation of unearned revenue requires creativity and a thorough understand of the underlying business activity.

Appraisals of cash basis corporations with accounts receivable usually include a calculation of a "Deferred Income Tax Liability." The liability for taxes on the collection of accounts receivable is equitable because the shareholder will eventually pay tax on these receivables either on the corporate or personal level. In corporations where profits are traditionally transformed into officer's salary, the tax on the accounts receivables will end up being paid on the individual level.

Line 3: Inventories Because the year-end for which ending inventory is determined is often close to the time at which the appraisal is performed, the relevant documentation for intensive research and analysis of this account is usually readily available. If an actual inventory count is taken, copies of the supporting detail should be obtained and reviewed. The procedures employed to make the count should be analyzed. Less analysis of procedures and valuation methodology is required if the taking of the inventory was observed by certified public accountants in conjunction with a certified audit.

Unreported sale of inventory ("inventory going out the back door") during the post-separation period is a frequent allegation made by non-shareholder spouses. Testing of gross profit ratios with industry percentages and against prior years' percentages for the corporation may support such allegations. Testing mark-up percentages against gross profit is another tool available in some cases to spot irregularities in inventory value.

The method by which inventory is valued may significantly affect the marital value of the corporate interest. Inventories are frequently undervalued in order to report lower taxable profit. Greater motivation to manipulate inventory exists in divorce cases because lower profitability from lower inventory benefits the shareholder/spouse via a lower business valuation and less income available for support.

Inventory valuation methods are important factors in determining the appropriate amount of inventory. The method used must conform to the best accounting practice in the particular trade or business. "Cost" means that the inventory is valued at the price paid. "Lower of cost or market" means that the cost of inventory, on an item by item basis, is compared to respective market value. The lower of the two values is used.

LIFO (last-in, first-out) and FIFO (first-in, first-out) are terms often used in connection with inventory valuation. If a LIFO method of costing inventory is used in an inflationary period, book value will tend to be understated. The FIFO method of costing inventory provides a more accurate representation of actual market value of the inventory because ending inventory is "costed" by reference to the most recent purchases of inventory.

Any changes in inventory accounting between prior years and the year of separation and subsequent period should be carefully investigated. Unusually large negative adjustments to inventory also warrant investigation.

Line 4: U.S. Government Obligations The IRS requires identification of assets held in this form. This kind of asset is known as a "Cash Equivalent." Investment interest income on U.S. government obligations should be accrued at the valuation date to insure that the full value of the corporation's interest is calculated.

Line 5: Tax-Exempt Securities As in the case of U.S. government obligations, the IRS requires identification of assets held in this form. This asset is also a "Cash Equivalent." Interest from tax-exempt securities is reported on Line 7 of the Schedule M-1 on Page 4 of the return. While not subject to federal income tax, the amount represents additional income available to the corporation.

Additional asset value may be uncovered through a calculation of interest and/or dividend income receivable for earnings that should have been accrued on these investments.

Line 6: Other Current Assets Other current assets are usually listed by type and amount on supporting schedules attached to the return. Typical examples of other current assets are loans to employees, prepaid expenses, and marketable securities.

Analysis of these assets may disclose that they are undervalued. Marketable securities that have appreciated will require an upward adjustment from historical to fair market value. The brokerage statement(s) at year-end should contain the appropriate fair market value information.

A review of the rent, taxes and insurance accounts in the general ledger may reveal that certain expenses have been paid for in advance. January rent for the following year paid in December of the current year is an example of an expense that causes an understatement of annual income and cash flow.

Line 7: Loans to Stockholders It is common to find stockholders of closely held corporations borrowing money from the corporation during a fiscal year. Often, loans to the stockholder represent distributions in lieu of salary if the stockholder is also an employee of the corporation. Since payroll taxes must be paid if salary is distributed, officer/shareholders of closely held corporations find this form of distribution during the year convenient.

When an interest in a corporation is valued as of the date of separation, the amount of the stockholder loan is offset by a marital liability of equal value. Under the circumstances, the appraisal of the corporate interest may be reduced by the amount of the loan. If this is done, no recognition of a liability to the corporation by the marital estate is required. Alternatively, if the asset is included in arriving at the value of the marital corporate interest, the marital liability to the corporation should not be overlooked.

Greater complexity arises when corporate interests are valued close to the time of trial. Under these circumstances, it is prudent to account for the loan as an asset of the corporation and recognize any loans payable to the corporation at the date of separation as a marital liability.

Line 8: Mortgage and Real Estate Loans Secured loans frequently result from the sale of corporate real estate. Research concerning the origin of the loan may lead to useful discovery. It may be important for the forensic accountant to investigate the propriety of the disposition of prior assets owned by the corporation.

Interest income should be compared with the outstanding loan balance(s) to ascertain that all income has been reported and collections have been properly deposited to the corporation.

The collectability of the loans needs to be ascertained for valuation purposes. For example, a potential bad debt, not recognized for tax purposes until the asset is deemed completely worthless, will nevertheless reduce the fair market value of the loan.

Another valuation adjustment is appropriate if the loan interest rate is either well below or above current market. Just as in the case of corporate bonds, the value of the secured loans will be a function of how the stated interest compares to market interest.

Line 9: Other Investments Investments in other corporations or partnerships are the most common types of assets in this category. The values indicated on the corporation balance sheet often do not reflect fair market value for these investments.

Where an investment in another enterprise is a significant corporate asset, a separate appraisal of the other entity may be required in order to arrive at fair market value of the corporation interest therein.

Line 10a and b: Building and Other Depreciable Assets Less Accumulated Depreciation As stated previously, historical cost is the basis for the amounts shown for assets. Consequently, capitalized real and personal property is presented at original cost. Annual depreciation expense taken is deducted from the cost to arrive at the "Book Value" of the fixed asset. Because depreciation expense is governed by tax guidelines, not actual asset deterioration and obsolescence, book value of fixed assets is usually not equal to fair market value.

Adjustment of fixed assets to fair market value is one of the most common appraisal procedures. Real estate is often restated to market based on an appraisal of the property performed by a real property expert. Automobiles are restated pursuant to "Blue Book" values. The value of other assets (equipment, machinery, furniture, and furnishings) may also be restated pursuant to appraisals prepared by experts.

The amount of cost and effort put into the restating of capital assets is a subjective determination depending on facts and circumstances. The materiality of the restatement involved is the primary factor to consider. Like many other decisions made in marital dissolution proceedings, the cost and benefit of the additional appraisals need to be assessed by the lawyer, the client and forensic accountant.

General ledger expense accounts, such as "Repairs and Maintenance," "Computer Expense," and "Office Expense" may contain payments for assets that should have been capitalized. Failure to restate these items as capital expenditures will understate assets. Income will also be understated when capital expenditures are charged to expense.

Line 11a and b: Depletable Assets Less Accumulated Depletion Like depreciation, depletion deductions for natural resources are often not representative of the actual exhaustion of the resource. The fair market value of the remaining reserves should be determined where practical and meaningful to the spouses involved in the divorce. Thus, if the interest of the marital estate is relatively small, and the cost of determining value of the resource substantial, book value may be the most practical value to use. If the interest is material, an expert may be hired to provide an opinion of value.

Line 12: Land Land is not a depreciable asset; however, costs incurred to acquire land, such as prepaid interest ("Points"), may be amortized (deducted over time) rather than entirely expensed in the year paid even if the corporation is on a cash basis.

Like other fixed assets, land is recorded at historical cost. Restating land to fair market value is a common appraisal adjustment affecting valuation of the corporation interest. Adjustments to land value will not change income unless an installment sale of the land is imminent. Annual installment payments would ordinarily be treated as a continuing source of cash to the corporation.

Line 13a and b: Intangibles Assets Less Accumulated Amortization Amortization, like depreciation, refers to the deductibility of certain capital expenditures or organization costs ratably over time. The primary difference between amortization and depreciation is the nature of the capital expenditures to which amortization applies. Examples of amortization have already been mentioned, i.e., depletion and capitalized interest. Other kinds of capital expenditures subject to amortization include "Leasehold Improvements," "Research & Development Costs," "Pollution Control Facilities," and intangible assets.

The most well-known intangible asset in family law is "Goodwill." The calculation of goodwill in connection with the preparation of a business appraisal is common practice. For tax purposes and under generally accepted accounting principles, "Goodwill" only appears on the balance sheet when it is purchased. The difference between the price paid for a business and the fair market value of the tangible assets and other intangibles purchased is goodwill. Acquired goodwill may be amortized over a 15-year period under IRS Code Section 197.

If amortization of intangibles appears on the corporation balance sheet, the origin of the asset should be investigated. Understanding the nature and cost of the asset will determine how it should be handled in a marital dissolution appraisal. The purchase price paid for goodwill may also represent a comparable sale that may be relevant evidence of value of certain or all assets of the corporation.

Certain intangibles have no independent market value and are generally embodied in the calculation of goodwill. Examples included covenants not to compete, patents, copyrights, and licenses. Rights such as these are generally incorporated into the concept of appraised goodwill. Rarely will independent calculation of the value of intangibles other than goodwill appear in a business appraisal prepared for marital dissolution purposes.

Line 14: Other Assets Non-current assets for which no line item has been provided on the balance sheet are generally listed on supporting schedules whose total is carried to this line. Examples of other assets include "Deposits" and "Notes Receivable."

Although improper for tax reporting, it is common practice for cash basis corporations to deduct lease and utility deposits. The value of a corporation will be understated unless these costs are listed as assets. Examination of relevant underlying documentation, such as facilities leases, will usually disclose the amount of the deposits.

Another asset often found listed in this section is secured and unsecured notes receivable. Secured and unsecured promissory notes are stated at historical cost for tax purposes. No reduction in value is permitted under tax law unless the note becomes worthless. These instruments need to be restated to fair market value for appraisal purposes. The most common factors evaluated by experts when determining fair market value of notes receivable are the implicit interest rates in comparison to market rates, the credit-worthiness of the borrower, and the underlying collateral. Use of these factors as a basis for comparison with notes traded in the marketplace may allow forensic accountants to estimate appraisal values.

LINE 15: TOTAL ASSETS Summation of all of the assets appears here for both the current and prior year-ends. This amount is also shown on Page 1, Box D. Total assets should equal total liabilities and stockholders' equity.

LIABILITIES AND CAPITAL

LINE 16: ACCOUNTS PAYABLE Accrual basis corporations enter the amounts due vendors at fiscal year-end here. No entry will appear on this line for cash basis corporations.

Accounts payable for cash basis corporations should be determined for business appraisal purposes. Forensic CPAs determine accounts payable for cash basis corporations by reviewing payments to vendors made after year-end. All payments for goods and services purchased during the tax year but not yet paid for represent the accounts payable of the corporation.

Failure to compute the accounts payable results in an overstatement of the value of the corporate interest. Conversely, overstated accounts payable will understate the value of the corporation.

LINE 17: MORTGAGES, NOTES, BONDS PAYABLE IN LESS THAN ONE YEAR The short-term portion of these liabilities is presented here. Further investigation of the books and records of the corporation is usually required in order to ascertain the nature and scope of these liabilities.

Please refer to the discussion of Line 20 for additional information about analyzing this liability.

LINE 18: OTHER CURRENT LIABILITIES Accrued expenses, payroll taxes payable, and unpaid retirement plan contributions are examples of other current liabilities. Cash basis corporations may deduct accrued payroll taxes and retirement plan contributions even if unpaid at year-end. Consequently, such other current liabilities may appear on a cash basis corporation's balance sheet. Accuracy of the accruals may be ascertained by examination of the pension plan contribution calculations and payroll tax returns.

Accrued expenses may reflect the amount of overhead that has been incurred but is unpaid at year-end. Unpaid telephone and utility bills are common examples of expenses that may be accrued. Proper valuation procedures require inclusion of such liabilities. Income available for support is generally unaffected by these expenses because the actual outflow of cash will occur in a future period.

Unearned income and deferred income taxes are current liabilities that do not appear on cash basis balance sheets but need to be considered in many business appraisals. Unearned income results from advances (e.g., retainers for lawyers) from clients or customers for work that has not yet been earned.

Deferred income taxes exist when a tax is created in the current period that will have to be paid in later years. In divorce cases, the most common type of deferred income tax is associated with the inclusion of accounts receivable on the balance sheet of cash basis corporations. Calculation of the amount of the deferred income tax is often at issue. To be persuasive, forensic accountants need to have reasonable support for the tax rates employed in their deferred income tax calculations.

LINE 19: LOANS FROM STOCKHOLDERS It is common to find stockholders of closely held corporations loaning money to their corporation. Often, loans from the stockholder occur when corporations require an infusion of capital but do not wish to borrow from conventional lenders.

Stockholder loans to the corporation should be eliminated from the corporate balance sheet if the corporate interest is valued as of the date of separation. Under these circumstances, the appraised value of the corporation may be increased by the elimination of the liability to the stockholder. If this is done, no recognition of a receivable from the corporation by the marital estate is required. Alternatively, if the liability is recognized in arriving at the corporate value, the marital receivable from the corporation should not be overlooked.

Greater complexity arises when corporate interests are valued close to the time of trial. Under these circumstances, it is prudent to account for the loan as a liability of the corporation and recognize any loans receivable from the corporation at the date of separation as a marital asset.

LINE 20: MORTGAGES, NOTES, BONDS PAYABLE IN MORE THAN ONE YEAR The long-term portion of such liabilities is presented here. Further investigation of the books and records of the corporation is usually required in order to ascertain the nature and scope of these liabilities.

The accuracy and authenticity of long-term liabilities need to be analyzed in the appraisal process. Liabilities may be inaccurate if the interest and principal on loan payments have not been allocated properly. The authenticity of liabilities may be suspect in some instances, e.g., liabilities to relatives who do not demand payment and have never received payment.

Certain liabilities may not be included on Schedule L but may be shown on Schedule M-1. Examples include liabilities under lease obligations and legal liability that has not been adjudicated. Such liabilities may reduce the value of the corporate interest even if the amount of the ultimate liability cannot be ascertained.

If a corporation is liable on a lease even though it has moved out of a facility or no longer uses the original leased asset, the liability under the lease should be computed at present value for appraisal purposes. Failure to reduce value for such liability overstates the value of the corporate interest.

LINE 21: OTHER LIABILITIES Other long-term liabilities are presented in supporting schedules with a total shown on this line. The amount presented reflects unsecured liabilities that may not have to be paid in the next fiscal year. Examples of other liabilities are the obligation to pay for goods or services under long-term contracts, and warranty liability for corporations engaged in manufacturing.

Understanding the nature of the enterprise is essential to locating all possible liabilities. Exploration of this area with corporate management through interview or deposition is advisable.

LINE 22 AND 23: CAPITAL STOCK AND PAID-IN CAPITAL Amounts originally used to capitalize the corporation and additional amounts of capital contributed from time to time will be reflected in this section.

LINE 24 AND 25: RETAINED EARNINGS Retained earnings represent the accumulated undistributed profits of the corporation since inception and by itself is not a significant element of corporate appraisal or cash flow. It merely represents corporate assets minus liabilities and minus capital and paid-in capital. Any adjustments on Line 25 should be thoroughly investigated to determine whether such items are relevant to the issues of appraisal or income available for support.

LINE 27: TREASURY STOCK If an entry appears here, investigation is warranted. Treasury stock represents stock purchased by the corporation from stockholders. The reason for the purchase may be relevant to the appraisal of the corporate interest. For example, if the stock purchase resulted from a stock redemption relating to the sale of a stockholder's interest in the corporation, evidence of the market value of the corporation may be obtained.

LINE 28: TOTAL LIABILITIES AND STOCKHOLDERS' EQUITY The amount shown here is merely a total of all of the liability and stockholder equity accounts and should be equal to the total assets of the corporation.

Schedule M-1: Reconciliation of Income (Loss) per Books with Income (Loss) per Return

Line 1: Net Income (Loss) Per Books The profit or loss shown on a corporation's financial statements (books) is entered on this line. Financial statements of the corporation will usually show a different profit or loss than the tax return because of timing differences in the recording of income and expense and the fact that certain book expense items are not deducted in arriving at corporate taxable income. Likewise, certain revenue and expense items not recognized in arriving at financial statement profit are included in arriving at taxable income.

Line 2: Federal Income Tax Although deductible in arriving at financial statement profit or loss, the amount paid for corporate federal income tax is not deductible on the tax return. As in the case of individual income taxation, state income tax payments are deductible. To reconcile book profit or loss to tax profit or loss, federal income tax paid during the year is added back to book profit or loss.

As mentioned previously in this text, payment of federal corporate income taxes is an appropriate reduction of income available to the shareholders because the tax paid limits the amount of cash available for corporate salary, dividends, or officer loans.

Line 3: Excess of Capital Losses Over Capital Gains Unlike individual taxpayers who may deduct up to $3,000 of capital losses per year, corporate capital loss deductions can only be deducted to offset capital gains. Thus, if corporate capital losses exceed capital gains, the book income will be lower than the tax income by the amount of the net capital. As a result, net capital losses are added back to book profit or loss to arrive at taxable income. Capital losses may be carried back or forward to offset prior or future capital gains. As such, capital losses represent a contingent non-balance sheet asset of both cash-basis and accrual basis corporations. The existence of the asset is contingent on the recognition of future capital gains.

Capital gains and losses are usually not considered in computing representative cash flow when the transaction(s) giving rise to the gains or losses are not recurring.

Line 4: Income Subject to Tax not Recorded on Books this Year Entries in this category should be investigated to determine which presentation is more appropriate for valuation and income available for support purposes. An example of an item that would appear here is the amount of advance payments received from customers for goods and services.

Line 5: Expenses Recorded on Books this Year not Deducted on this Return The three most common types of expenses of this kind are "Depreciation," "Contribution Carryovers," and "Meals and Entertainment."

Accelerated depreciation taken in prior years' tax returns may result in more depreciation per books than for tax in the current year because assets may have been entirely depreciated for tax purposes and not fully depreciated for financial statement purposes. Amounts shown here may indicate that depreciation expense should be added back to income to arrive at true income available for support.

While a legitimate tax deduction, charitable contributions made by a corporation may not be a legitimate reduction of cash flow. The test is whether the contribution has a reasonable and necessary business purpose. In any event, corporations may not deduct contributions in excess of 10% of taxable income in any year. However, a special COVID provision did allow corporations to deduct up to 25% for tax year 2021. The excess may be carried over. Like net operating losses, the carryover of a deduction represents an asset that may not appear on a balance sheet. Typically, the amount involved in this area is not material enough to warrant extensive investigation.

Under current tax rules, only 50% of business-related meals expenses are deductible for tax purposes (note that with the passage of the Tax Cut and Jobs Act in 2017, business entertainment is no longer deductible). Also note that for tax years 2021 and 2022, a special COVID provision allows a 100% deduction for meals purchased from a restaurant. However, 100% of these expenses are deducted for financial statement profit; accordingly, a reconciliation of this expense is always necessary when it exists. Travel expenses may also differ on financial statements because of a variety of statutory tax limitations. The type of limitation will depend on the nature of the expense. Generally, reasonable and necessary business-related travel expenses are deductible. Amounts shown here suggest the possibility of perquisites. Personal travel deducted by a corporation is common.

Another common non-deductible expense is officer's life insurance. While not deductible, this expense may be a legitimate reduction of cash flow if another shareholder, other than the shareholder/spouse, or the corporation is the beneficiary.

Line 7: Income Recorded on Books this Year not Included on this Return Tax-exempt interest is the most common example of book income excluded from taxation. However, tax-exempt income should be included in computing representative cash flow. Existence of such income should alert the reader to tax-exempt investments owned by the corporation.

Line 8: Deductions Included on this Return not Charged Against Book Income this Year Depreciation is the most prominent example of this kind of expense. MACRS and other forms of accelerated depreciation allowed for tax purposes can result in tax depreciation being larger than depreciation on the books.

Depletion is another expense that can be higher for tax than on the financial statements.

A contribution carryover from a prior year will reduce taxable income. Since the decrease results from a prior period cash outlay, it is proper to add the contribution carryover back to taxable income to arrive at representative income for the period.

Line 10: Income (Loss) The amount arrived at through the reconciliation should match line 28 of Page 1. This is the total ordinary taxable income or loss of the corporation.

Schedule M-2: Analysis of Unappropriated Retained Earnings per Books

Reconciliation of year-end retained earnings with beginning retained earnings is the primary purpose of this section. In most cases, the only adjustment to retained earnings is the book profit or loss of the corporation. However, dividends made by the corporation during the year will affect ending retained earnings.

Dividends to the shareholders may affect cash flow and valuation. Historical dividends should be analyzed in order to determine the basis of the distributions. With the understanding gained from this analysis, it may be possible to form an opinion of a representative amount of dividends that should be added to income available for alimony and/or child support.

Distributions of property other than cash should be scrutinized to determine whether fair market value was assigned to the property especially if the shareholder spouse takes control of the property. Distributions of appreciated property result in gain to the corporation.

FORM 1120S: S CORPORATION TAX RETURNS

Page 1: U.S. Income Tax Return for an S Corporation

S Corporations generally are required to report on a calendar year unless a business purpose for such non-calendar year-end can be established to the satisfaction of the IRS. The criteria include the nature of the underlying business activity and its natural year. Special rules (including a tax deposit) govern the use of a fiscal year causing non-calendar year S corporations to be rarely seen by forensic accountants.

Greater complexity in the preparation of income available for child support and spousal support (which the IRS and many states call "alimony") is more likely to exist where substantial income, loss or cash flow is derived from activities of an S Corporation that reports on a fiscal year other than December 31. A thorough discussion of these complexities is presented in the Overview of Partnership Taxation. Please refer to that section as it applies equally to S Corporations.

Line A: S Election Effective Date In order to avoid double taxation at the corporate level, shareholders may elect to be treated as an S Corporation instead of a C Corporation. The election is only available under specific circumstances to domestic corporations. In general, to qualify as an S Corporation, the corporation must consist of 100 or fewer shareholders (none of whom are non-resident aliens), and have only one class of stock issued and outstanding. In addition, none of the shareholders may be a corporation, a partnership, or a trust.

Line B: Business Activity Code Business code numbers are used by the government to compile statistical economic information. A listing of such codes can be accessed through the IRS website, www.IRS.gov.

Line C: Check if M-3 Attached The Schedule M-3 is a reconciliation of net income or loss for corporations with assets of $10 million or more. Control of large corporations by one spouse is not that common in marital dissolutions. Large corporations are typically audited annually by their CPA firms. The audited financial statements provide greater transparency regarding transactional activity than the unaudited financial statements typically produced by CPAs engaged by smaller corporations. As a result, perquisite analyses and other investigations designed to discover the true income of the corporation are not usually needed in these instances.

Line D: Employer Identification Number S Corporations may obtain an "Employer ID Number" by filing Form SS-4. The ID number is reflected on all payroll tax forms the corporation is required to file.

Line E: Date Incorporated The date of incorporation provides an appraiser of the length of time the company has been in business.

Line F: Total Assets "Total Assets" shown here should be the same as the total assets on Page 4, Schedule L, Line 15. A quick idea of the size of the business can be gleaned from this number.

Lines G and H: Provide information about whether the S corporation election was made or terminated in the current year and any other changes in corporate status. Any changes noted should prompt additional inquiry as to the underlying reasons for the change.

Line I: Number of Shareholders Changes in the number of shareholders may affect cash flow and appraised value. As a result, comparison of the amount of shareholders shown with the amount shown on prior years' returns is recommended.

INCOME

Line 1a: Gross Receipts or Sales Gross receipts or sales, commonly referred to as the business's "Gross," is usually a very significant statistics for valuation purposes. Non-accountants frequently use the terms "Income," "Revenue," and "Gross Income" interchangeably. This is a common area of confusion that lawyers should avoid. The gross receipts are synonymous with revenue for a corporation that operates on a cash basis. If the corporation operates on an accrual basis, gross cash receipts may not be the same amount as corporate revenue even though they are placed on the same line on the tax return. In the case of accrual basis corporations, the revenue represents what the business has billed or sold while the cash receipts are the collections of its accounts receivable. "Income" is the difference between revenue and expenses. It is synonymous with "Profit" or the "Bottom Line."

Straight Edge, Inc.'s tax return, shown at the end of this section, is an example of an "S" corporation that reports on an accrual basis. The $943,098 shown on Line 1 represents corporate sales that have been billed to customers. The amount is obtained from a summary of yearly sales contained in the company's general ledger and sales journal. The amount of sales does not equate to the amount collected on its accounts receivable.

The "Gross" is an important element of tax return analysis. Often, a business or practice is sold on the basis of multiples of gross receipts. Comparison with prior years "Gross" will provide information for a historical trend analysis of sales or fees. If a decrease in revenue in the current period has occurred, the cause for the reduction should be ascertained through interview, deposition, or document inspection. The concern generally focuses on whether the decrease was the result of lower productivity engendered by the divorce or just market conditions. Whether this decrease was caused by the psychological effects of the divorce or by a willful slowdown are possibilities requiring investigation.

A trend analysis is also appropriate for corporate income analysis. Revenue and income trends are important factors to consider in appraising a commercial business. Divorce effects may be highlighted by reference to such analyses.

Many closely held cash basis corporations commit tax evasion by depositing checks received in December into the business bank account in January of the following year. Under the law, any checks received in December are considered constructively received and must be reported in the fiscal year that the month of December falls. If a corporation has just begun this practice of holding checks in December of 2022, the "Gross" of the business is understated by the amount of the held checks. This results in a lower amount of corporation taxable income allocable to the officer/shareholder and a lower apparent income for that spouse. If this practice of holding checks has been consistently followed for years, an analysis of the amounts involved for the prior versus the current year will provide the most accurate representation of annual gross receipts.

Unusually low amounts of reported gross in corporations that handle cash, particularly retail businesses such as restaurants, may indicate unreported income. Analysis of cash register tapes and other business records may be helpful in determining the amount of unreported income in some circumstances. When information required for such an analysis is unavailable, other procedures are employed by forensic accountants to assist in quantifying the unreported income.

One such procedure relies upon statistical gross profit information for the industry to suggest appropriate levels of gross receipts. The quantification of what the "Gross" should be is achieved by dividing the actual "Cost of Goods Sold" of the subject business by the industry percentage for "Cost of Goods Sold." Comparing the gross profit ("Revenue" less "Cost of Goods Sold"—also known as "Gross Margin") of the subject business to industry statistical information provides a quick method for determining the probability of unreported income.

An analysis of the mark-up on the company's merchandise may also be revealing. If the typical mark-up is 25% (let's say $1.25 on goods that cost $1.00), then the gross profit to be expected is 20% ($.25 divided by $1.25). If the corporation tax return reflects a materially lower "Gross Profit" enhanced scrutiny is advisable. The value of this type of approach is substantially reduced in corporations that have a large product mix or in cases where merchandise is frequently discounted.

Another way of proving unreported income exists, albeit more time-consuming and costly than those mentioned, is the lifestyle analysis. A disparity between the parties' lifestyle and their adjusted gross income for the period reported on the individual income tax return (this would include salary from and dividends paid by the closely held corporation) may provide a reasonable estimate of unreported income under certain circumstances. If the unreported income is stored in a safe deposit box and not exhausted on living expenses, the lifestyle analysis will not prove very useful. The lifestyle approach requires an accounting for all sources and uses of cash for a particular period. The accounting should include deposits to the parties' personal accounts that may have emanated from gifts, inheritance, borrowing, or prior year loan repayments. Cash balances at both the beginning and the end of the period need to be ascertained in order to calculate the amount of cash flow funded by savings on hand at the beginning of the period. Classification of recorded expenditures by the parties during the particular period under scrutiny may reveal expenditures well in excess of reported income. Additionally, such classification may disclose either small or nonexistent expenditures for known costs of living such as housekeeper costs and grocery expenses. An estimate of the reasonable monthly cost of such expenditures may then be added to the reported cost of living to arrive at the total lifestyle of the parties.

Line 1b: Returns and Allowances This represents sold merchandise that has been returned or, in the case of a personal service corporations, a refund of an overpayment. While seemingly similar, "Returns and Allowances" should not be confused with "Bad Debts" discussed in the following.

Line 2: Cost of Goods Sold Professional practice and service corporations typically report nothing on this line. Commercial businesses with inventories report the cost relating to the products sold on this line. Schedule A is the portion of the S corporation tax return in which additional information relative to "Cost of Goods Sold" is reported. A more detailed explanation of this area is included in the discussion of Form 1125-A presented later.

Line 3: Gross Profit The gross profit is the difference between "Gross receipts or sales" ("Revenue") and the cost of merchandise sold. Reference to the percentage of "Gross Profit" to "Revenue" is an important indicator of corporate economic trends. A decline in the gross profit percentage may indicate greater price competition in the industry or higher raw material costs. Variances in the year of divorce warrant concern and scrutiny. Both "Revenue" and "Cost of Goods Sold" may impact this percentage. As mentioned previously, a divergence from industry norms creates an inference that the corporation is not reporting revenue. More on "Gross Profit" (also known as "Gross Margin") is presented in the discussion of Schedule A.

Line 4: Net Gain or (Loss) from Form 4797 Gain from disposition of real or personal property used in the business activity that results in ordinary income to the S corporation is reflected here. An entry on this line indicates that a sale or conversion of assets has taken place during the year. For cash flow purposes, a sale of business assets generally is not a recurring business activity. Consequently, a representative cash flow analysis for the year should exclude these proceeds. Form 4797 is used to determine the capital gain versus ordinary income portion of gain from sale of business-related capital assets.

Line 5: Other Income (Loss) This line reflects miscellaneous sources of income not specifically delineated in Lines 1 through 4. Typically, income that does not recur annually is inserted on this line. Examples of income that would appear here are proceeds from successfully litigated lawsuits and insurance proceeds. Non-recurring sources of income are usually not considered cash available for support. But large amounts of cash generated by such income that remain within the corporation will result in an increase in investment income. All investment and other passive income passed through to the shareholders of an S Corporation.

Line 6: Total Income (Loss) This line is merely the summation of the above and, standing alone, is not as significant from an analytical perspective as are its components. Of note is the fact that, unlike a C Corporation, income from interest, dividends, rents, royalties, and capital gains do not appear in this section. They appear on the shareholders' K-1s as pass through items that are reported on the individual shareholders' tax returns.

DEDUCTIONS

Expenses are often converted into percentages and compared with prior years. Anomalies and deviations can be more easily identified through use of analysis of comparative percentages (also known as "Common Size" comparative income statements).

Line 7: Compensation of Officers The amount of compensation received by the spouse is one of the most important factors in both cash flow and valuation analyses. Historical compensation summaries are useful in the determination of representative and reasonable compensation. Representative compensation is a key factor in cash flow analyses. Reasonable compensation may be a critical component of a goodwill analysis.

In addition to salary, a shareholder of an S Corporation must report his or her share of the corporate profit or loss. The effect of reportable profit or loss on income must be evaluated on a case by case basis. In temporary support situations, reference should be made to recent historical precedent. In permanent support situations, a longer term analysis may be more representative of a spouse's income from the S Corporation.

If the S Corporation has distributed profits historically, the allocable profit of the shareholder spouse should be included in cash flow. Losses that require no funds to be transferred from stockholder to corporation should only be considered reductions to income if the facts and circumstances suggest that such treatment would be equitable.

Current business conditions may make historical precedent irrelevant. That is why it is important for the forensic accountant to dig deeper than the books and records of the business to form a reliable opinion of income.

Line 8: Salary and Wages Are friends and relatives on payroll who do not really perform full services for compensation received? Inspection of payroll tax returns and, where available, payroll journals will identify those persons on payroll. To the extent that "Salary and Wages" are overstated, conclusions as to the value of the enterprise and cash flow available for support are understated.

Closely related, but usually not included in "Salary and Wages," are payments to independent contractors. Corporations are required to file IRS Form 1099 to report all payments to independent contractors in excess of $600 per year. Observation of the payees listed on the 1099 forms may disclose payments to friends or relatives.

Line 9: Repairs and Maintenance In closely held corporations where the officer/shareholder has unfettered control of all expenditures, closer scrutiny of this expense item is advised. Frequently, personal residence repairs and improvements are run through this account. Vendors who provide goods or services to the corporation may also provide additional *personal* goods or services. The "out-spouse" may be helpful in identifying companies or individuals who have provided good or services for the parties personally that have been paid for out of the corporation.

Capital expenditures that are written off as an expense of the period are often classified as repair expense. The effect of improper recording of capital assets is the understatement of business income. If the asset was purchased outright, actual cash flow for the period may be properly reflected; however, income available for support reports should contain an adjustment for this item. Appropriate adjustment to income requires that the amount of capital expenditures charged to expense be added back. By this means, projected future cash flow does not include the non-recurring costs of asset acquisitions. If, on the other hand, it is common practice for the corporation to regularly upgrade and replace assets, no adjustment, or only a partial adjustment, may be necessary.

Line 10: Bad Debts Cash basis corporations are allowed to deduct bad debt only to the extent that they have been previously reported as income to the enterprise or as a loan to a customer. This is a rare occurrence. Corporations seeking to suppress income may report bad debts from friends and relatives that are not true business debts, or they may write off debts in the year of a pending divorce suit and then report them as income in a later tax year. In either event, the profitability of the business is understated. The understatement affects both the appraisal of the corporation and the calculation of a spouse's cash flow from the corporation.

Accrual basis corporations must use the specific charge-off method to deduct business bad debts. Only direct write-offs are allowed. In terms of income or business value, this means that receivables reported on the corporate tax return may be overvalued and income overstated because the tax law does not allow a deduction pursuant to a reserve for bad debts. Income of accrual basis corporations should be adjusted for anticipated bad debts in order to derive a more accurate income conclusion.

Line 11: Rents In some cases, inquiry should be made concerning the identity of the lessor and the fair market value of the rental payment. If the lessor is a friend or relative of the officer/shareholder of a closely held corporation, the probability of overstated rent that reduces profitability is enhanced. Examination of the facility lease is generally an integral part of the appraisal process. A bargain lease has the effect of overstating profitability; accordingly, an adjustment should be made to restate the annual rental to market.

A bargain lease suggests an asset with value that typically will not be disclosed in any discovery materials. Real estate experts are able to render opinions of value for leases whose stated rent is lower than market.

Line 12: Taxes and Licenses Real estate, personal property, and payroll taxes are reported here. Examination of tax bills and other supporting documentation may disclose unreported assets or misstated values.

Line 13: Interest An amount shown here evidences the existence of either secured or unsecured loans. Note that the Tax Cut and Jobs Act implemented a limitation to the amount of deductible interest to 30% of the businesses adjusted taxable income. As a result, the interest listed here may not reflect the interest the business actually paid. Loan application files may be obtained from lenders. This documentation may help to confirm or uncover the existence of certain marital assets. Opinions of value are also found in these files. While the individual officer/shareholder's opinion of the value of the real estate and/or the corporation may carry little weight at trial, it may be useful for settlement purposes. Personal financial statements from the officer/shareholder spouse may be found in the loan file. The officer's opinions of value of other marital assets may also appear in the loan file. This information may promote settlement and save expert witness appraisal costs. In summary, loan files may contain application forms and other informative documents that provide a cross-reference for checking the accuracy of marital asset values. The loan application usually includes a sworn statement of earning ability, an amount that can be compared with the income reported for the same period on the corporation tax return and on the officer/shareholder's individual tax return. The spouse's credibility as a witness may be impaired by presenting evidence of major inconsistencies between the income shown on the loan application and the tax return income.

Line 14: Depreciation Reported depreciation must be analyzed with a view to the impact of this expense on income. Page 4 of the S Corporation tax return contains a balance sheet that includes a summary of the cost of depreciable property and the accumulated depreciation.

Analysis of depreciation and asset history may be provided either wholly or partially on Form 4562 and supporting schedules included in the return of a corporation claiming depreciation expense. Probative information concerning the assets of the business, including date of acquisition and original cost, are usually available on this form and supporting detail schedules that may be included in the return. More asset information may be obtained from a corporation's internally prepared depreciation schedule or the work papers maintained by its independent certified public accounting firm.

Depreciation schedules aid in identifying assets that have been written off but still have value. In addition to providing relevant data for determining the fair market value of the fixed assets, the depreciation schedule is also useful for evaluating claimed cash flow needs of the business for investment in new equipment.

The first $1,080,000 of personal property additions in 2022 (increasing to $1,160,000 in 2023 and subsequent years) can generally be currently deducted under Internal Revenue Code (IRC) Section 179. In S Corporations, this expense is a flow through item that appears on the individual shareholder's K-1s. The immediate deduction of all or a substantial part of the cost of an asset may require an adjustment to arrive at representative income. In other words, Section 179 depreciation is typically not considered a reduction in income available for support.

Depreciation rates appearing on the tax return should be compared to financial statement depreciation. Differences between the tax return and financial depreciation are noted on Page 5, Schedule M-1, Lines 3a and 6a. Entries on these lines warrant further analysis because rapid depreciation write-offs usually result in overstatement of annual operating costs and corresponding understatement of value for the business (especially when a capitalization of earnings method is used to value the business or its goodwill).

LINE 15: DEPLETION Depletion is "depreciation" for natural resources. It represents a deduction for the capital investment that the corporation receives pro rata over the estimated productive life of the resource. Different tax methods, such as cost depletion and percentage depletion, are allowed for computation of the deduction.

Like depreciation, analysis of actual cash flow related to this expense is required to determine "true" cash flow. Generally, the capital investment providing the basis for depreciation is not a recurring cost of the corporation; accordingly, depletion expense is considered a non-cash expense that is usually added back to profit to arrive at representative cash flow for the corporation.

LINE 16: ADVERTISING Amounts shown here should be evaluated for perquisite possibility. Misclassification of personal travel and entertainment may be included in the total expense. Examination of supporting accounting records such as general ledgers and journals will reveal whether perks are included in advertising expense.

LINE 17: PENSION, PROFIT-SHARING, ETC., PLANS Entries on this line denote the existence of a corporate retirement plan. The amount shown represents payments made on behalf of both the officer/shareholder and other employees. Determination of the value of the marital portion of the officer/shareholder's interest in retirement plans is essential for property division purposes.

Qualified plans (those that meet IRS standards for deductibility) require the annual filing of IRS Forms in the 5500 series. These tax returns generally reveal substantial probative information of trust value. Participant statements for the officer/shareholder may usually be obtained from the retirement plan administrators.

The funding of nonqualified plans (nondeductible because they allow discrimination, i.e., non-inclusion of employees other than the business owner) will not be reported on the corporation income tax return. The existence of such a plan may be disclosed in the reconciliation of tax and book income shown on Schedule M-1 on Page 5 of the S Corporation tax return. If business records are properly maintained, the nonqualified plan balances should appear on the business balance sheet as an asset.

The amount contributed to the retirement plan on behalf of the officer/shareholder may be added back to arrive at income available for support if the contribution is discretionary and/or controllable by the spouse. Frequently, in the case of temporary support orders, the shareholder spouse does not have the discretion and control to avoid making the contribution. Under these circumstances, the retirement plan contribution on the spouse's behalf should not be added back arrive at income available for support. In all other circumstances, contributions to retirement plans represent nontaxable compensation that may be considered perquisites.

Line 18: Employee Benefit Programs Employee benefit programs are in addition to any retirement contributions reported on Line 24. Employee benefits may include life and health insurance, dental insurance, and dependent care assistance programs. If employee benefits are claimed, a careful investigation should be made to determine whether the officer/shareholder is benefiting from these payments or if non-employee friends or relatives are in collusion to divert funds. In other words, this category of expense provides an opportunity to disguise personal expenditures as a business expense.

Line 19: Other Deductions The total of all other deductible expenses for which no room has been allocated on Page 1 of Form 1120S is entered on this line. The expense categories that may be included here are numerous and vary with the corporation's business activity. "Other Deductions" may contain perquisites. Examples of "Other Deductions" that frequently contain perquisites are presented below. Each of the hypothetical returns contains supporting detail summaries of these deductions.

Analysis of corporation general ledgers and journals may be very useful in spotting "perks" (perquisites or personal expense items). Some general ledgers contain complete details of all payees receiving corporation checks. Most, businesses computerize their accounting. Computerization facilitates the inspection of account detail in a general ledger. If the payees listed in an account do not appear proper, investigation of underlying supporting documentation, such as canceled checks and vendor's invoices, merits consideration.

Line 20: Total Deductions The sum total of all of the deductions listed above it is entered here.

Line 21: Ordinary Income (Loss) Income or loss shown on this line is the starting point for the analysis of profitability. Reference should also be made to Page 3 (Schedule K) when assessing income because that page generally contains additional income or expense items that do not appear on Page 1 because tax law requires special treatment for those items, many of which are items that flow through to and must be reported on the shareholder's individual income tax returns.

Correct adjustments to income for perquisites and other items needed to restate income on a representative basis will result in "true profitability" produced by the trade or business activity of the corporation. "True profitability" is the profit concept used for valuation and income available for support analyses. Historical analysis of true profitability is mandatory for valuation purposes under IRS Revenue Ruling 59-60. Revenue Ruling 59-60 contains a thorough explanation of all factors and considerations necessary and appropriate for valuation of closely held businesses. Familiarity with the contents of this Revenue Ruling is essential for forensic accountants and other business appraisers.

The issue of whether or not to include the S Corporation's ordinary income in income available for support is often hotly contested when the spouse is a controlling shareholder. Consideration should be given to the availability of cash generated by earnings that have not been distributed to shareholders. The amount of discretion and control over income generated by operations may be construed differently based on whether the issue is permanent or temporary alimony and/or child support. In temporary support situations, the undistributed earnings should not be considered if the corporation's ability to make additional distributions is impaired by legitimate business cash flow requirements. A recent California appellate case held that legitimate reinvestment of current year's profit into the corporation was a reasonable basis for excluding such profit from income availability for support. As a general rule in all other cases, the undistributed income should be attributable to the officer/shareholder as cash flow available for alimony and child support.

Note the $73,075 of ordinary income shown on the tax return of Straight Edge, Inc. and the $50,000 of compensation of officers. The salary paid to the officer/shareholder and the ordinary income represents primary components of Matthew Collins's cash flow. Depreciation and perquisites may be additional components of income in this case. The $100,000 distributed to Mr. Collins during the year, as shown on Page 3, Line 16d, was probably partially used to pay quarterly estimated personal income taxes on 2022 S Corporation ordinary income that flows through to the shareholder. As such, it is not necessarily an additional component of income irrespective of the fact that a cash distribution was made. The amount of available cash at year-end and the working capital needs of the business usually determine whether a forensic accountant will rely on corporate income or distributions in forming an opinion of income available for support.

Distributions made to shareholders at or around April 15 is a common occurrence in S Corporations (often referred to as "tax distributions"). Because shareholders are taxed personally on their share of S Corporation income, whether or not distributed, corporate funds are often required to be distributed to shareholders at this time of year to pay personal income taxes.

Line 22 to 27: Corporate Level Tax Cases in which S Corporations have a tax liability are not very common because, as previously mentioned, the S Corporation is a flow through entity. Exceptions to the general rule exist primarily with respect to corporations that have changed from C to S status. Built in gain taxes are triggered when assets with built in gains as of the date of conversion from a C to an S Corporation are sold. If the S Corporation does pay a corporate level tax, the amount should be analyzed to determine the propriety of reducing cash flow. Facts and circumstances will dictate whether this expense is recurring or not.

FORM 1125-A: COST OF GOODS SOLD

Line 1: Inventory at Beginning of Year This is the starting point for analyzing the cost of goods sold. The amount should match the ending inventory reported in the prior year's tax return. If it does not, the matter requires investigation.

Reporting a higher than actual opening inventory will understate profit. As a result, analysis of last year's return and accompanying supporting documentation to verify the reliability of the opening inventory is recommended.

Line 2: Purchases The cost of inventory items purchased for sale by retailers and wholesalers appears on this line. If a corporation manufactures goods, the amount shown will represent raw material purchases.

Timing of expense is an important element in determining the reliability of the amount shown. Typically, businesses with inventories report on the accrual basis; accordingly, the date of purchase or delivery of the goods, not the date of payment for the goods, is the point at which the expense is recorded. Criteria for determining the date of purchase follow legal guidelines reflected in the Uniform Commercial Code. The contractual time at which goods change hands determines when goods are considered purchased under the accrual basis of accounting.

Consistency in reporting transactional activity with regular vendors is indicative of reliability in the timing of the expense. Inconsistency merits further analysis.

Accountants preparing audited or reviewed financial statements will test year-end transactions to determine appropriate reporting of purchases at the cut-off date, December 31 for all calendar year corporations. This accounting technique provides enhanced reliability of the amount reported.

The corporation's "Accounts Payable" is a balance sheet item that is closely associated with the recordation of purchases. In many businesses an accounts payable or purchases journal is maintained. Monthly summations of additions to accounts payable for purchases of goods or raw materials constitute the "Purchases" account reflected on the general ledger, and, ultimately, the tax return.

Inspection of the purchases journal and the cash disbursement journal is recommended when suspicion exists that personal items have been paid for by the business. Examples of corporations that warrant analysis for inventory used personally are restaurants, electronics retailers, computer stores, and clothing outlets.

Line 3: Cost of Labor Generally, this line is used by businesses that manufacture goods. Only direct labor costs of manufacturing are included.

Administrative salaries should not be included in this area of the return. As pointed out in the discussion of Line 8 of Page 1, "Salaries and wages," obtaining the names of all employees is advisable to ascertain whether friends and relatives who do not actually perform real services for compensation received are on payroll. Inspection of payroll tax returns and, where available, payroll journals will identify those persons on payroll. To the extent that there is an overstatement of "Wages," conclusions as to the value of the enterprise and income available for support are understated.

Line 4: Additional Section 263a Costs Corporations that manufacture or resell a product are subject to "Uniform Capitalization Rules." Resellers with gross receipts of less than $27 million on average in the last three years are exempt from this rule. Under the IRS regulations, indirect costs attributable to the cost of inventory are added to inventory. This type of cost is rarely an issue in marital dissolution matters because it generally does not arise in those corporations where manipulation of income is an issue.

Line 5: Other Costs Generally, "Other Costs" refers to overhead, also known as indirect costs of manufacturing. An entire branch of accounting, known as "Cost Accounting," is devoted to the study of allocating overhead expenses not directly related to the manufacture of the product. Portions of the rent, utilities, administrative labor, and property taxes are examples of types of indirect manufacturing expenses that are allocated to the cost of manufactured goods.

Line 7: Inventory at End of Year A thorough discussion of this expense item is presented in the discussion of the C Corporation. Please refer to that section as it applies equally to S Corporations.

Line 8: Cost of Goods Sold Cost of goods is carried forward to Page 1, Line 2.

Line 9a to f: Methods Used to Value Closing Inventory The method by which inventory is valued may significantly affect the corporation valuation. Inventories are frequently undervalued in order to report lower taxable profit. Greater motivation to manipulate inventory exists in divorce cases because lower profitability from lower inventory benefits the officer/shareholder spouse via a lower business valuation and less cash flow available for support.

Inventory valuation methods are important factors in determining the appropriate amount of inventory. The method must conform to the best accounting practice in the particular trade or business. "Cost" means that the inventory is valued at the price paid. "Lower of cost or market" means that the cost of inventory, on an item by item basis, is compared to respective market value. The lower of the two values is then applied.

LIFO (last-in, first-out) and FIFO (first-in, first-out) are terms often used in connection with inventory valuation. If a LIFO method of costing inventory is used in an inflationary period, book value will tend to be understated. The FIFO method of costing inventory provides a more accurate representation of actual market value of the inventory because ending inventory is "costed" by reference to the most recent purchases.

Any changes in inventory accounting between prior years and the year of separation and the subsequent period should be carefully investigated. Unusually large negative adjustments to inventory also warrant research.

Page 2: Schedule B: Other Information

Line 1: Method of Accounting The two most common accounting methods are the "cash basis" and "accrual basis." When a corporation is on a cash basis, revenue is reported in the year in which it is actually or constructively received in the form of cash. Deductions are taken only for expenses actually paid during the year. In contrast, accrual basis corporations report revenue when it is earned (when the right to receive it is created). Thus, if a customer was billed for an item received on December 31, 2022 but the customer did not pay for until February 1, 2023, the business reporting on an accrual basis would still record the income in 2022 even though the merchandise was paid for in the subsequent year. On the accrual basis, expenses may be deducted when incurred, whether paid or not in the tax year.

If the accounting method changes from cash to accrual or vice versa between two tax years, adjustments to taxable income resulting from the change should have no effect on income. The accounting transition is merely a change in form that does not change the underlying economic reality.

Corporations whose business activity includes the sale of inventory must use the accrual basis of accounting unless their average annual gross receipts do not exceed $27 million or more during the three preceding years. Service corporations, such as professional practices, generally are on a cash basis. A cash basis corporation does not report accounts receivables on its Schedule L (Page 4). As a result, for purposes of valuation, forensic accountants must obtain this information from the corporation's non-tax accounting records. Discovery of the net realizable value of accounts receivable is important for valuation purposes as it is often one of the largest assets of a business or practice.

Receivables present an interesting problem when cash basis corporations are valued in family law matters if the spouse charged with the accounts receivables will also be required to pay support from the collection of the same receivables. The perceived "double-dip" may appear particularly inequitable in property divisions where one party is awarded the corporation and is paying support while assets of equal stated value are awarded to the other spouse.

The "double-dip" effect, while appearing inequitable, can be better understood in terms of accrual basis accounting. On an accrual basis, the paying spouse is actually providing support from current accrual basis earnings. This can be illustrated by a hypothetical in which it is assumed that the business or practice is terminated at date of separation and the shareholder/spouse finds a job as an employee. In this situation, no apparent inequity exists if the spousal support is based on wages that are received currently because the corporate accounts receivable in this situation would be allocated to both parties based on their equal ownership interest in the corporation.

In cases where the corporation will be valued at date of separation, the "double-dip" effect may be eliminated through a segregation of collections of pre- and post-separation accounts receivable. The payer spouse may accomplish this result by creating a new corporation for all post-separation activity. As a result, both parties will report their share of income emanating from pre-separation activity. The tax advantages and disadvantages of this procedure must be evaluated on a case by case basis. If economically feasible, the segregation facilitates the presentation of "true" income from current operations because collection of prior period receivables will not affect cash basis income. Despite the frequency of the "double-dip" scenario, such segregation of accounts receivable is rare.

Another manner of reporting revenue and expense is known as "Percentage of Completion." Used primarily in the construction industries, the percentage of completion method dictates that revenue and expenses be recognized in conjunction with the progress of the construction project(s). Under this method, advance payments in anticipation of completion of certain percentages of a project are recorded as liabilities rather than as revenue until the completion of the construction phase. When the construction phase is completed, the liability is extinguished and the revenue earned in connection with the phase is recognized.

The completed contract method is another accounting method for reporting income and expenses in the construction industry. Under this method, income and expenses of a project are reported in the year that a contract is completed.

Line 2A and B: The box provided for "Business Activity" and the other box for "Product or Service" are self-explanatory. The hypothetical S Corporation tax return shown at the end of the narrative contains an example of how the questions are answered.

Lines 4: Subsidiaries and Affiliates If a corporation owned more than a 50% interest in another corporation, information concerning the other corporation must be provided to the IRS. An S corporation may own other S corporations and combine their income in a single S corporation tax return.

An S Corporation may also own more than 80% of the stock of a C corporation. But the C Corporation must file a separate tax return. An understanding of relationships between affiliated corporations is important for the preparation of appraisal reports and cash flow analysis in family law matters. A separate appraisal of the subsidiary is usually required under these circumstances. The appraised value of the subsidiary may then be included as an asset of a parent corporation.

Evaluation of cash flow for shareholders of corporations with subsidiaries and /or affiliates also poses a challenging task for forensic accountants. The degree of control a parent corporation exercises over the subsidiary may ultimately dictate how the subsidiary's earnings will be construed for cash flow purposes. Even if the subsidiary has never paid dividends, cash flow to the parent may be imputed if it is anticipated that such earnings will be distributed during the alimony and/or child support period.

Line 5: Affirmative responses to questions regarding restricted stock, sometimes referred to as RSUs, and stock options should prompt additional investigation of assets with the potential of future income. Future gains from the exercise of RSUs and options may be relevant in determining child and spousal support in future years.

Line 6: Reportable Transaction The inquiries in this section alert the IRS to transactions that might have the potential for tax avoidance or evasion.

Line 7: Offering Original Issue Discount Debt Instruments Generally, an original issue discount is the difference between the issue price of a bond and its redemption price. The discount is amortized as interest income to the purchaser (interest expense to the issuer) over the life of the bond. Original issue discounts may also be used in other situations where the stated interest rate is below market. It may be described as imputed interest income or expense, depending on which side of the transaction the corporation is on.

Line 8: Net Unrealized Built-In Gains C Corporations that elected to become S Corporations may have owned appreciated property at the time of the election. The appreciation is called a built-in gain and is subject to special tax recognition rules. The appearance of an entry here may denote that historical book value is not indicative of the fair market value of certain of the corporate fixed assets.

Line 11: Exception to Schedules L and M-1 If the corporation can answer these questions affirmatively it is not required to complete schedules L and M-1, which leaves out a lot of valuable information for your review.

Line 12: An affirmative response regarding cancellation or forgiveness of non-shareholder debt should prompt investigation. Diversion of funds to relatives and friends through loans that may never be repaid may be a way of siphoning funds out of the corporation and thereby reducing its value and reducing its ability to make distribution or pay officer salaries.

Lines 13 to 14: The lines are self-explanatory.

Schedule K: Shareholders' Pro Rata Share Items

The primary purpose of this page is to disclose certain income and expense items that require special tax treatment by shareholders. Most of the line items on this page exactly match the total shown for those items on each of the shareholders' individual K-1s. Straight Edge, Inc. only has one shareholder. Accordingly, the same amounts for the entries on Schedule K appear on Matthew T. Collins's K-1.

A complete explanation for each of the entries on this page is included in the portion of the text dealing with the Schedule K-1 discussed later in this section.

Page 4: Schedule L: Balance Sheets Per Books

The opening and closing assets and liabilities of the corporation, and the related supporting schedules, are reflected in this section of the S Corporate tax return. The balance sheet is frequently the starting point for appraising a corporate interest. The value of the shareholder/spouse's interest is generally a function of the fair market value of assets and the stated amount of the liabilities shown on the balance sheet.

Because assets are stated at historical cost, which is frequently not the same as fair market value, forensic accountant and other business appraisers must adjust assets using marketplace factors. Unrealized appreciation in the value of assets is not recognized on the corporate return except when an asset is sold. At that point, the appreciation is transformed into recognizable gain. Such gains, whether capital or not, are recognized as taxable events by the S Corporation.

ASSETS

Line 1: Cash Very little adjustment is generally required for this asset. Bank reconciliation worksheets are standard supporting documentation. The financial statements of the corporation, if available, may provide additional details concerning the location of the institutions at which funds are maintained.

Unusually high accumulations of cash may impact both cash flow and valuation. From a cash flow perspective, the accumulation may deprive the spouse of current disposable cash flow from which to pay support. Whether or not the accumulation is a willful attempt to keep cash flow at a minimum may be at issue.

When an unnecessarily high amount of cash is on hand, the appraiser must take this fact into consideration when preparing the business valuation. Under certain appraisal techniques, such as the "Excess Earnings Method," a return on the use of the net assets of the corporation is deducted from average earnings to arrive at the capitalizable excess earnings used to compute goodwill. Failure to adjust for excess cash not required for business operations will have the effect of reducing the intangible value (goodwill) of the corporation computed under the excess earnings method.

Lines 2a and b: Accounts Receivable Less Allowance for Bad Debts Accounts receivable is a material asset of many corporations. If the corporation reports on an accrual basis, an entry will be found on these lines. The allowance for bad debt is deducted from the receivables. The fair market value of the accounts receivable is known as its "net realizable value." Analysis of the underlying accounts is essential for this determination. The net accounts receivable shown on corporate tax returns often do not represent net realizable value because of limitations imposed by tax law.

Cash basis corporations may also have accounts receivable, even though no reference is made to them on the corporate return. Personal service corporations are the most common examples of cash basis corporations with accounts receivable.

Determination of fair market value of accounts receivable requires a reasonable estimate of collectability. An estimate may be obtained by testing subsequent cash receipts in order to ascertain how much of the receivables were actually collected over time. In cases where insufficient time has elapsed to perform such testing, estimates based on past experience must be used. An "aging" of the receivables into 30-, 60-, 90-, 120-, and over 120-day groups provide guidance in repairing such estimates. Most businesses maintain aging analyses on a monthly basis.

Sometimes the accounts receivable valuation is not easily accomplished because of the unique nature of the underlying business. Examples include personal injury lawyers representing plaintiffs, criminal defense lawyers, and orthodontists.

An incorporated personal injury lawyer typically has no accounts receivable; however, a similar asset known as work in progress (also known as work in process) amounts to somewhat the same thing from a marital dissolution perspective. A detailed analysis of the disposition of cases begun during marriage must be undertaken to compute the marital interest in the funds received from those cases that result in the collection of contingent fees. The methods used to arrive at value are beyond the scope of this text but, needless to say, much creativity is required to make such an analysis persuasive.

The incorporated law firm that specializes in criminal defense is an example of a practice that will typically contain accounts receivable at a negative value. The negative accounts receivable are liabilities that accountants refer to as "Unearned Revenue." Criminal defense practitioners generally require the fee for their services to be paid either wholly or partially in advance. The fee is then earned with future services. As in the case of work in progress of personal injury attorneys, calculation of unearned revenue requires creativity and a thorough understand of the underlying business activity.

Appraisals of cash basis corporations with accounts receivable usually include a calculation of a "Deferred Income Tax Liability." The liability for taxes on the collection of accounts receivable is equitable because the shareholder will eventually pay tax on these receivables either on the corporate or personal level. In corporations where profits are traditionally transformed into officer's salary, the tax on the accounts receivables will end up being paid on the individual level.

Line 3: Inventories Because the year-end for which ending inventory is determined is often close to the time at which the appraisal is performed, the relevant documentation for intensive research and analysis of this account is usually readily available. If an actual inventory count is taken, copies of the supporting detail should be obtained and reviewed. The procedures employed to make the count should be analyzed. Less analysis of procedures and valuation methodology is required if the taking of the inventory was observed by certified public accountants in conjunction with a certified audit.

Unreported sale of inventory ("inventory going out the back door") during the post-separation period is a frequent allegation made by non-shareholder spouses. Testing of gross profit ratios with industry percentages and against prior years' percentages for the corporation may support such allegations. Testing mark-up percentages against gross profit is another tool available in some cases to spot irregularities in inventory value.

The method by which inventory is valued may significantly affect the marital value of the corporate interest. Inventories are frequently undervalued in order to report lower taxable profit. Greater motivation to manipulate inventory exists in divorce cases because lower profitability from lower inventory benefits the shareholder/spouse via a lower business valuation and less income available for support.

Inventory valuation methods are important factors in determining the appropriate amount of inventory. The method used must conform to the best accounting practice in the particular trade or business. "Cost" means that the inventory is valued at the price paid. "Lower of cost or market" means that the cost of inventory, on an item by item basis, is compared to respective market value. The lower of the two values is used.

LIFO (last-in, first-out) and FIFO (first-in, first-out) are terms often used in connection with inventory valuation. If a LIFO method of costing inventory is used in an inflationary period, book value will tend to be understated. The FIFO method of costing inventory provides a more accurate representation of actual market value of the inventory because ending inventory is "costed" by reference to the most recent purchases of inventory.

Any changes in inventory accounting between prior years and the year of separation and subsequent period should be carefully investigated. Unusually large negative adjustments to inventory also warrant investigation.

Line 4: U.S. Government Obligations The IRS requires identification of assets held in this form. This kind of asset is known as a "Cash Equivalent." Investment interest income on U.S. government obligations should be accrued at the valuation date to insure that the full value of the corporation's interest is calculated.

Line 5: Tax-Exempt Securities As in the case of U.S. government obligations, the IRS requires identification of assets held in this form. This asset is also a "Cash Equivalent." Interest from tax-exempt securities is reported on Line 17 of the Schedule K on Page 3 of the return and the individual shareholder K-1s. While not subject to federal income tax, the amount may represent additional cash flow available to the corporation.

Additional asset value may be uncovered through a calculation of interest and/or dividend income receivable for earnings that should have been accrued on these investments.

Line 6: Other Current Assets Other current assets are usually listed by type and amount on supporting schedules attached to the return. Typical examples of other current assets are loans to employees, prepaid expenses, and marketable securities.

Analysis of these assets may disclose that they are undervalued. Marketable securities that have appreciated will require an upward adjustment from historical to fair market value. The brokerage statement(s) at year-end should contain the appropriate fair market value information.

A review of the rent, taxes and insurance accounts in the general ledger may reveal that certain expenses have been paid for in advance. January rent for the following year paid in December of the current year is an example of an expense that causes an understatement of annual income and cash flow.

Line 7: Loans to Stockholders It is common to find stockholders of closely held S Corporations borrowing money from the corporation during a fiscal year. Often, loans to the stockholder represent distributions in lieu of salary if the stockholder is also an employee of the corporation. Since payroll taxes must be paid if salary is distributed, officer/shareholders of closely held corporations find this form of distribution in midyear convenient.

When an interest in a corporation is valued as of the date of separation, the amount of the stockholder loan is offset by a marital liability of equal value. Under these circumstances, the appraisal of the corporate interest may be reduced by the amount of the loan. If this is done, no recognition of a liability to the corporation by the marital estate is required. Alternatively, if the asset is counted in arriving at the marital corporate interest, the marital liability to the corporation should not be overlooked.

Greater complexity arises when corporate interests are valued close to the time of trial. Under these circumstances, it is prudent to account for the loan as an asset of the corporation and recognize any loans payable to the corporation at the date of separation as a marital liability.

LINE 8: MORTGAGE AND REAL ESTATE LOANS Secured loans frequently result from the sale of corporate real estate. Research concerning the origin of the loan may lead to useful discovery. It may be important for the forensic accountant to investigate the propriety of the disposition of prior assets owned by the corporation.

Interest income reported on Line 4a of Schedule K on Page 3 should be compared with the outstanding loan balance(s) to ascertain that all income has been reported and collections have been properly deposited to the corporation.

The collectability of the loans needs to be ascertained for valuation purposes. For example, a potential bad debt, not recognized for tax purposes until the asset is deemed completely worthless, will nevertheless reduce the fair market value of the loan.

Another valuation adjustment is appropriate if the loan interest rate is either well below or above current market. Just as in the case of corporate bonds, the value of the secured loans will be a function of how the stated interest compares to market interest.

LINE 9: OTHER INVESTMENTS Investments in other corporations or partnerships are the most common types of assets in this category. The values indicated on the corporation balance sheet often do not reflect fair market value for these investments.

Where an investment in another enterprise is a significant corporate asset, a separate appraisal of the other entity may be required in order to arrive at fair market value of the corporation interest therein.

LINE 10A AND B: BUILDING AND OTHER DEPRECIABLE ASSETS LESS ACCUMULATED DEPRECIATION As stated previously, historical cost is the basis for the amounts shown for assets. Consequently, capitalized real and personal property is presented at original cost. Annual depreciation expense taken is deducted from the cost to arrive at the "Book Value" of the fixed asset. Because depreciation expense is governed by tax guidelines, not actual asset deterioration and obsolescence, book value of fixed assets is usually not equal to fair market value.

Adjustment of fixed assets to fair market value is one of the most common appraisal procedures. Real estate is often restated to market based on an appraisal of the property performed by a real property expert. Automobiles are restated pursuant to "Blue Book" values. The value of other assets (equipment, machinery, furniture, and furnishings) may also be restated pursuant to appraisals prepared by experts.

The amount of cost and effort put into the restating of capital assets is a subjective determination depending on facts and circumstances. The materiality of the restatement involved is the primary factor to consider. Like many other decisions made in marital dissolution proceedings, the cost and benefit of the additional appraisals need to be assessed by the lawyer, the client and forensic accountant.

General ledger expense accounts, such as "Repairs and Maintenance," "Computer Expense," and "Office Expense" may contain payments for assets that should have been capitalized. Failure to restate these items as capital expenditures will understate assets. Income will also be understated when capital expenditures are charged to expense.

LINE 11A AND B: DEPLETABLE ASSETS LESS ACCUMULATED DEPLETION Like depreciation, depletion deductions for natural resources are often not representative of the actual exhaustion of the resource.

The fair market value of the remaining reserves should be determined where practical and meaningful to the spouses involved in the divorce. Thus, if the interest of the marital estate is relatively small, and the cost of determining value of the resource substantial, book value may be the most practical value to use. If the interest is material, an expert may be hired to provide an opinion of value.

Line 12: Land Land is not a depreciable asset; however, costs incurred to acquire land, such as prepaid interest ("Points"), may be amortized (deducted over time) rather than entirely expensed in the year paid even if the corporation is on a cash basis.

Like other fixed assets, land is recorded at historical cost. Restating land to fair market value is a common appraisal adjustment affecting valuation of the corporation interest. Adjustments to land value will not change income unless an installment sale of the land is imminent. Annual installment payments would ordinarily be treated as a continuing source of cash to the corporation.

Line 13a and b: Intangibles Assets Less Accumulated Amortization Amortization, like depreciation, refers to the deductibility of certain capital expenditures or organization costs ratably over time. The primary difference between amortization and depreciation is the nature of the capital expenditures to which amortization applies. Examples of amortization have already been mentioned, i.e., depletion and capitalized interest. Other kinds of capital expenditures subject to amortization include "Leasehold Improvements," "Research & Development Costs," "Pollution Control Facilities," and intangible assets.

The most well-known intangible asset in family law is "Goodwill." The calculation of goodwill in connection with the preparation of a business appraisal is common practice. For tax purposes and under generally accepted accounting principles, "Goodwill" only appears on the balance sheet when it is purchased. The difference between the price paid for a business and the fair market value of the tangible assets and other intangibles purchased is goodwill. Acquired goodwill may be amortized over a 15-year period under IRS Code Section 197.

If amortization of intangibles appears on the corporation balance sheet, the origin of the asset should be investigated. Understanding the nature and cost of the asset will determine how it should be handled in a marital dissolution appraisal. The purchase price paid for goodwill may also represent a comparable sale that may be relevant evidence of value of certain or all assets of the corporation.

Certain intangibles have no independent market value and are generally embodied in the calculation of goodwill. Examples included covenants not to compete, patents, copyrights, and licenses. Rights such as these are generally incorporated into the concept of appraised goodwill. Rarely will independent calculation of the value of intangibles other than goodwill appear in a business appraisal prepared for marital dissolution purposes.

Line 14: Other Assets Non-current assets for which no line item has been provided on the balance sheet are generally listed on supporting schedules whose total is carried to this line. Examples of other assets include "Deposits," and "Notes Receivable."

Although improper for tax reporting, it is common practice for cash basis corporations to deduct lease and utility deposits. The value of a corporation will be understated unless these costs are listed as assets. Examination of relevant underlying documentation, such as facilities leases, will usually disclose the amount of the deposits.

Another asset often found listed in this section is secured and unsecured notes receivable. Secured and unsecured promissory notes are stated at historical cost for tax purposes. No reduction in value is permitted under tax law unless the note becomes worthless. These instruments need to be restated to fair market value for appraisal purposes. The most common factors evaluated by experts when determining fair market value of notes receivable are the implicit interest rates in comparison to market rates, the creditworthiness of the borrower, and the underlying collateral. Use of the above factors as a basis for comparison with notes traded in the marketplace may allow forensic accountants to estimate appraisal values.

Line 15: Total Assets Summation of all of the assets appears here for both the current and prior year-ends. This amount is also shown on Page 1, Box D. Total assets should equal total liabilities and stockholders' equity.

LIABILITIES AND CAPITAL

Line 16: Accounts Payable Accrual basis corporations enter the amounts due vendors at fiscal year-end here. No entry will appear on this line for cash basis corporations.

Accounts payable for cash basis corporations should be determined for business appraisal purposes. Forensic CPAs determine accounts payable for cash basis corporations by reviewing payments to vendors made after year-end. All payments for goods and services purchased during the tax year but not yet paid for represent the accounts payable of the corporation.

Failure to compute the accounts payable results in an overstatement of the value of the corporate interest. Conversely, overstated accounts payable will understate the value of the corporation.

Line 17: Mortgages, Notes, Bonds Payable in Less than One Year The short-term portion of these liabilities is presented here. Further investigation of the books and records of the corporation is usually required in order to ascertain the nature and scope of these liabilities.

Please refer to the discussion of Line 20 for additional information about analyzing this liability.

Line 18: Other Current Liabilities Accrued expenses, payroll taxes payable, and unpaid retirement plan contributions are examples of other current liabilities. Cash basis corporations may deduct current year payroll taxes and retirement plan contributions even if unpaid at year-end. Consequently, such other current liabilities may appear on a cash basis corporation's balance sheet. Accuracy of the accruals may be ascertained by examination of the pension plan contribution calculations and payroll tax returns.

Accrued expenses reflect the amount of overhead that has been incurred but is unpaid at year-end. Unpaid telephone and utility bills are common examples of expenses that may be accrued. Proper valuation procedures require inclusion of such liabilities. Income available for support is generally unaffected by these expenses because the actual outflow of cash will occur in a future period.

Unearned income and deferred income taxes are current liabilities that do not appear on cash basis balance sheets but need to be considered in many business appraisals. Unearned income results from advances (e.g., retainers for lawyers) from clients or customers for work that has not yet been earned.

Deferred income taxes exist when a tax is created in the current period that will have to be paid in later years. In divorce cases, the most common type of deferred income tax is associated with the inclusion of accounts receivable on the balance sheet of cash basis corporations. Calculation of the amount of the deferred income tax is often at issue. To be persuasive, forensic accountants need to have reasonable support for the tax rates employed in their deferred income tax calculations.

Line 19: Loans from Stockholders It is common to find stockholders of closely held corporations loaning money to their corporation. Often, loans from the stockholder occur when corporations require an infusion of capital but do not wish to borrow from conventional lenders.

Stockholder loans to the corporation should be eliminated from the corporate balance sheet if the corporate interest is valued as of the date of separation. Under these circumstances, the appraised value of the corporation may be increased by the elimination of the liability to the stockholder. If this is done, no recognition of a receivable from the corporation by the marital estate is required.

Alternatively, if the liability is recognized in arriving at the corporate value, the marital receivable from the corporation should not be overlooked.

Greater complexity arises when corporate interests are valued close to the time of trial. Under these circumstances, it is prudent to account for the loan as a liability of the corporation and recognize any loans receivable from the corporation at the date of separation as a marital asset.

Line 20: Mortgages, Notes, Bonds Payable in More than One Year The long-term portion of such liabilities is presented here. Further investigation of the books and records of the corporation is usually required in order to ascertain the nature and scope of these liabilities.

The accuracy and authenticity of long-term liabilities need to be analyzed in the appraisal process. Liabilities may be inaccurate if the interest and principal on loan payments have not been allocated properly. The authenticity of liabilities may be suspect in some instances, e.g., liabilities to relatives who do not demand payment and have never received payment.

Certain liabilities may not be included on corporation balance sheets for tax purposes. Examples include liabilities under lease obligations and legal liability that has not been adjudicated. Such liabilities may reduce the value of the corporate interest even if the amount of the ultimate liability cannot be ascertained.

If a corporation is liable on a lease even though it has moved out of a facility or no longer uses the original leased asset, the liability under the lease should be computed at present value for appraisal purposes. Failure to reduce value for such liability overstates the value of the corporate interest.

Line 21: Other Liabilities Other long-term liabilities are presented in supporting schedules with a total shown on this line. The amount presented reflects unsecured liabilities that may not have to be paid in the next fiscal year. Examples of other liabilities are the obligation to pay for goods or services under long-term contracts, and warranty liability for corporations engaged in manufacturing.

Understanding the nature of the enterprise is essential to locating all possible liabilities. Exploration of this area with corporate management through interview or deposition is advisable.

Line 22 and 23: Capital Stock and Paid-In Capital Amounts originally used to capitalize the corporation and additional amounts of capital contributed from time to time will be reflected in this section.

Line 24: Retained Earnings Retained earnings represent the accumulated undistributed profits of the corporation since inception and by itself is not a significant element of corporate appraisal or cash flow. It merely represents corporate assets minus liabilities and minus capital and paid-in capital.

Line 25: Adjustments to Shareholders' Equity Any adjustments on Line 25 should be thoroughly investigated to determine whether such items are relevant to the issues of appraisal or income available for support.

Line 26: Treasury Stock If an entry appears here, investigation is warranted. Treasury stock represents stock purchased by the corporation from stockholders. The reason for the purchase may be relevant to the appraisal of the corporate interest. For example, evidence of the market value of the corporation may be obtained if the stock purchase resulted from a stock redemption relating to the sale of a stockholder's interest in the corporation.

Line 27: Total Liabilities and Shareholders' Equity The amount shown here is merely a total of all of the liability and stockholder equity accounts and should be equal to the total assets of the corporation.

Page 5
Schedule M-1: Reconciliation of Income (Loss) Per Books With Income (Loss) Per Return

Line 1: Net Income (Loss) Per Books The profit or loss shown on a corporation's financial statements is entered on this line. Financial statements of the corporation will usually show a different profit or loss than the tax return because certain revenue and expense items are not recognized in arriving at corporate taxable income. Likewise, certain revenue and expense items not recognized in arriving at financial statement profit are included in arriving at taxable income.

Line 2: Income Included on Schedule K, Lines 1 through 10, not Recorded on Books this Year Entries in this category should be investigated to determine which presentation is more appropriate for valuation and income available for support purposes. An example of an item that would appear here is the amount of advance payments received from customers for goods and services.

Line 3: Expenses Recorded on Books this Year not Included on Schedule K, Lines 1 Through 12 and 14l The two most common types of expenses of this kind are "Depreciation," and "Meals and Entertainment."

Accelerated depreciation taken in prior years' tax returns may result in more depreciation per books than for tax in the current year because assets may have been entirely depreciated for tax purposes and not fully depreciated for financial statement purposes. Amounts shown here may indicate that depreciation expense should be added back to income to arrive at true cash flow for the corporation.

Under current tax rules, only 50% of business-related entertainment expenses are deductible for tax purposes (note that with the passage of the Tax Cut and Jobs Act in 2017 business entertainment is no longer deductible). Also note that for tax years 2021 and 2022, a special COVID provision allows a 100% deduction for meals purchased from a restaurant. However, 100% of these expenses are deducted for financial statement profit; accordingly, a reconciliation of this expense is always necessary when it exists. Travel expenses may also differ on financial statements because of a variety of statutory tax limitations. The type of limitation will depend on the nature of the expense. Generally, reasonable and necessary business-related travel expenses are deductible. Amounts shown here suggest the possibility of perquisites. Personal travel deducted by a corporation is common.

Another common non-deductible expense is officer's life insurance. While not deductible, this expense may be a legitimate reduction of income available for support if a shareholder, other than the shareholder/spouse and unrelated to the shareholder/spouse, or the corporation is the beneficiary.

Line 4: Add Lines 1 through 3 This line item is self-explanatory.

Line 5: Income Recorded on Books this Year not Included on Schedule K, Lines 1 through 10 Tax-exempt interest is the most common example of book income excluded from taxation. However, tax-exempt income should be included in computing representative income available for support. Existence of such income should also alert the reader to tax-exempt investments owned by the corporation.

Line 6: Deductions Included on Schedule K, Lines 1 through 12 and 14l, not Charged Against Book Income this Year Depreciation is the most prominent example of this kind of expense. MACRS and other forms of accelerated depreciation allowed for tax purposes can result in tax depreciation being larger than depreciation on the books.

Depletion is another expense that can be higher for tax than on the financial statements.

Line 7: Add Lines 5 and 6 This line item is self-explanatory.

LINE 8: INCOME (LOSS) (SCHEDULE K, LINE 18) This amount arrived at through the reconciliation should match line 18 of Page 4. This is the total taxable income or loss of the corporation.

Schedule M-2: Analysis of Accumulated Adjustments Account, Other Adjustments Account, and Shareholders' Undistributed Taxable Income Previously Taxed

This section of the S Corporation income tax return tracks undistributed S corporation income.

Because a working knowledge of these rules is generally not significant for family law purposes, a detailed explanation of the tax law in this regard is not presented here. Forensic accountants familiar with S Corporation tax treatment should be consulted if questions arise in this area.

Line 7, distributions other than dividend distributions, is a relevant line item for determining income available for support because the amount of distributions made to the shareholders during the year is presented. Inquiry concerning the facts and circumstances of the distribution should be made. The nature and purpose of the distributions may be relevant to the calculation of income available for support. Where distributions appear more relevant to the issues of child and spousal support, a forensic accountant may use distributions to the shareholder/spouse as a better indicator of income than the reported S corporation income for the period. Whether a forensic accountant determines cash flow available for support based on S Corporation income or, alternatively, on distributions is based on a number of factors. If sufficient cash is on hand at year-end to meet the working capital needs of the corporation, S Corporation income may be more indicative of cash flow than actual distributions. The reason is that the cash was available to make the distribution of reported income but the shareholders exercised their discretion not to do so. This situation illustrates that distributions are discretionary and may be manipulated, especially by a 100% shareholder during a divorce. S corporation income may also be manipulated (by the write-off of personal expenses) but usually not to the same extent as distributions. The forensic accountant considers the interplay of many factors in arriving at a conclusion of income available for support when analyzing S corporation activities.

Schedule K-1: Shareholder's Share of Income, Credits, Deductions, Etc.

As stated previously, the S Corporation usually does not pay income taxes. The tax liability arising from corporate income flows through to the individual shareholders' tax returns. The K-1 is the vehicle through which this flow-through is accomplished.

The K-1 provides abundant information concerning an individual shareholder's interest in the corporation. It is generally the most important basis for computing income available for support from the corporation to the shareholder. The shareholders' K-1s for a few years should be examined to observe changes in percentages of ownership equity.

Each K-1 includes the name and identification number (social security number if the shareholder is an individual) of a shareholder and the corporation. A shareholder's pro rata share of the taxable income or loss generated by the corporation is disclosed on the K-1, Line 1. The K-1 amount is then reported on the shareholder's personal income tax return.

PART I: INFORMATION ABOUT THE CORPORATION

LINES A TO D: The IRS center where the return is filed will vary with the location in which the corporation activity takes place.

PART II: INFORMATION ABOUT THE SHAREHOLDER

LINES E TO I: Stock ownership and shareholder loan information is presented here. Comparison with the prior year is recommended so that any ownership change may be spotted quickly.

Tax shelter issues may be present when evaluating K-1s for prior years. Abuses involving deductibility of certain expenses in past years led to tax reform laws that focused the IRS's attention on S Corporations that come under the definition of tax shelters. Generally, a tax shelter is an investment in which individual shareholders obtain a write-off of their capital investment in a greater than two to one ratio.

PART III: SHAREHOLDER'S SHARE OF CURRENT YEAR INCOME, DEDUCTIONS, CREDITS, AND OTHER ITEMS

This section of the K-1 lists all of the pass-through items of income or loss, deductions, preference items, credits, and other pass-through tax amounts that are required for the preparation of the shareholders' individual tax returns.

1. "ORDINARY BUSINESS INCOME (LOSS)" It is reported on Schedule E of the shareholder's individual tax return. Income from service corporations usually reflects the shareholder's share of the corporation income shown on Page 1 of the return. Multiplying the shareholder's percentage of profit and loss by the corporation profit or loss should result in the same amount as shown on this line.

In those cases in which the corporation represents the spouse's primary work activity, a shareholder's share of income is a significant factor in determining income available for support. The amount reflects the latest historical operating income of the business. Comparison with prior years may be helpful in establishing trends that might influence the court's decision concerning the amount of support.

However, a shareholder's share of S Corporation income is not considered earnings subject to self-employment tax. I.R.C. Section 911(d)(2)(A), which defines earned income, specifically excludes "that part of the compensation derived by the taxpayer for personal services rendered by him to a corporation which represents a distribution of earnings or profits." S corporation income is thus not earned income.

In this respect, partnerships and S corporations differ. All income earned by a general partner is earned income subject to self-employment tax. The Partnership K-1 provides for the reporting of net earnings from self-employment. In contrast, the S corporation K-1 has no such line item. This is indicative of the fact that S corporation income is not subject to self-employment tax because it is not considered earned income.

This distinction may also be important in arguments concerning the character of S corporation distributions from separate property corporations. Since the S corporation income is considered the income of the corporation and not the individual, an argument can be made that such distributions are the separate property of the shareholder/spouse that owns the separate interest in the S corporation (assuming the shareholder/spouse received a reasonable salary).

2. "NET RENTAL REAL ESTATE INCOME OR (LOSS)" If the corporation has income or loss from rental real estate, each shareholder is allocated his or her share. The allocation is required because of limitations on deductibility of rental losses. Shareholders who materially participate in rental activity and report less than $150,000 in adjusted gross income on their personal return may be entitled to deduct up to $25,000 in losses for the year. Otherwise, rental activity is considered to be a passive activity subject to passive loss limitations.

Rental revenue and expenses are listed on supplemental schedules. Typically, income available for support from rental real estate is generally derived by adding depreciation back to rental income or loss and subtracting principal payments on mortgages. Depreciation information is usually provided either on the rental schedule or other supplemental schedules to the return.

3. "OTHER NET INCOME (LOSS)" Losses generated from other than rental activities are passive losses.

4. TO 8. "INTEREST, DIVIDENDS, ROYALTIES, AND CAPITAL GAINS AND LOSSES" is often referred to as "portfolio income" and may not be netted against passive losses but need to be reported on separate

forms of the shareholder's personal income tax return.

Portfolio income is not part of the corporate income shown on Page 1 because it is not generated from the income producing business activities of the corporation. Portfolio income should be matched with the size of investment type assets shown on the balance sheet on Page 4 of the return to see if a correlation exists. If not, examination of mid-year activity through inspection of bank statements, brokerage statements, or the general ledger of the corporation may be advisable.

Ascertaining the nature and purpose of any dispositions of large amounts of liquid assets during the year may uncover diversions of capital made in contemplation of divorce.

Capital gains and losses are identified and explained in supporting schedules attached to the S Corporation return. Capital gain items usually reflect one-time sales of assets and will not represent a source of continuing income; however, certain recurring capital gains, such as those from installment sales, should be included in determining income available for support.

9. "NET SECTION 1231 GAIN (LOSS)" A section 1231 gain or loss results from the sale of business personal or real property. Here again, the K-1 provides for splitting tax items to allow appropriate reporting in the individual returns. Section 1231 gains or losses need to be netted against other section 1231 gains and losses, not necessarily related to the S corporation, on the shareholder's individual return.

10. "OTHER INCOME" "Other income" is a designated area for pass through income not elsewhere described. Examples of income not subject to self-employment tax because the income was not generated from the business activity include insurance recovery, lawsuit settlements, and involuntary conversion proceeds.

11. "SECTION 179 EXPENSE DEDUCTION" It is the election to write-off a maximum of $1,080,000 (increasing to $1,160,000 in subsequent years) of depreciation for certain fixed assets acquired during the year. Each shareholder may only take a pro rata share of the $1,080,000. If a shareholder purchases depreciable property used in other unincorporated businesses or rental activities, no more than $1,080,000 of aggregated Section 179 may be deducted on his or her personal return. A shareholder's pro rata share of Section 179 depreciation is taken as an offset to S corporation income on Schedule E of the individual income tax return.

As noted previously, depreciation must be analyzed with a view to the impact of this expense on income available for support. The Balance Sheet on Page 4 of the S corporation tax return includes a summary of the cost of depreciable property and the accumulated depreciation.

Analysis of depreciation and asset history is provided either wholly or partially on Form 4562 that is required to be included in the return of an S corporation claiming depreciation expense. Probative information concerning the assets of the business, including date of acquisition and original cost, are usually available on this form and supporting detail schedules that may be included in the return. More asset information may be obtained from a corporation's "Depreciation Schedule" or the work papers maintained by its independent certified public accounting firm.

Depreciation schedules aid in identifying assets that have been written off but still have value. In addition to providing relevant data for determining the fair market value of the fixed assets, the depreciation schedule is also useful for evaluating claimed cash flow needs of the business for investment in new equipment.

12. "OTHER DEDUCTIONS" "Other deductions" represent other pass through items that are reported on the tax returns of the individual shareholders. Because of limitations on deductibility, certain expenses are passed through to the individual shareholder's personal tax return via this line item on the K-1.

The instructions for Page 2 of the K-1 may be obtained through an Internet search. The instructions include letter identification codes for various types of deductions that are reported as "Other deduction." For example, in the instructions under "Other deductions" letter **A** through **G** relates to charitable contributions. A shareholder adds these contributions to other contributions made from personal funds and reports the total donations as an itemized deduction on the personal tax return. Sometimes donations, though not deductible against the income of an S corporation, may be considered a reduction in income available for support. This may be the case when the donations are made to organizations many of whose members are clients or customers of the corporation. Arguably, the donation is a form of marketing expense.

Another example of an "Other deduction" is investment interest expense. Investment interest expense is a pass through item that is reported on the tax returns of the individual shareholder. Interest expense deductions for individuals are limited to interest paid on personal residence mortgages and investment interest. Interest expense is deducted as investment interest if related to debts that are allocable to property held for investment. If, for example, the corporation invests in marketable securities on margin, the margin interest expense may be deducted against any passive interest and dividends earned by the corporation.

The existence of this line item indicates that the corporation owns investment property. Examination of other portions of the tax return, particularly the balance sheet on Page 4 and supporting schedules thereto, may reveal some information about the nature of the investments. If not, appropriate discovery should uncover supporting documentation, such as brokerage account statements, which might provide a basis for the determination of the fair market value of the investments.

13. "Credits" This portion of the K-1 is devoted to pass through credits. If credits relating to low income housing and real estate rehabilitation expenditures appear on the K-1, the amount of tax payable by the individual shareholder will be reduced. This factor should be considered in arriving at income available for support. Material credits affecting the calculation of the shareholder's personal income taxes are relevant to the calculation of alimony and child support. The tax effects of credits should be highlighted in declarations or other forms of evidence presented to the court.

14. "Foreign transactions" As of tax year 2022, this section has been replaced with separate Forms K-2 and/or K-3 and this line is used simply to note whether or not Schedule K-3 is included. The IRS provides certain exceptions eliminating the need for the S corporation to prepare and include such forms. Because a working knowledge of these rules is generally not significant for family law purposes, a detailed explanation of the tax law in this regard is not presented here. The forms include foreign income and tax credits and are flow through items reported on the shareholder's individual income tax. An entry here should alert the reader to a possible diversion of funds outside the country.

Business activity abroad provides another possibility for hiding income. The impracticality and cost of performing discovery in a foreign country may require creativity in dealing with such a situation. Foreign forensic accountants may be employed to assist if the amounts are material.

15. "Alternative minimum tax (AMT) items" Code A shown on Page 2 of the K-1 indicates "Post -1986 depreciation adjustment." Major tax legislation was enacted in 1986 that introduced the "Modified Accelerated Cost Recovery System" commonly referred to as MACRS. Differences may exist between shareholders relative to the amount of depreciation to which each shareholder is entitled under MACRS. These differences are noted in this section for tax preference purposes. A tax preference is an addition to alternate minimum taxable income subject to alternative minimum tax on the personal return. The minimum tax is an attempt by the government to insure that liberal

deductions do not completely eliminate a taxpayer's tax liability.

16. "ITEMS AFFECTING SHAREHOLDER BASIS" **"Tax-exempt interest income"** is not taxable for federal income tax but may represent additional income available to the shareholder.

Additional asset value may be uncovered through a calculation of interest and/or dividend income receivable for earnings on these investments not reported on a cash basis.

"Nondeductible expenses." The most common expense in this category is the nondeductible 50% portion of meals and entertainment expense. Though nondeductible, this expense may very well be an important aspect of the business activity of the corporation. Under such circumstances, the nondeductible portion may be considered as a reduction in income if the expense is shown to be business related.

The nature and purpose of any entry here should be examined with regard to the effect on income available for support. It may be an error to assume that because an expense is not deductible, it does not reduce cash flow.

"Property Distributions." Cash or other property distributed to a shareholder is coded with a **D.** The most important aspects of property distributions from a family law perspective include the determination of (1) the fair market value of the property, (2) the reason for the distribution, and (3) the frequency of such distributions. Where the fair market value of the property distributed is greater than the corporate basis, a taxable disposition occurs triggering a gain reportable on Schedule K.

Cash distributions should be analyzed for income available for support purposes on the basis of historical precedent viewed in light of current economic conditions affecting the corporation. No general rule governs the amount of income available for support from S Corporation distributions. Frequently, however, historical cash flow is the most persuasive evidence of representative income.

Whether a forensic accountant determines income available for support based on S Corporation income or, alternatively, on distributions is based on a number of factors. If sufficient cash is on hand at year-end to meet the working capital needs of the corporation, S Corporation income may be more indicative of income available for support than actual distributions. The reason is that the cash was available to make the distribution but the shareholders decided not to do so. This situation illustrates that distributions are discretionary and may be manipulated, especially by a 100% shareholder during a divorce. S corporation income may also be manipulated (by the discretionary write-off of personal expenses) but usually not to the same extent as distributions. Consequently, the forensic accountant must consider many factors in arriving at a conclusion of income available for support when analyzing S corporation activities.

17. "OTHER INFORMATION" An analysis of whether the investment income or expense will be the same from year to year may be relevant to determining income available for support. An examination of the nature of and activity within the underlying portfolio should help in arriving at expected income from this source. Passive portfolios are more predictable than portfolios in which there is frequent trading activity. In most cases, the amount of passive income and related deductions are small enough to warrant assuming the same amount will recur annually; however, if amounts are material, thorough investigation may lead to other conclusions.

12/31/22 **2022 FEDERAL DEPRECIATION SCHEDULE** **PAGE 1**

CLIENT FASHIONA **FASHION APPAREL, INC.** **95-2222222**

1/24/23 08:00AM

NO.	DESCRIPTION	DATE ACQUIRED	DATE SOLD	COST/ BASIS	BUS. PCT.	CUR 179 BONUS	SPECIAL DEPR. ALLOW.	PRIOR 179/ BONUS/ SP. DEPR.	PRIOR DEC. BAL DEPR.	SALVAG /BASIS REDUCT	DEPR. BASIS	PRIOR DEPR.	METHOD	LIFE	RATE	CURRENT DEPR.
FORM 1120																
	FURNITURE AND FIXTURES															
2	OFFICE FURNITURE	1/04/21		3,000							3,000	429	200DB HY	7	.24490	735
4	FURNITURE	6/25/21		4,330							4,330	619	200DB HY	7	.24490	1,060
	TOTAL FURNITURE AND FIXTURE			7,330		0	0	0	0	0	7,330	1,048				1,795
	MACHINERY AND EQUIPMENT															
1	COMPUTER	2/01/22		2,200		2,200					0		200DB HY	5		0
3	OFFCIE EQUIPMENT	7/07/17		2,500							2,500	2,356	200DB HY	5	.05760	144
	TOTAL MACHINERY AND EQUIPME			4,700		2,200	0	0	0	0	2,500	2,356				144
	TOTAL DEPRECIATION			12,030		2,200	0	0	0	0	9,830	3,404				1,939
	GRAND TOTAL DEPRECIATION			12,030		2,200	0	0	0	0	9,830	3,404				1,939

Form **1120**
Department of the Treasury Internal Revenue Service

U.S. Corporation Income Tax Return

For calendar year 2022 or tax year beginning ________, 2022, ending ________, ________
Go to *www.irs.gov/Form1120* for instructions and the latest information.

OMB No. 1545-0123
2022

A Check if:
1a Consolidated return (attach Form 851) ☐
b Life/nonlife consolidated return ☐
2 Personal holding co. (attach Sch. PH) ☐
3 Personal service corp. (see instrs) ☐
4 Schedule M-3 attached ☐

TYPE OR PRINT
FASHION APPAREL, INC.
6789 PENN ST., SUITE 400
LOS ANGLES, CA 91234

B Employer identification number: 95-2222222
C Date incorporated: 1/10/2011
D Total assets (see instructions): $ 691,480.

E Check if: (1) ☐ Initial return (2) ☐ Final return (3) ☐ Name change (4) ☐ Address change

INCOME	1a	Gross receipts or sales	1a	1,147,545.		
	b	Returns and allowances	1b			
	c	Balance. Subtract line 1b from line 1a			1c	1,147,545.
	2	Cost of goods sold (attach Form 1125-A)			2	755,753.
	3	Gross profit. Subtract line 2 from line 1c			3	391,792.
	4	Dividends and inclusions (Schedule C, line 23)			4	
	5	Interest			5	2,512.
	6	Gross rents			6	
	7	Gross royalties			7	
	8	Capital gain net income (attach Schedule D (Form 1120))			8	
	9	Net gain or (loss) from Form 4797, Part II, line 17 (attach Form 4797) FORM 4684			9	-5,834.
	10	Other income (see instructions – attach statement) SEE STATEMENT 1			10	1,523.
	11	**Total income.** Add lines 3 through 10			11	389,993.
DEDUCTIONS (SEE INSTRUCTIONS FOR LIMITATIONS ON DEDUCTIONS)	12	Compensation of officers (see instructions – attach Form 1125-E)			12	15,000.
	13	Salaries and wages (less employment credits)			13	70,136.
	14	Repairs and maintenance			14	
	15	Bad debts			15	6,825.
	16	Rents			16	15,024.
	17	Taxes and licenses			17	1,553.
	18	Interest (see instructions)			18	5,821.
	19	Charitable contributions			19	
	20	Depreciation from Form 4562 not claimed on Form 1125-A or elsewhere on return (attach Form 4562)			20	4,139.
	21	Depletion			21	
	22	Advertising			22	482.
	23	Pension, profit-sharing, etc., plans			23	
	24	Employee benefit programs			24	
	25	Reserved for future use			25	
	26	Other deductions (attach statement) SEE STATEMENT 2			26	253,349.
	27	**Total deductions.** Add lines 12 through 26			27	372,329.
	28	Taxable income before net operating loss deduction and special deductions. Subtract line 27 from line 11			28	17,664.
	29a	Net operating loss deduction (see instructions) SEE ST 3	29a	17,664.		
	b	Special deductions (Schedule C, line 24)	29b			
	c	Add lines 29a and 29b			29c	17,664.
TAX, REFUNDABLE CREDITS, AND PMTS	30	**Taxable income.** Subtract line 29c from line 28. See instructions			30	0.
	31	Total tax (Schedule J, Part I, line 11)			31	0.
	32	Reserved for future use			32	
	33	Total payments and credits (Schedule J, Part III, line 23)			33	0.
	34	Estimated tax penalty. See instructions. Check if Form 2220 is attached ☐			34	
	35	**Amount owed.** If line 33 is smaller than the total of lines 31 and 34, enter amount owed			35	0.
	36	**Overpayment.** If line 33 is larger than the total of lines 31 and 34, enter amount overpaid			36	
	37	Enter amount from line 36 you want: **Credited to 2023 estimated tax**		**Refunded**	37	

Sign Here
Under penalties of perjury, I declare that I have examined this return, including accompanying schedules and statements, and to the best of my knowledge and belief, it is true, correct, and complete. Declaration of preparer (other than taxpayer) is based on all information of which preparer has any knowledge.

Signature of officer | Date | PRESIDENT (Title)

May the IRS discuss this return with the preparer shown below? See instructions. ☒ Yes ☐ No

Paid Preparer Use Only

Print/Type preparer's name	Preparer's signature	Date	Check ☒ if self-employed	PTIN
RON E. THOMPSON	RON E. THOMPSON	1/24/23		P00166602

Firm's name: WHITE ZUCKERMAN WARSAVSKY LUNA HUNT LLP — Firm's EIN: 95-4115549
Firm's address: 15490 VENTURA BLVD 3RD FL, SHERMAN OAKS, CA 91403 — Phone no. (818) 981-4226

BAA For Paperwork Reduction Act Notice, see separate instructions. Form **1120** (2022)

CPCA0205 10/04/22

Form 1120 (2022) FASHION APPAREL, INC. 95-2222222 Page **2**

Schedule C **Dividends, Inclusions, and Special Deductions** (see instructions)	**(a)** Dividends and inclusions	**(b)** Percentage	**(c)** Special deductions **(a) x (b)**
1 Dividends from less-than-20%-owned domestic corporations (other than debt-financed stock)		50	
2 Dividends from 20%-or-more-owned domestic corporations (other than debt-financed stock)		65	
3 Dividends on certain debt-financed stock of domestic and foreign corporations		See instructions	
4 Dividends on certain preferred stock of less-than-20%-owned public utilities		23.3	
5 Dividends on certain preferred stock of 20%-or-more-owned public utilities		26.7	
6 Dividends from less-than-20%-owned foreign corporations and certain FSCs		50	
7 Dividends from 20%-or-more-owned foreign corporations and certain FSCs		65	
8 Dividends from wholly owned foreign subsidiaries		100	
9 **Subtotal.** Add lines 1 through 8. See instructions for limitations		See instructions	
10 Dividends from domestic corporations received by a small business investment company operating under the Small Business Investment Act of 1958		100	
11 Dividends from affiliated group members		100	
12 Dividends from certain FSCs		100	
13 Foreign-source portion of dividends received from a specified 10%-owned foreign corporation (excluding hybrid dividends) (see instructions)		100	
14 Dividends from foreign corporations not included on line 3, 6, 7, 8, 11, 12, or 13 (including any hybrid dividends)			
15 Reserved for future use			
16a Subpart F inclusions derived from the sale by a controlled foreign corporation (CFC) of the stock of a lower-tier foreign corporation treated as a dividend (attach Form(s) 5471) (see instructions)		100	
b Subpart F inclusions derived from hybrid dividends of tiered corporations (attach Form(s) 5471) (see instructions)			
c Other inclusions from CFCs under subpart F not included on line 16a, 16b, or 17 (attach Form(s) 5471) (see instructions)			
17 Global Intangible Low-Taxed Income (GILTI) (attach Form(s) 5471 and Form 8992)			
18 Gross-up for foreign taxes deemed paid			
19 IC-DISC and former DISC dividends not included on line 1, 2, or 3			
20 Other dividends			
21 Deduction for dividends paid on certain preferred stock of public utilities			
22 Section 250 deduction (attach Form 8993)			
23 **Total dividends and inclusions.** Add column (a), lines 9 through 20. Enter here and on page 1, line 4			
24 **Total special deductions.** Add column (c) lines 9 through 22. Enter here and on page 1, line 29b			

Form **1120** (2022)

CPCA0212 10/04/22

Form 1120 (2022) FASHION APPAREL, INC. 95-2222222 Page **3**

Schedule J **Tax Computation and Payment** (see instructions)

Part I – Tax Computation

1	Check if the corporation is a member of a controlled group (attach Schedule O (Form 1120)). See instructions ☐				
2	Income tax. See instructions			2	0.
3	Base erosion minimum tax amount (attach Form 8991)			3	
4	Add lines 2 and 3			4	0.
5a	Foreign tax credit (attach Form 1118)	5a			
b	Credit from Form 8834 (see instructions)	5b			
c	General business credit (attach Form 3800)	5c			
d	Credit for prior year minimum tax (attach Form 8827)	5d			
e	Bond credits from Form 8912	5e			
6	**Total credits.** Add lines 5a through 5e			6	
7	Subtract line 6 from line 4			7	
8	Personal holding company tax (attach Schedule PH (Form 1120))			8	
9a	Recapture of investment credit (attach Form 4255)	9a			
b	Recapture of low-income housing credit (attach Form 8611)	9b			
c	Interest due under the look-back method – completed long-term contracts (attach Form 8697)	9c			
d	Interest due under the look-back method – income forecast method (attach Form 8866)	9d			
e	Alternative tax on qualifying shipping activities (attach Form 8902)	9e			
f	Interest/tax due under section 453A(c) and/or section 453(l)	9f			
g	Other (see instructions – attach statement)	9g			
10	**Total.** Add lines 9a through 9g			10	
11	**Total tax.** Add lines 7, 8, and 10. Enter here and on page 1, line 31			11	0.

Part II – Reserved for Future Use

12	Reserved for future use	12	

Part III – Payments and Refundable Credits

13	2021 overpayment credited to 2022			13	
14	2022 estimated tax payments			14	
15	2022 refund applied for on Form 4466			15	( )
16	Combine lines 13, 14, and 15			16	0.
17	Tax deposited with Form 7004			17	
18	Withholding (see instructions)			18	
19	**Total payments.** Add lines 16, 17, and 18			19	0.
20	Refundable credits from:				
a	Form 2439	20a			
b	Form 4136	20b			
c	Reserved for future use	20c			
d	Other (attach statement – see instructions)	20d			
21	**Total credits.** Add lines 20a through 20d			21	
22	Reserved for future use			22	
23	**Total payments and credits.** Add lines 19 and 21. Enter here and on page 1, line 33			23	0.

Form **1120** (2022)

Form 1120 (2022) FASHION APPAREL, INC. 95-2222222 Page 4

Schedule K **Other Information** (see instructions)

		Yes	No
1	Check accounting method: a ☐ Cash b ☒ Accrual c ☐ Other (specify)		
2	See the instructions and enter the:		
	a Business activity code no. 448190		
	b Business activity SALES		
	c Product or service APPAREL		
3	Is the corporation a subsidiary in an affiliated group or a parent-subsidiary controlled group? If "Yes," enter name and EIN of the parent corporation		X
4	At the end of the tax year:		
	a Did any foreign or domestic corporation, partnership (including any entity treated as a partnership), trust, or tax-exempt organization own directly 20% or more, or own, directly or indirectly, 50% or more of the total voting power of all classes of the corporation's stock entitled to vote? If "Yes," complete Part I of Schedule G (Form 1120) (attach Schedule G)		X
	b Did any individual or estate own directly 20% or more, or own, directly or indirectly, 50% or more of the total voting power of all classes of the corporation's stock entitled to vote? If "Yes," complete Part II of Schedule G (Form 1120) (attach Schedule G)	X	
5	At the end of the tax year, did the corporation:		
	a Own directly 20% or more, or own, directly or indirectly, 50% or more of the total voting power of all classes of stock entitled to vote of any foreign or domestic corporation not included on **Form 851,** Affiliations Schedule? For rules of constructive ownership, see instructions. If "Yes," complete (i) through (iv) below.		X

(i) Name of Corporation	(ii) Employer Identification Number (if any)	(iii) Country of Incorporation	(iv) Percentage Owned in Voting Stock

	Yes	No
b Own directly an interest of 20% or more, or own, directly or indirectly, an interest of 50% or more in any foreign or domestic partnership (including an entity treated as a partnership) or in the beneficial interest of a trust? For rules of constructive ownership, see instructions. If "Yes," complete (i) through (iv) below.		X

(i) Name of Entity	(ii) Employer Identification Number (if any)	(iii) Country of Organization	(iv) Maximum Percentage Owned in Profit, Loss, or Capital

		Yes	No
6	During this tax year, did the corporation pay dividends (other than stock dividends and distributions in exchange for stock) in excess of the corporation's current and accumulated earnings and profits? See sections 301 and 316. If "Yes," file **Form 5452**, Corporate Report of Nondividend Distributions. See the instructions for Form 5452. If this is a consolidated return, answer here for the parent corporation and on Form 851 for each subsidiary.		X
7	At any time during the tax year, did one foreign person own, directly or indirectly, at least 25% of the total voting power of all classes of the corporation's stock entitled to vote or at least 25% of the total value of all classes of the corporation's stock? For rules of attribution, see section 318. If "Yes," enter: (a) Percentage owned ______ and (b) Owner's country ______ (c) The corporation may have to file **Form 5472,** Information Return of a 25% Foreign-Owned U.S. Corporation or a Foreign Corporation Engaged in a U.S. Trade or Business. Enter the number of Forms 5472 attached ______		X
8	Check this box if the corporation issued publicly offered debt instruments with original issue discount ☐ If checked, the corporation may have to file **Form 8281**, Information Return for Publicly Offered Original Issue Discount Instruments.		
9	Enter the amount of tax-exempt interest received or accrued during the tax year $ NONE		
10	Enter the number of shareholders at the end of the tax year (if 100 or fewer) 1		
11	If the corporation has an NOL for the tax year and is electing to forego the carryback period, check here (see instructions) ☐ If the corporation is filing a consolidated return, the statement required by Regulations section 1.1502-21(b)(3) must be attached or the election will not be valid.		
12	Enter the available NOL carryover from prior tax years (do not reduce it by any deduction reported on page 1, line 29a.) $ 27,270.		

Form **1120** (2022)

CPCA0234 10/05/22

Form 1120 (2022) FASHION APPAREL, INC. 95-2222222 Page **5**

Schedule K **Other Information** *(continued from page 4)*

		Yes	No
13	Are the corporation's total receipts (page 1, line 1a, plus lines 4 through 10) for the tax year **and** its total assets at the end of the tax year less than $250,000?		X
	If "Yes," the corporation is not required to complete Schedules L, M-1, and M-2. Instead, enter the total amount of cash distributions and the book value of property distributions (other than cash) made during the tax year $		
14	Is the corporation required to file Schedule UTP (Form 1120), Uncertain Tax Position Statement? See instructions. If "Yes," complete and attach Schedule UTP.		X
15a	Did the corporation make any payments in 2022 that would require it to file Form(s) 1099?		X
b	If "Yes," did or will the corporation file required Form(s) 1099?		
16	During this tax year, did the corporation have an 80%-or-more change in ownership, including a change due to redemption of its own stock?		X
17	During or subsequent to this tax year, but before the filing of this return, did the corporation dispose of more than 65% (by value) of its assets in a taxable, non-taxable, or tax deferred transaction?		X
18	Did the corporation receive assets in a section 351 transfer in which any of the transferred assets had a fair market basis or fair market value of more than $1 million?		X
19	During the corporation's tax year, did the corporation make any payments that would require it to file Forms 1042 and 1042-S under chapter 3 (sections 1441 through 1464) or chapter 4 (sections 1471 through 1474) of the Code?		X
20	Is the corporation operating on a cooperative basis?		X
21	During the tax year, did the corporation pay or accrue any interest or royalty for which the deduction is not allowed under section 267A? See instructions		X
	If "Yes," enter the total amount of the disallowed deductions $		
22	Does the corporation have gross receipts of at least $500 million in any of the 3 preceding tax years? (See sections 59A(e)(2) and (3))		X
	If "Yes," complete and attach Form 8991.		
23	Did the corporation have an election under section 163(j) for any real property trade or business or any farming business in effect during the tax year? See instructions		X
24	Does the corporation satisfy one or more of the following? See instructions		X
a	The corporation owns a pass-through entity with current, or prior year carryover, excess business interest expense.		
b	The corporation's aggregate average annual gross receipts (determined under section 448(c)) for the 3 tax years preceding the current tax year are more than $27 million and the corporation has business interest expense.		
c	The corporation is a tax shelter and the corporation has business interest expense.		
	If "Yes," complete and attach Form 8990.		
25	Is the corporation attaching Form 8996 to certify as a Qualified Opportunity Fund?		X
	If "Yes," enter amount from Form 8996, line 15 $		
26	Since December 22, 2017, did a foreign corporation directly or indirectly acquire substantially all of the properties held directly or indirectly by the corporation, and was the ownership percentage (by vote or value) for purposes of section 7874 greater than 50% (for example, the shareholders held more than 50% of the stock of the foreign corporation)? If "Yes," list the ownership percentage by vote and by value. See instructions		X
	Percentage: By Vote Percentage: By Value		

Form **1120** (2022)

CPCA0234 10/05/22

Form 1120 (2022) FASHION APPAREL, INC. 95-2222222 Page **6**

Schedule L Balance Sheets per Books

Assets	Beginning of tax year (a)	(b)	End of tax year (c)	(d)
1 Cash		1,240.		1,250.
2a Trade notes and accounts receivable	115,712.		124,897.	
b Less allowance for bad debts	( )	115,712.	( )	124,897.
3 Inventories		570,846.		560,846.
4 U.S. government obligations				
5 Tax-exempt securities (see instructions)				
6 Other current assets (attach statement)				
7 Loans to shareholders				
8 Mortgage and real estate loans				
9 Other investments (attach statement)				
10a Buildings and other depreciable assets	9,830.		12,030.	
b Less accumulated depreciation	(3,404.)	6,426.	(7,543.)	4,487.
11a Depletable assets				
b Less accumulated depletion	( )		( )	
12 Land (net of any amortization)				
13a Intangible assets (amortizable only)	1,000.		1,000.	
b Less accumulated amortization	(833.)	167.	(1,000.)	
14 Other assets (attach statement)				
15 Total assets		694,391.		691,480.
Liabilities and Shareholders' Equity				
16 Accounts payable		39,611.		45,276.
17 Mortgages, notes, bonds payable in less than 1 year				
18 Other current liabilities (attach stmt) SEE ST 4		32,351.		28,111.
19 Loans from shareholders		658,000.		636,000.
20 Mortgages, notes, bonds payable in 1 year or more				
21 Other liabilities (attach statement) SEE ST 5		39,528.		39,528.
22 Capital stock: a Preferred stock				
b Common stock	10,000.	10,000.	10,000.	10,000.
23 Additional paid-in capital				
24 Retained earnings — Approp (att stmt)				
25 Retained earnings — Unappropriated		-85,099.		-67,435.
26 Adjmt to shareholders' equity (att stmt)				
27 Less cost of treasury stock		( )		( )
28 Total liabilities and shareholders' equity		694,391.		691,480.

Schedule M-1 **Reconciliation of Income (Loss) per Books With Income per Return**
Note: The corporation may be required to file Schedule M-3. See instructions.

1 Net income (loss) per books	17,664.	7 Income recorded on books this year not included on this return (itemize): Tax-exempt interest $	
2 Federal income tax per books			
3 Excess of capital losses over capital gains			
4 Income subject to tax not recorded on books this year (itemize):		8 Deductions on this return not charged against book income this year (itemize): a Depreciation $ b Charitable contribns $	
5 Expenses recorded on books this year not deducted on this return (itemize): a Depreciation $ b Charitable contributions $ c Travel & entertainment $			
		9 Add lines 7 and 8	0.
6 Add lines 1 through 5	17,664.	10 Income (page 1, line 28) — line 6 less line 9	17,664.

Schedule M-2 **Analysis of Unappropriated Retained Earnings per Books (Schedule L, Line 25)**

1 Balance at beginning of year	-85,099.	5 Distributions a Cash	
2 Net income (loss) per books	17,664.	b Stock c Property	
3 Other increases (itemize):		6 Other decreases (itemize):	
		7 Add lines 5 and 6	
4 Add lines 1, 2, and 3	-67,435.	8 Balance at end of year (line 4 less line 7)	-67,435.

Form **1120** (2022)

CPCA0234 10/04/22

Form **1125-A** (Rev. November 2018) Department of the Treasury Internal Revenue Service

Cost of Goods Sold

► Attach to Form 1120, 1120-C, 1120-F, 1120S, or 1065.
► Go to *www.irs.gov/Form1125A* for the latest information.

OMB No. 1545-0123

Name	Employer identification number
FASHION APPAREL, INC.	95-2222222

1	Inventory at beginning of year	1	570,846.
2	Purchases	2	745,753.
3	Cost of labor	3	
4	Additional section 263A costs (attach schedule)	4	
5	Other costs (attach schedule)	5	
6	**Total.** Add lines 1 through 5	6	1,316,599.
7	Inventory at end of year	7	560,846.
8	**Cost of goods sold.** Subtract line 7 from line 6. Enter here and on Form 1120, page 1, line 2 or the appropriate line of your tax return. See instructions	8	755,753.

9 a Check all methods used for valuing closing inventory:

(i) ☐ Cost

(ii) ☒ Lower of cost or market

(iii) ☐ Other (Specify method used and attach explanation.) ►

b Check if there was a writedown of subnormal goods ► ☐

c Check if the LIFO inventory method was adopted this tax year for any goods (if checked, attach Form 970) ► ☐

d If the LIFO inventory method was used for this tax year, enter amount of closing inventory computed under LIFO **9d**

e If property is produced or acquired for resale, do the rules of section 263A apply to the entity? See instructions ☐ Yes ☒ No

f Was there any change in determining quantities, cost, or valuations between opening and closing inventory? If "Yes," attach explanation ☐ Yes ☒ No

BAA For Paperwork Reduction Act Notice, see instructions. Form **1125-A** (Rev. 11-2018)

CPCZ0401L 09/26/18

SCHEDULE G
(Form 1120)
(Rev December 2011)
Department of the Treasury
Internal Revenue Service

Information on Certain Persons Owning the Corporation's Voting Stock

► Attach to Form 1120.
► See instructions.

OMB No. 1545-0123

Name: FASHION APPAREL, INC.

Employer identification number (EIN): 95-2222222

Part I **Certain Entities Owning the Corporation's Voting Stock.** (Form 1120, Schedule K, Question 4a). Complete columns (i) through (v) below for any foreign or domestic corporation, partnership (including any entity treated as a partnership), trust, or tax-exempt organization that owns directly 20% or more, or owns, directly or indirectly, 50% or more of the total voting power of all classes of the corporation's stock entitled to vote (see instructions).

(i) Name of Entity	(ii) Employer Identification Number (if any)	(iii) Type of Entity	(iv) Country of Organization	(v) Percentage Owned in Voting Stock

Part II **Certain Individuals and Estates Owning the Corporation's Voting Stock.** (Form 1120, Schedule K, Question 4b). Complete columns (i) through (iv) below for any individual or estate that owns directly 20% or more, or owns, directly or indirectly, 50% or more of the total voting power of all classes of the corporation's stock entitled to vote (see instructions).

(i) Name of Individual or Estate	(ii) Identifying Number (if any)	(iii) Country of Citizenship (see instructions)	(iv) Percentage Owned in Voting Stock
CATHERINE P ANDERSON	123-45-6789	UNITED STATES	100.00%

BAA For Paperwork Reduction Act Notice, see the Instructions for Form 1120. CPCA1901L 06/02/11 Schedule G (Form 1120) (Rev 12-2011)

Form **1125-E**
(Rev October 2016)
Department of the Treasury
Internal Revenue Service

Compensation of Officers

► **Attach to Form 1120, 1120-C, 1120-F, 1120-REIT, 1120-RIC, or 1120S.**
► **Information about Form 1125-E and its separate instructions is at *www.irs.gov/form1125e*.**

OMB No. 1545-0123

Name	Employer identification number
FASHION APPAREL, INC.	95-2222222

Note: Complete Form 1125-E only if total receipts are $500,000 or more. See instructions for definition of total receipts.

1 (a) Name of officer	(b) Social security number	(c) Percent of time devoted to business	Percent of stock owned		(f) Amount of compensation
			(d) Common	(e) Preferred	
CATHERINE P ANDERSON	123-45-6789	100 %	100 %	0.00 %	15,000.
		%	%	%	
		%	%	%	
		%	%	%	
		%	%	%	
		%	%	%	
		%	%	%	
		%	%	%	
		%	%	%	
		%	%	%	
		%	%	%	
		%	%	%	
		%	%	%	
		%	%	%	
		%	%	%	
		%	%	%	
		%	%	%	
		%	%	%	
		%	%	%	
		%	%	%	

2	Total compensation of officers	15,000.
3	Compensation of officers claimed on Form 1125-A or elsewhere on return	
4	Subtract line 3 from line 2. Enter the result here and on Form 1120, page 1, line 12 or the appropriate line of your tax return	15,000.

BAA For Paperwork Reduction Act Notice, see separate instructions. Form **1125-E** (Rev 10-2016)

CPCA2101L 08/18/16

Form **4562** — Department of the Treasury, Internal Revenue Service

Depreciation and Amortization
(Including Information on Listed Property)

Attach to your tax return.
Go to *www.irs.gov/Form4562* for instructions and the latest information.

OMB No. 1545-0172
2022
Attachment Sequence No. **179**

Name(s) shown on return: FASHION APPAREL, INC.
Identifying number: 95-2222222
Business or activity to which this form relates: FORM 1120

Part I — Election To Expense Certain Property Under Section 179
Note: If you have any listed property, complete Part V before you complete Part I.

1	Maximum amount (see instructions)	1	1,080,000.
2	Total cost of section 179 property placed in service (see instructions)	2	2,200.
3	Threshold cost of section 179 property before reduction in limitation (see instructions)	3	2,700,000.
4	Reduction in limitation. Subtract line 3 from line 2. If zero or less, enter -0-	4	0.
5	Dollar limitation for tax year. Subtract line 4 from line 1. If zero or less, enter -0-. If married filing separately, see instructions	5	1,080,000.

6 (a) Description of property	(b) Cost (business use only)	(c) Elected cost
5-YEAR COMPUTER	2,200.	2,200.

7	Listed property. Enter the amount from line 29	7	0.
8	Total elected cost of section 179 property. Add amounts in column (c), lines 6 and 7	8	2,200.
9	Tentative deduction. Enter the **smaller** of line 5 or line 8	9	2,200.
10	Carryover of disallowed deduction from line 13 of your 2021 Form 4562	10	0.
11	Business income limitation. Enter the smaller of business income (not less than zero) or line 5. See instrs	11	19,864.
12	Section 179 expense deduction. Add lines 9 and 10, but don't enter more than line 11	12	2,200.
13	Carryover of disallowed deduction to 2023. Add lines 9 and 10, less line 12	13	0.

Note: Don't use Part II or Part III below for listed property. Instead, use Part V.

Part II — Special Depreciation Allowance and Other Depreciation (**Don't** include listed property. See instructions.)

14	Special depreciation allowance for qualified property (other than listed property) placed in service during the tax year. See instructions	14	
15	Property subject to section 168(f)(1) election	15	
16	Other depreciation (including ACRS)	16	

Part III — MACRS Depreciation (**Don't** include listed property. See instructions.)

Section A

17	MACRS deductions for assets placed in service in tax years beginning before 2022	17	1,939.
18	If you are electing to group any assets placed in service during the tax year into one or more general asset accounts, check here ☐		

Section B – Assets Placed in Service During 2022 Tax Year Using the General Depreciation System

(a) Classification of property	(b) Month and year placed in service	(c) Basis for depreciation (business/investment use only — see instructions)	(d) Recovery period	(e) Convention	(f) Method	(g) Depreciation deduction
19a 3-year property						
b 5-year property						
c 7-year property						
d 10-year property						
e 15-year property						
f 20-year property						
g 25-year property			25 yrs		S/L	
h Residential rental property			27.5 yrs	MM	S/L	
			27.5 yrs	MM	S/L	
i Nonresidential real property			39 yrs	MM	S/L	
				MM	S/L	

Section C – Assets Placed in Service During 2022 Tax Year Using the Alternative Depreciation System

(a)	(b)	(c)	(d)	(e)	(f)	(g)
20a Class life					S/L	
b 12-year			12 yrs		S/L	
c 30-year			30 yrs	MM	S/L	
d 40-year			40 yrs	MM	S/L	

Part IV — Summary (See instructions.)

21	Listed property. Enter amount from line 28	21	
22	**Total.** Add amounts from line 12, lines 14 through 17, lines 19 and 20 in column (g), and line 21. Enter here and on the appropriate lines of your return. Partnerships and S corporations — see instructions	22	4,139.
23	For assets shown above and placed in service during the current year, enter the portion of the basis attributable to section 263A costs	23	

Form 4684 (2022) Attachment Sequence No. **26** Page **2**

Name(s) shown on tax return. Do not enter name and identifying number if shown on page 1.

FASHION APPAREL, INC.

Identifying number 95-2222222

SECTION B – Business and Income-Producing Property

Part I Casualty or Theft Gain or Loss (Use a separate Part I for each casualty or theft.)

19 Description of properties (show type, location, and date acquired for each property). Use a separate line for each property lost or damaged from the same casualty or theft. **See instructions if claiming a loss due to a Ponzi-type investment scheme and Section C is not completed.**

Property **A** VARIOUS THEFT OF INVENTORY (AT COST) 1/15/2021

Property **B**

Property **C**

Property **D**

		Properties A	B	C	D
20 Cost or adjusted basis of each property	20	5,834.			
21 Insurance or other reimbursement (whether or not you filed a claim). See the instructions for line 3. **Note:** If ln 20 is **more** than ln 21, skip ln 22.	21				
22 Gain from casualty or theft. If line 21 is **more** than line 20, enter the difference here and on line 29 or line 34, column (c), except as provided in the instructions for line 33. Also, skip lines 23 through 27 for that column. See the instructions for line 4 if line 21 includes insurance or other reimbursement you did not claim, or you received payment for your loss in a later tax year	22				
23 Fair market value **before** casualty or theft	23	5,834.			
24 Fair market value **after** casualty or theft	24	0.			
25 Subtract line 24 from line 23	25	5,834.			
26 Enter the **smaller** of line 20 or line 25. **Note:** If the property was totally destroyed by casualty or lost from theft, enter on line 26 the amount from line 20.	26	5,834.			
27 Subtract ln 21 from ln 26. If zero or less, enter -0-	27	5,834.			

28 Casualty or theft loss. Add the amounts on line 27. Enter the total here and on line 29 **or** line 34. See instructions. | 28 | 5,834.

Part II Summary of Gains and Losses (from separate Parts I)

(a) Identify casualty or theft	(b) Losses from casualties or thefts (i) Trade, business, rental, or royalty property	(b) (ii) Income-producing property	(c) Gains from casualties or thefts includible in income
Casualty or Theft of Property Held One Year or Less			
29 VARIOUS THEFT OF INVENTORY (AT COST)	(5,834.)	( )	
	( )	( )	
30 Totals. Add the amounts on line 29 — 30	(5,834.)	( )	
31 Combine line 30, columns (b)(i) and (c). Enter the net gain or (loss) here and on Form 4797, line 14. If Form 4797 is not otherwise required, see instructions — 31			-5,834.
32 Enter the amount from line 30, column (b)(ii), here. Individuals, enter the amount from income-producing property on Schedule A (Form 1040), line 16; or Schedule A (Form 1040-NR), line 7. (Do not include any loss on property used as an employee.) Estates and trusts, partnerships, and S corporations, see instructions — 32			
Casualty or Theft of Property Held More Than One Year			
33 Casualty or theft gains from Form 4797, line 32 — 33			
34	( )	( )	
	( )	( )	
35 Total losses. Add amounts on line 34, columns (b)(i) and (b)(ii) — 35	( )	( )	
36 Total gains. Add lines 33 and 34, column (c) — 36			
37 Add amounts on line 35, columns (b)(i) and (b)(ii) — 37			
38 If the loss on line 37 is **more** than the gain on line 36:			
a Combine line 35, column (b)(i), and line 36, and enter the net gain or (loss) here. Partnerships and S corporations, see the *Note* below. All others, enter this amount on Form 4797, line 14. If Form 4797 is not otherwise required, see instructions — 38a			
b Enter the amount from line 35, column (b)(ii), here. Individuals, enter the amount from income-producing property on Schedule A (Form 1040), line 16; or Schedule A (Form 1040-NR), line 7. (Do not include any loss on property used as an employee.) Estates and trusts, enter on the "Other deductions" line of your tax return. Partnerships and S corporations, see the *Note* below — 38b			
39 If the loss on line 37 is **less** than or **equal** to the gain on line 36, combine lines 36 and 37 and enter here. Partnerships, see the *Note* below. All others, enter this amount on Form 4797, line 3 — 39			

Note: Partnerships, enter the amount from line 38a, 38b, or 39 on Form 1065, Schedule K, line 11. S corporations, enter the amount from line 38a or 38b on Form 1120-S, Schedule K, line 10.

2022	FEDERAL STATEMENTS	PAGE 1
CLIENT FASHIONA	FASHION APPAREL, INC.	95-2222222
1/24/23		08:00AM

STATEMENT 1
FORM 1120, LINE 10
OTHER INCOME

MISCELLANEOUS ORDINARY INCOME	$	1,523.
TOTAL	$	1,523.

STATEMENT 2
FORM 1120, LINE 26
OTHER DEDUCTIONS

ACCOUNTING	$	12,000.
AMORTIZATION		167.
ARTIST/DESIGN		1,900.
BANK CHARGES		3,840.
BUSINESS GIFTS		2,260.
COMMISSIONS		5,508.
CONSULTING FEES		10,000.
DUES AND SUBSCRIPTIONS		842.
INSURANCE		6,640.
LEGAL AND PROFFESIONAL		10,000.
MISCELLANEOUS		3,259.
OFFICE EXPENSE		4,926.
OFFICE SUPPLIES		2,653.
OUTSIDE SERVICE		5,000.
POSTAGE		1,898.
PRINTING		2,560.
PROMOTIONAL EXPENSE		11,003.
ROYALTY EXPENSE		42,577.
TELEPHONE		19,843.
TRADE SHOWS		14,694.
TRAVEL		91,779.
TOTAL	$	253,349.

STATEMENT 3
FORM 1120, LINE 29A
NET OPERATING LOSS DEDUCTION

CARRYOVER GENERATED FROM YEAR END	12/31/15		$ 33,860.	
AMOUNT UTILIZED IN		33,860.		
TOTAL UTILIZATION			$ 33,860.	
AVAILABLE FOR CARRYOVER TO 2022				0.
CARRYOVER GENERATED FROM YEAR END	12/31/17		$ 22,165.	
AVAILABLE FOR CARRYOVER TO 2022				22,165.
CARRYOVER GENERATED FROM YEAR END	12/31/18		$ 1,196.	
AVAILABLE FOR CARRYOVER TO 2022				1,196.

2022 **FEDERAL STATEMENTS** **PAGE 2**

CLIENT FASHIONA **FASHION APPAREL, INC.** **95-2222222**

1/24/23 08:00AM

STATEMENT 3 (CONTINUED)
FORM 1120, LINE 29A
NET OPERATING LOSS DEDUCTION

CARRYOVER GENERATED FROM YEAR END	12/31/19	$ 2,205.	
AVAILABLE FOR CARRYOVER TO 2022			2,205.
CARRYOVER GENERATED FROM YEAR END	12/31/20	$ 1,704.	
AVAILABLE FOR CARRYOVER TO 2022			1,704.
NET OPERATING LOSSES AVAILABLE IN 2022			$ 27,270.
TAXABLE INCOME			17,664.
NET OPERATING LOSS DEDUCTION FOR PRE-2018 LOSSES (LIMITED TO TI)			17,664.
TOTAL NET OPERATING LOSS DEDUCTION			17,664.

STATEMENT 4
FORM 1120, SCHEDULE L, LINE 18
OTHER CURRENT LIABILITIES

	BEGINNING	ENDING
OTHER CURRENT LIABILITIES	$ 32,351.	$ 28,111.
TOTAL	$ 32,351.	$ 28,111.

STATEMENT 5
FORM 1120, SCHEDULE L, LINE 21
OTHER LIABILITIES

	BEGINNING	ENDING
OTHER LIABILITIES	$ 39,528.	$ 39,528.
TOTAL	$ 39,528.	$ 39,528.

12/31/22 **2022 FEDERAL DEPRECIATION SCHEDULE** **PAGE 1**

CLIENT LEDGERPA **LEDGER & POST, AN ACCOUNTANCY CORP.** **95-3333333**

1/24/23 08:42AM

NO.	DESCRIPTION	DATE ACQUIRED	DATE SOLD	COST/ BASIS	BUS. PCT.	CUR 179 BONUS	SPECIAL DEPR. ALLOW.	PRIOR 179/ BONUS/ SP. DEPR.	PRIOR DEC. BAL DEPR.	SALVAG /BASIS REDUCT	DEPR. BASIS	PRIOR DEPR.	METHOD	LIFE	RATE	CURRENT DEPR.
	FORM 1120															
	FURNITURE AND FIXTURES															
1	OFFICE FURNITURE	3/15/20		4,500							4,500	1,745	200DB HY	7	.17490	787
2	FURNITURE	7/08/22		10,000		10,000					0		200DB HY	7		0
	TOTAL FURNITURE AND FIXTURE			14,500		10,000	0	0	0	0	4,500	1,745				787
	MACHINERY AND EQUIPMENT															
3	OFFICE EQUIPMENT	11/13/19		2,500							2,500	1,406	200DB HY	7	.12490	312
4	COMPUTER	12/01/19		2,000							2,000	1,780	200DB HY	5	.11520	220
5	COMPUTER	2/07/22		2,500		2,500					0		200DB HY	5		0
	TOTAL MACHINERY AND EQUIPME			7,000		2,500	0	0	0	0	4,500	3,186				532
	TOTAL DEPRECIATION			21,500		12,500	0	0	0	0	9,000	4,931				1,319
	GRAND TOTAL DEPRECIATION			21,500		12,500	0	0	0	0	9,000	4,931				1,319

Form **1120**
Department of the Treasury
Internal Revenue Service

U.S. Corporation Income Tax Return

For calendar year 2022 or tax year beginning ________, 2022, ending ________, ______

Go to *www.irs.gov/Form1120* for instructions and the latest information.

OMB No. 1545-0123

2022

A Check if:	TYPE OR PRINT		
1a Consolidated return (attach Form 851) ☐		LEDGER & POST, AN ACCOUNTANCY CORP.	B Employer identification number: 95-3333333
b Life/nonlife consolidated return ☐		8765 CREDIT AVE	C Date incorporated: 1/01/1987
2 Personal holding co. (attach Sch. PH) ☐		LOS ANGELES, CA 91234	D Total assets (see instructions): $ 283,554.
3 Personal service corp. (see instrs) ☐			
4 Schedule M-3 attached ☐			

E Check if: (1) ☐ Initial return (2) ☐ Final return (3) ☐ Name change (4) ☐ Address change

INCOME	1a	Gross receipts or sales	1a	2,020,967.		
	b	Returns and allowances	1b			
	c	Balance. Subtract line 1b from line 1a			1c	2,020,967.
	2	Cost of goods sold (attach Form 1125-A)			2	
	3	Gross profit. Subtract line 2 from line 1c			3	2,020,967.
	4	Dividends and inclusions (Schedule C, line 23)			4	
	5	Interest			5	4,632.
	6	Gross rents			6	
	7	Gross royalties			7	
	8	Capital gain net income (attach Schedule D (Form 1120))			8	
	9	Net gain or (loss) from Form 4797, Part II, line 17 (attach Form 4797)			9	
	10	Other income (see instructions — attach statement)			10	
	11	**Total income.** Add lines 3 through 10			11	2,025,599.
DEDUCTIONS (SEE INSTRUCTIONS FOR LIMITATIONS ON DEDUCTIONS)	12	Compensation of officers (see instructions — attach Form 1125-E)			12	586,200.
	13	Salaries and wages (less employment credits)			13	885,517.
	14	Repairs and maintenance			14	3,655.
	15	Bad debts			15	
	16	Rents			16	201,080.
	17	Taxes and licenses			17	74,441.
	18	Interest (see instructions)			18	
	19	Charitable contributions			19	
	20	Depreciation from Form 4562 not claimed on Form 1125-A or elsewhere on return (attach Form 4562)			20	13,819.
	21	Depletion			21	
	22	Advertising			22	
	23	Pension, profit-sharing, etc., plans			23	
	24	Employee benefit programs			24	26,394.
	25	Reserved for future use			25	
	26	Other deductions (attach statement) SEE STATEMENT 1			26	226,133.
	27	**Total deductions.** Add lines 12 through 26			27	2,017,239.
	28	Taxable income before net operating loss deduction and special deductions. Subtract line 27 from line 11			28	8,360.
	29a	Net operating loss deduction (see instructions)	29a			
	b	Special deductions (Schedule C, line 24)	29b			
	c	Add lines 29a and 29b			29c	
TAX, REFUNDABLE CREDITS, AND PMTS	30	**Taxable income.** Subtract line 29c from line 28. See instructions			30	8,360.
	31	Total tax (Schedule J, Part I, line 11)			31	1,756.
	32	Reserved for future use			32	
	33	Total payments and credits (Schedule J, Part III, line 23)			33	0.
	34	Estimated tax penalty. See instructions. Check if Form 2220 is attached ☐			34	
	35	**Amount owed.** If line 33 is smaller than the total of lines 31 and 34, enter amount owed			35	1,756.
	36	**Overpayment.** If line 33 is larger than the total of lines 31 and 34, enter amount overpaid			36	
	37	Enter amount from line 36 you want: **Credited to 2023 estimated tax**		**Refunded**	37	

Sign Here

Under penalties of perjury, I declare that I have examined this return, including accompanying schedules and statements, and to the best of my knowledge and belief, it is true, correct, and complete. Declaration of preparer (other than taxpayer) is based on all information of which preparer has any knowledge.

Signature of officer | Date | PRESIDENT (Title)

May the IRS discuss this return with the preparer shown below? See instructions. ☒ **Yes** ☐ **No**

Paid Preparer Use Only				
Print/Type preparer's name: RON E. THOMPSON	Preparer's signature: RON E. THOMPSON	Date: 1/24/23	Check ☒ if self-employed	PTIN: P00166602
Firm's name: WHITE ZUCKERMAN WARSAVSKY LUNA HUNT LLP			Firm's EIN: 95-4115549	
Firm's address: 15490 VENTURA BLVD 3RD FL, SHERMAN OAKS, CA 91403			Phone no. (818) 981-4226	

BAA For Paperwork Reduction Act Notice, see separate instructions. Form **1120** (2022)

CPCA0205 10/04/22

Form 1120 (2022) LEDGER & POST, AN ACCOUNTANCY CORP. 95-3333333 Page **2**

Schedule C **Dividends, Inclusions, and Special Deductions** (see instructions)	**(a)** Dividends and inclusions	**(b)** Percentage	**(c)** Special deductions **(a)** x **(b)**
1 Dividends from less-than-20%-owned domestic corporations (other than debt-financed stock)		50	
2 Dividends from 20%-or-more-owned domestic corporations (other than debt-financed stock)		65	
3 Dividends on certain debt-financed stock of domestic and foreign corporations		See instructions	
4 Dividends on certain preferred stock of less-than-20%-owned public utilities		23.3	
5 Dividends on certain preferred stock of 20%-or-more-owned public utilities		26.7	
6 Dividends from less-than-20%-owned foreign corporations and certain FSCs		50	
7 Dividends from 20%-or-more-owned foreign corporations and certain FSCs		65	
8 Dividends from wholly owned foreign subsidiaries		100	
9 **Subtotal.** Add lines 1 through 8. See instructions for limitations		See instructions	
10 Dividends from domestic corporations received by a small business investment company operating under the Small Business Investment Act of 1958		100	
11 Dividends from affiliated group members		100	
12 Dividends from certain FSCs		100	
13 Foreign-source portion of dividends received from a specified 10%-owned foreign corporation (excluding hybrid dividends) (see instructions)		100	
14 Dividends from foreign corporations not included on line 3, 6, 7, 8, 11, 12, or 13 (including any hybrid dividends)			
15 Reserved for future use			
16a Subpart F inclusions derived from the sale by a controlled foreign corporation (CFC) of the stock of a lower-tier foreign corporation treated as a dividend (attach Form(s) 5471) (see instructions)		100	
b Subpart F inclusions derived from hybrid dividends of tiered corporations (attach Form(s) 5471) (see instructions)			
c Other inclusions from CFCs under subpart F not included on line 16a, 16b, or 17 (attach Form(s) 5471) (see instructions)			
17 Global Intangible Low-Taxed Income (GILTI) (attach Form(s) 5471 and Form 8992)			
18 Gross-up for foreign taxes deemed paid			
19 IC-DISC and former DISC dividends not included on line 1, 2, or 3			
20 Other dividends			
21 Deduction for dividends paid on certain preferred stock of public utilities			
22 Section 250 deduction (attach Form 8993)			
23 **Total dividends and inclusions.** Add column (a), lines 9 through 20. Enter here and on page 1, line 4			
24 **Total special deductions.** Add column (c) lines 9 through 22. Enter here and on page 1, line 29b			

Form **1120** (2022)

CPCA0212 10/04/22

Form 1120 (2022) LEDGER & POST, AN ACCOUNTANCY CORP. 95-3333333 Page 3

Schedule J **Tax Computation and Payment** (see instructions)

Part I – Tax Computation

1	Check if the corporation is a member of a controlled group (attach Schedule O (Form 1120)). See instructions ☐			
2	Income tax. See instructions		2	1,756.
3	Base erosion minimum tax amount (attach Form 8991)		3	
4	Add lines 2 and 3		4	1,756.
5a	Foreign tax credit (attach Form 1118)	5a		
b	Credit from Form 8834 (see instructions)	5b		
c	General business credit (attach Form 3800)	5c		
d	Credit for prior year minimum tax (attach Form 8827)	5d		
e	Bond credits from Form 8912	5e		
6	**Total credits.** Add lines 5a through 5e		6	
7	Subtract line 6 from line 4		7	1,756.
8	Personal holding company tax (attach Schedule PH (Form 1120))		8	
9a	Recapture of investment credit (attach Form 4255)	9a		
b	Recapture of low-income housing credit (attach Form 8611)	9b		
c	Interest due under the look-back method – completed long-term contracts (attach Form 8697)	9c		
d	Interest due under the look-back method – income forecast method (attach Form 8866)	9d		
e	Alternative tax on qualifying shipping activities (attach Form 8902)	9e		
f	Interest/tax due under section 453A(c) and/or section 453(l)	9f		
g	Other (see instructions – attach statement)	9g		
10	**Total.** Add lines 9a through 9g		10	
11	**Total tax.** Add lines 7, 8, and 10. Enter here and on page 1, line 31		11	1,756.

Part II – Reserved for Future Use

12	Reserved for future use		12	

Part III – Payments and Refundable Credits

13	2021 overpayment credited to 2022		13	
14	2022 estimated tax payments		14	
15	2022 refund applied for on Form 4466		15	( )
16	Combine lines 13, 14, and 15		16	0.
17	Tax deposited with Form 7004		17	
18	Withholding (see instructions)		18	
19	**Total payments.** Add lines 16, 17, and 18		19	0.
20	Refundable credits from:			
a	Form 2439	20a		
b	Form 4136	20b		
c	Reserved for future use	20c		
d	Other (attach statement – see instructions)	20d		
21	**Total credits.** Add lines 20a through 20d		21	
22	Reserved for future use		22	
23	**Total payments and credits.** Add lines 19 and 21. Enter here and on page 1, line 33		23	0.

Form **1120** (2022)

CPCA0234 10/05/22

Form 1120 (2022) LEDGER & POST, AN ACCOUNTANCY CORP. 95-3333333 Page 4

Schedule K **Other Information** (see instructions)

		Yes	No
1	Check accounting method: **a** [X] Cash **b** [ ] Accrual **c** [ ] Other (specify)		
2	See the instructions and enter the:		
	a Business activity code no. 541211		
	b Business activity SERVICE		
	c Product or service ACCOUNTING		
3	Is the corporation a subsidiary in an affiliated group or a parent-subsidiary controlled group? If "Yes," enter name and EIN of the parent corporation		X
4	At the end of the tax year:		
	a Did any foreign or domestic corporation, partnership (including any entity treated as a partnership), trust, or tax-exempt organization own directly 20% or more, or own, directly or indirectly, 50% or more of the total voting power of all classes of the corporation's stock entitled to vote? If "Yes," complete Part I of Schedule G (Form 1120) (attach Schedule G)		X
	b Did any individual or estate own directly 20% or more, or own, directly or indirectly, 50% or more of the total voting power of all classes of the corporation's stock entitled to vote? If "Yes," complete Part II of Schedule G (Form 1120) (attach Schedule G)	X	
5	At the end of the tax year, did the corporation:		
	a Own directly 20% or more, or own, directly or indirectly, 50% or more of the total voting power of all classes of stock entitled to vote of any foreign or domestic corporation not included on **Form 851,** Affiliations Schedule? For rules of constructive ownership, see instructions. If "Yes," complete (i) through (iv) below.		X

(i) Name of Corporation	**(ii)** Employer Identification Number (if any)	**(iii)** Country of Incorporation	**(iv)** Percentage Owned in Voting Stock

		Yes	No
	b Own directly an interest of 20% or more, or own, directly or indirectly, an interest of 50% or more in any foreign or domestic partnership (including an entity treated as a partnership) or in the beneficial interest of a trust? For rules of constructive ownership, see instructions. If "Yes," complete (i) through (iv) below.		X

(i) Name of Entity	**(ii)** Employer Identification Number (if any)	**(iii)** Country of Organization	**(iv)** Maximum Percentage Owned in Profit, Loss, or Capital

		Yes	No
6	During this tax year, did the corporation pay dividends (other than stock dividends and distributions in exchange for stock) in excess of the corporation's current and accumulated earnings and profits? See sections 301 and 316. If "Yes," file **Form 5452**, Corporate Report of Nondividend Distributions. See the instructions for Form 5452. If this is a consolidated return, answer here for the parent corporation and on Form 851 for each subsidiary.		X
7	At any time during the tax year, did one foreign person own, directly or indirectly, at least 25% of the total voting power of all classes of the corporation's stock entitled to vote or at least 25% of the total value of all classes of the corporation's stock? For rules of attribution, see section 318. If "Yes," enter: **(a)** Percentage owned ______ and **(b)** Owner's country ______ **(c)** The corporation may have to file **Form 5472,** Information Return of a 25% Foreign-Owned U.S. Corporation or a Foreign Corporation Engaged in a U.S. Trade or Business. Enter the number of Forms 5472 attached ______		X
8	Check this box if the corporation issued publicly offered debt instruments with original issue discount [ ] If checked, the corporation may have to file **Form 8281**, Information Return for Publicly Offered Original Issue Discount Instruments.		
9	Enter the amount of tax-exempt interest received or accrued during the tax year $ NONE		
10	Enter the number of shareholders at the end of the tax year (if 100 or fewer) 2		
11	If the corporation has an NOL for the tax year and is electing to forego the carryback period, check here (see instructions) [ ] If the corporation is filing a consolidated return, the statement required by Regulations section 1.1502-21(b)(3) must be attached or the election will not be valid.		
12	Enter the available NOL carryover from prior tax years (do not reduce it by any deduction reported on page 1, line 29a.) $ NONE		

Form **1120** (2022)

CPCA0234 10/05/22

Form 1120 (2022) LEDGER & POST, AN ACCOUNTANCY CORP. 95-3333333 Page **5**

Schedule K **Other Information** *(continued from page 4)*

		Yes	No
13	Are the corporation's total receipts (page 1, line 1a, plus lines 4 through 10) for the tax year **and** its total assets at the end of the tax year less than $250,000?		X
	If "Yes," the corporation is not required to complete Schedules L, M-1, and M-2. Instead, enter the total amount of cash distributions and the book value of property distributions (other than cash) made during the tax year $		
14	Is the corporation required to file Schedule UTP (Form 1120), Uncertain Tax Position Statement? See instructions.		X
	If "Yes," complete and attach Schedule UTP.		
15a	Did the corporation make any payments in 2022 that would require it to file Form(s) 1099?		X
b	If "Yes," did or will the corporation file required Form(s) 1099?		
16	During this tax year, did the corporation have an 80%-or-more change in ownership, including a change due to redemption of its own stock?		X
17	During or subsequent to this tax year, but before the filing of this return, did the corporation dispose of more than 65% (by value) of its assets in a taxable, non-taxable, or tax deferred transaction?		X
18	Did the corporation receive assets in a section 351 transfer in which any of the transferred assets had a fair market basis or fair market value of more than $1 million?		X
19	During the corporation's tax year, did the corporation make any payments that would require it to file Forms 1042 and 1042-S under chapter 3 (sections 1441 through 1464) or chapter 4 (sections 1471 through 1474) of the Code?		X
20	Is the corporation operating on a cooperative basis?		X
21	During the tax year, did the corporation pay or accrue any interest or royalty for which the deduction is not allowed under section 267A? See instructions		X
	If "Yes," enter the total amount of the disallowed deductions $		
22	Does the corporation have gross receipts of at least $500 million in any of the 3 preceding tax years? (See sections 59A(e)(2) and (3))		X
	If "Yes," complete and attach Form 8991.		
23	Did the corporation have an election under section 163(j) for any real property trade or business or any farming business in effect during the tax year? See instructions		X
24	Does the corporation satisfy one or more of the following? See instructions		X
a	The corporation owns a pass-through entity with current, or prior year carryover, excess business interest expense.		
b	The corporation's aggregate average annual gross receipts (determined under section 448(c)) for the 3 tax years preceding the current tax year are more than $27 million and the corporation has business interest expense.		
c	The corporation is a tax shelter and the corporation has business interest expense.		
	If "Yes," complete and attach Form 8990.		
25	Is the corporation attaching Form 8996 to certify as a Qualified Opportunity Fund?		X
	If "Yes," enter amount from Form 8996, line 15 $		
26	Since December 22, 2017, did a foreign corporation directly or indirectly acquire substantially all of the properties held directly or indirectly by the corporation, and was the ownership percentage (by vote or value) for purposes of section 7874 greater than 50% (for example, the shareholders held more than 50% of the stock of the foreign corporation)? If "Yes," list the ownership percentage by vote and by value. See instructions		X
	Percentage: By Vote Percentage: By Value		

Form **1120** (2022)

CPCA0234 10/05/22

Form 1120 (2022) LEDGER & POST, AN ACCOUNTANCY CORP. 95-3333333 Page 6

Schedule L Balance Sheets per Books

Assets	Beginning of tax year (a)	Beginning of tax year (b)	End of tax year (c)	End of tax year (d)
1 Cash		272,835.		280,804.
2a Trade notes and accounts receivable				
b Less allowance for bad debts	( )		( )	
3 Inventories				
4 U.S. government obligations				
5 Tax-exempt securities (see instructions)				
6 Other current assets (attach statement)				
7 Loans to shareholders				
8 Mortgage and real estate loans				
9 Other investments (attach statement)				
10a Buildings and other depreciable assets	9,000.		21,500.	
b Less accumulated depreciation	(4,931.)	4,069.	(18,750.)	2,750.
11a Depletable assets				
b Less accumulated depletion	( )		( )	
12 Land (net of any amortization)				
13a Intangible assets (amortizable only)				
b Less accumulated amortization	( )		( )	
14 Other assets (attach statement)				
15 Total assets		276,904.		283,554.
Liabilities and Shareholders' Equity				
16 Accounts payable				
17 Mortgages, notes, bonds payable in less than 1 year				
18 Other current liabilities (attach stmt)				
19 Loans from shareholders				
20 Mortgages, notes, bonds payable in 1 year or more				
21 Other liabilities (attach statement)				
22 Capital stock: a Preferred stock				
b Common stock	1,000.	1,000.	1,000.	1,000.
23 Additional paid-in capital				
24 Retained earnings — Approp (att stmt)				
25 Retained earnings — Unappropriated		275,904.		282,554.
26 Adjmt to shareholders' equity (att stmt)				
27 Less cost of treasury stock		( )		( )
28 Total liabilities and shareholders' equity		276,904.		283,554.

Schedule M-1 **Reconciliation of Income (Loss) per Books With Income per Return**

Note: The corporation may be required to file Schedule M-3. See instructions.

1 Net income (loss) per books	6,650.	7 Income recorded on books this year not included on this return (itemize): Tax-exempt interest $	
2 Federal income tax per books			
3 Excess of capital losses over capital gains			
4 Income subject to tax not recorded on books this year (itemize):		8 Deductions on this return not charged against book income this year (itemize): a Depreciation $ b Charitable contribns $	
5 Expenses recorded on books this year not deducted on this return (itemize): a Depreciation $ b Charitable contributions $ c Travel & entertainment $ 1,710.	1,710.	9 Add lines 7 and 8	0.
6 Add lines 1 through 5	8,360.	10 Income (page 1, line 28) — line 6 less line 9	8,360.

Schedule M-2 **Analysis of Unappropriated Retained Earnings per Books (Schedule L, Line 25)**

1 Balance at beginning of year	275,904.	5 Distributions: a Cash	
2 Net income (loss) per books	6,650.	b Stock	
		c Property	
3 Other increases (itemize):		6 Other decreases (itemize):	
		7 Add lines 5 and 6	
4 Add lines 1, 2, and 3	282,554.	8 Balance at end of year (line 4 less line 7)	282,554.

Form 1120 (2022)

CPCA0234 10/04/22

SCHEDULE G
(Form 1120)
(Rev December 2011)
Department of the Treasury
Internal Revenue Service

Information on Certain Persons Owning the Corporation's Voting Stock

► **Attach to Form 1120.**
► **See instructions.**

OMB No. 1545-0123

Name	Employer identification number (EIN)
LEDGER & POST, AN ACCOUNTANCY CORP.	95-3333333

Part I **Certain Entities Owning the Corporation's Voting Stock.** (Form 1120, Schedule K, Question 4a).
Complete columns (i) through (v) below for any foreign or domestic corporation, partnership (including any entity treated as a partnership), trust, or tax-exempt organization that owns directly 20% or more, or owns, directly or indirectly, 50% or more of the total voting power of all classes of the corporation's stock entitled to vote (see instructions).

(i) Name of Entity	(ii) Employer Identification Number (if any)	(iii) Type of Entity	(iv) Country of Organization	(v) Percentage Owned in Voting Stock

Part II **Certain Individuals and Estates Owning the Corporation's Voting Stock.** (Form 1120, Schedule K, Question 4b).
Complete columns (i) through (iv) below for any individual or estate that owns directly 20% or more, or owns, directly or indirectly, 50% or more of the total voting power of all classes of the corporation's stock entitled to vote (see instructions).

(i) Name of Individual or Estate	(ii) Identifying Number (if any)	(iii) Country of Citizenship (see instructions)	(iv) Percentage Owned in Voting Stock
KENNETH LEDGER	123-45-6789	UNITED STATES	50.00%
JOYCE POST	987-65-4321	UNITED STATES	50.00%

Form **1125-E**
(Rev October 2016)
Department of the Treasury
Internal Revenue Service

Compensation of Officers

► **Attach to Form 1120, 1120-C, 1120-F, 1120-REIT, 1120-RIC, or 1120S.**
► **Information about Form 1125-E and its separate instructions is at *www.irs.gov/form1125e.***

OMB No. 1545-0123

Name: LEDGER & POST, AN ACCOUNTANCY CORP.

Employer identification number: 95-3333333

Note: Complete Form 1125-E only if total receipts are $500,000 or more. See instructions for definition of total receipts.

1 **(a)** Name of officer	**(b)** Social security number	**(c)** Percent of time devoted to business	Percent of stock owned		**(f)** Amount of compensation
			(d) Common	**(e)** Preferred	
KENNETH LEDGER	123-45-6789	100 %	50.00 %	0.00 %	250,000.
JOYCE POST	987-65-4321	100 %	50.00 %	0.00 %	150,000.
		%	%	%	
		%	%	%	
		%	%	%	
		%	%	%	
		%	%	%	
		%	%	%	
		%	%	%	
		%	%	%	
		%	%	%	
		%	%	%	
		%	%	%	
		%	%	%	
		%	%	%	
		%	%	%	
		%	%	%	
		%	%	%	
		%	%	%	
		%	%	%	

2	Total compensation of officers	400,000.
3	Compensation of officers claimed on Form 1125-A or elsewhere on return	
4	Subtract line 3 from line 2. Enter the result here and on Form 1120, page 1, line 12 or the appropriate line of your tax return	586,200.

BAA For Paperwork Reduction Act Notice, see separate instructions. Form **1125-E** (Rev 10-2016)

CPCA2101L 08/18/16

Form **4562** — Department of the Treasury, Internal Revenue Service

Depreciation and Amortization
(Including Information on Listed Property)

Attach to your tax return.

Go to *www.irs.gov/Form4562* for instructions and the latest information.

OMB No. 1545-0172

2022

Attachment Sequence No. **179**

Name(s) shown on return: LEDGER & POST, AN ACCOUNTANCY CORP.

Identifying number: 95-3333333

Business or activity to which this form relates: FORM 1120

Part I Election To Expense Certain Property Under Section 179

Note: If you have any listed property, complete Part V before you complete Part I.

1	Maximum amount (see instructions)	1	1,080,000.
2	Total cost of section 179 property placed in service (see instructions)	2	12,500.
3	Threshold cost of section 179 property before reduction in limitation (see instructions)	3	2,700,000.
4	Reduction in limitation. Subtract line 3 from line 2. If zero or less, enter -0-	4	0.
5	Dollar limitation for tax year. Subtract line 4 from line 1. If zero or less, enter -0-. If married filing separately, see instructions	5	1,080,000.

6	(a) Description of property	(b) Cost (business use only)	(c) Elected cost
	7-YEAR FURNITURE	10,000.	10,000.
	5-YEAR COMPUTER	2,500.	2,500.
7	Listed property. Enter the amount from line 29	7	0.

8	Total elected cost of section 179 property. Add amounts in column (c), lines 6 and 7	8	12,500.
9	Tentative deduction. Enter the **smaller** of line 5 or line 8	9	12,500.
10	Carryover of disallowed deduction from line 13 of your 2021 Form 4562	10	0.
11	Business income limitation. Enter the smaller of business income (not less than zero) or line 5. See instrs	11	20,860.
12	Section 179 expense deduction. Add lines 9 and 10, but don't enter more than line 11	12	12,500.
13	Carryover of disallowed deduction to 2023. Add lines 9 and 10, less line 12	13	0.

Note: Don't use Part II or Part III below for listed property. Instead, use Part V.

Part II Special Depreciation Allowance and Other Depreciation (Don't include listed property. See instructions.)

14	Special depreciation allowance for qualified property (other than listed property) placed in service during the tax year. See instructions	14	
15	Property subject to section 168(f)(1) election	15	
16	Other depreciation (including ACRS)	16	

Part III MACRS Depreciation (Don't include listed property. See instructions.)

Section A

17	MACRS deductions for assets placed in service in tax years beginning before 2022	17	1,319.
18	If you are electing to group any assets placed in service during the tax year into one or more general asset accounts, check here ☐		

Section B – Assets Placed in Service During 2022 Tax Year Using the General Depreciation System

(a) Classification of property	(b) Month and year placed in service	(c) Basis for depreciation (business/investment use only – see instructions)	(d) Recovery period	(e) Convention	(f) Method	(g) Depreciation deduction
19a 3-year property						
b 5-year property						
c 7-year property						
d 10-year property						
e 15-year property						
f 20-year property						
g 25-year property			25 yrs		S/L	
h Residential rental			27.5 yrs	MM	S/L	
property			27.5 yrs	MM	S/L	
i Nonresidential real			39 yrs	MM	S/L	
property				MM	S/L	

Section C – Assets Placed in Service During 2022 Tax Year Using the Alternative Depreciation System

(a) Classification of property	(b)	(c)	(d)	(e)	(f)	(g)
20a Class life					S/L	
b 12-year			12 yrs		S/L	
c 30-year			30 yrs	MM	S/L	
d 40-year			40 yrs	MM	S/L	

Part IV Summary (See instructions.)

21	Listed property. Enter amount from line 28	21	
22	**Total.** Add amounts from line 12, lines 14 through 17, lines 19 and 20 in column (g), and line 21. Enter here and on the appropriate lines of your return. Partnerships and S corporations – see instructions	22	13,819.
23	For assets shown above and placed in service during the current year, enter the portion of the basis attributable to section 263A costs	23	

2022	**FEDERAL STATEMENTS**	**PAGE 1**
CLIENT LEDGERPA	**LEDGER & POST, AN ACCOUNTANCY CORP.**	**95-3333333**
1/24/23		08:43AM

STATEMENT 1
FORM 1120, LINE 26
OTHER DEDUCTIONS

AUTO AND TRUCK	$	24,947.
DUES AND SUBSCRIPTIONS		30,052.
GIFTS		385.
INSURANCE		13,681.
MEALS		1,710.
MISCELLANEOUS		656.
OFFICE EXPENSE		44,674.
OUTSIDE SERVICE		18,286.
PARKING AND TOLLS		17,235.
POSTAGE		4,735.
PROFFESIONAL FEES		12,296.
RESEARCH		28,506.
TELEPHONE		28,970.
TOTAL	$	226,133.

12/31/22 **2022 FEDERAL DEPRECIATION SCHEDULE** **PAGE 1**

CLIENT STRAIGHT **STRAIGHT EDGE, INC.** **95-4145770**

1/26/23 03:05PM

NO.	DESCRIPTION	DATE ACQUIRED	DATE SOLD	COST/ BASIS	BUS. PCT.	CUR 179 BONUS	SPECIAL DEPR. ALLOW.	PRIOR 179/ BONUS/ SP. DEPR.	PRIOR DEC. BAL DEPR.	SALVAG /BASIS REDUCT	DEPR. BASIS	PRIOR DEPR.	METHOD	LIFE	RATE	CURRENT DEPR.
	FORM 1120S															
	AUTO / TRANSPORT EQUIPMENT															
1	TRUCK **	10/25/19		40,000							40,000	28,480	200DB HY	5	.11520	4,608
	TOTAL AUTO / TRANSPORT EQUIP			40,000		0	0	0	0	0	40,000	28,480				4,608
	MACHINERY AND EQUIPMENT															
2	OFFICE EQUIPMENT **	2/05/18		5,277							5,277	3,628	200DB HY	7	.08930	471
3	COMPUTER **	11/06/19		1,500							1,500	1,068	200DB HY	5	.11520	173
4	OFFICE EQUIPMENT **	2/02/22		3,500		3,500					0		200DB HY	5		0
	TOTAL MACHINERY AND EQUIPME			10,277		3,500	0	0	0	0	6,777	4,696				644
	TOTAL DEPRECIATION			50,277		3,500	0	0	0	0	46,777	33,176				5,252
	GRAND TOTAL DEPRECIATION			50,277		3,500	0	0	0	0	46,777	33,176				5,252

**ASSET INCLUDED IN UNADJUSTED BASIS IMMEDIATELY AFTER ACQUISITION FOR THE QBI CALCULATION.

Form **1120-S**

Department of the Treasury
Internal Revenue Service

U.S. Income Tax Return for an S Corporation

Do not file this form unless the corporation has filed or is attaching Form 2553 to elect to be an S corporation.
Go to *www.irs.gov/Form1120S* for instructions and the latest information.

OMB No. 1545-0123

2022

For calendar year 2022 or tax year beginning , 2022, ending ,

A S election effective date: 1/01/2001	TYPE OR PRINT: STRAIGHT EDGE, INC. 3855 TAMPA AVE. TARZANA, CA 91356	**D** Employer identification number: 95-4145770
B Business activity code number (see instructions): 423800		**E** Date incorporated: 1/01/2001
C Check if Schedule M-3 attached ☐		**F** Total assets (see instructions): $ 768,254.

G Is the corporation electing to be an S corporation beginning with this tax year? See instructions. ☐ Yes ☒ No

H Check if: **(1)** ☐ Final return **(2)** ☐ Name change **(3)** ☐ Address change **(4)** ☐ Amended return **(5)** ☐ S election termination

I Enter the number of shareholders who were shareholders during any part of the tax year ... 1

J Check if corporation: **(1)** ☐ Aggregated activities for section 465 at-risk purposes **(2)** ☐ Grouped activities for section 469 passive activity purposes

Caution: Include **only** trade or business income and expenses on lines 1a through 21. See the instructions for more information.

INCOME	1a	Gross receipts or sales	1a	943,098.		
	b	Returns and allowances	1b			
	c	Balance. Subtract line 1b from line 1a			1c	943,098.
	2	Cost of goods sold (attach Form 1125-A)			2	574,081.
	3	Gross profit. Subtract line 2 from line 1c			3	369,017.
	4	Net gain (loss) from Form 4797, line 17 (attach Form 4797)			4	
	5	Other income (loss) (see instrs — att statement)			5	
	6	**Total income (loss).** Add lines 3 through 5			6	369,017.
DEDUCTIONS (SEE INSTRS)	7	Compensation of officers (see instructions – attach Form 1125-E)			7	50,000.
	8	Salaries and wages (less employment credits)			8	28,020.
	9	Repairs and maintenance			9	5,668.
	10	Bad debts			10	
	11	Rents			11	60,000.
	12	Taxes and licenses			12	11,202.
	13	Interest (see instructions)			13	
	14	Depreciation from Form 4562 not claimed on Form 1125-A or elsewhere on return (attach Form 4562)			14	5,252.
	15	Depletion **(Do not deduct oil and gas depletion.)**			15	
	16	Advertising			16	
	17	Pension, profit-sharing, etc., plans			17	
	18	Employee benefit programs			18	
	19	Other deductions (attach statement) SEE STATEMENT 1			19	135,800.
	20	**Total deductions.** Add lines 7 through 19			20	295,942.
	21	**Ordinary business income (loss).** Subtract line 20 from line 6			21	73,075.
TAX AND PAYMENTS	22a	Excess net passive income or LIFO recapture tax (see instructions)	22a			
	b	Tax from Schedule D (Form 1120-S)	22b			
	c	Add lines 22a and 22b (see instructions for additional taxes)			22c	
	23a	2022 estimated tax payments and 2021 overpayment credited to 2022	23a			
	b	Tax deposited with Form 7004	23b			
	c	Credit for federal tax paid on fuels (attach Form 4136)	23c			
	d	Add lines 23a through 23c			23d	
	24	Estimated tax penalty (see instructions). Check if Form 2220 is attached ☐			24	
	25	**Amount owed.** If line 23d is smaller than the total of lines 22c and 24, enter amount owed			25	0.
	26	**Overpayment.** If line 23d is larger than the total of lines 22c and 24, enter amount overpaid			26	
	27	Enter amount from line 26: **Credited to 2023 estimated tax** **Refunded**			27	

Sign Here

Under penalties of perjury, I declare that I have examined this return, including accompanying schedules and statements, and to the best of my knowledge and belief, it is true, correct, and complete. Declaration of preparer (other than taxpayer) is based on all information of which preparer has any knowledge.

Signature of officer | Date | Title: PRESIDENT

May the IRS discuss this return with the preparer shown below? See instructions. ☒ **Yes** ☐ **No**

Paid Preparer Use Only

Print/Type preparer's name	Preparer's signature	Date	Check ☒ if self-employed	PTIN
RON E. THOMPSON	RON E. THOMPSON	1/26/23	☒	P00166602

Firm's name: WHITE ZUCKERMAN WARSAVSKY LUNA HUNT LLP — Firm's EIN: 95-4115549

Firm's address: 15490 VENTURA BLVD 3RD FL, SHERMAN OAKS, CA 91403 — Phone no. (818) 981-4226

Form 1120-S (2022) STRAIGHT EDGE, INC. 95-4145770 Page **2**

Schedule B **Other Information** (see instructions)

		Yes	No
1	Check accounting method: **a** ☐ Cash **b** ☒ Accrual **c** ☐ Other (specify)		
2	See the instructions and enter the: **a** Business activity DISTRIBUTION **b** Product or service MACHINE TOOLS		
3	At any time during the tax year, was any shareholder of the corporation a disregarded entity, a trust, an estate, or a nominee or similar person? If "Yes," attach Schedule B-1, Information on Certain Shareholders of an S Corporation		X
4	At the end of the tax year, did the corporation: **a** Own directly 20% or more, or own, directly or indirectly, 50% or more of the total stock issued and outstanding of any foreign or domestic corporation? For rules of constructive ownership, see instructions. If "Yes," complete (i) through (v) below		X

(i) Name of Corporation	**(ii)** Employer Identification Number (if any)	**(iii)** Country of Incorporation	**(iv)** Percentage of Stock Owned	**(v)** If Percentage in (iv) is 100%, Enter the Date (if applicable) a Qualified Subchapter S Subsidiary Election Was Made

		Yes	No
b	Own directly an interest of 20% or more, or own, directly or indirectly, an interest of 50% or more in the profit, loss, or capital in any foreign or domestic partnership (including an entity treated as a partnership) or in the beneficial interest of a trust? For rules of constructive ownership, see instructions. If "Yes," complete (i) through (v) below		X

(i) Name of Entity	**(ii)** Employer Identification Number (if any)	**(iii)** Type of Entity	**(iv)** Country of Organization	**(v)** Maximum % Owned in Profit, Loss, or Capital

		Yes	No
5a	At the end of the tax year, did the corporation have any outstanding shares of restricted stock?		X
	If "Yes," complete lines (i) and (ii) below. **(i)** Total shares of restricted stock ______ **(ii)** Total shares of non-restricted stock ______		
b	At the end of the tax year, did the corporation have any outstanding stock options, warrants, or similar instruments?		X
	If "Yes," complete lines (i) and (ii) below. **(i)** Total shares of stock outstanding at the end of the tax year ______ **(ii)** Total shares of stock outstanding if all instruments were executed ______		
6	Has this corporation filed, or is it required to file, **Form 8918,** Material Advisor Disclosure Statement, to provide information on any reportable transaction?		X
7	Check this box if the corporation issued publicly offered debt instruments with original issue discount ☐ If checked, the corporation may have to file **Form 8281,** Information Return for Publicly Offered Original Issue Discount Instruments.		
8	If the corporation **(a)** was a C corporation before it elected to be an S corporation **or** the corporation acquired an asset with a basis determined by reference to the basis of the asset (or the basis of any other property) in the hands of a C corporation, **and (b)** has net unrealized built-in gain in excess of the net recognized built-in gain from prior years, enter the net unrealized built-in gain reduced by net recognized built-in gain from prior years. See instructions $______		
9	Did the corporation have an election under section 163(j) for any real property trade or business or any farming business in effect during the tax year? See instructions		X
10	Does the corporation satisfy one or more of the following? See instructions		X
	a The corporation owns a pass-through entity with current, or prior year carryover, excess business interest expense. **b** The corporation's aggregate average annual gross receipts (determined under section 448(c)) for the 3 tax years preceding the current tax year are more than $27 million and the corporation has business interest expense. **c** The corporation is a tax shelter and the corporation has business interest expense. If "Yes," complete and attach **Form 8990,** Limitation on Business Interest Expense Under Section 163(j).		
11	Does the corporation satisfy **both** of the following conditions?		X
	a The corporation's total receipts (see instructions) for the tax year were less than $250,000. **b** The corporation's total assets at the end of the tax year were less than $250,000. If "Yes," the corporation is not required to complete Schedules L and M-1.		

SPSA0112 09/14/22 Form **1120-S** (2022)

Form 1120-S (2022) STRAIGHT EDGE, INC. 95-4145770 Page **3**

Schedule B **Other Information** (see instructions) *(continued)*

		Yes	No
12	During the tax year, did the corporation have any non-shareholder debt that was canceled, was forgiven, or had the terms modified so as to reduce the principal amount of the debt?		X
	If "Yes," enter the amount of principal reduction . . . $		
13	During the tax year, was a qualified subchapter S subsidiary election terminated or revoked? If "Yes," see instructions		X
14a	Did the corporation make any payments in 2022 that would require it to file Form(s) 1099?		X
b	If "Yes," did or will the corporation file required Form(s) 1099?		
15	Is the corporation attaching Form 8996 to certify as a Qualified Opportunity Fund?		X
	If "Yes," enter the amount from Form 8996, line 15 . . . $		

Schedule K **Shareholders' Pro Rata Share Items**

					Total amount
Income (Loss)	1	Ordinary business income (loss) (page 1, line 21)		1	73,075.
	2	Net rental real estate income (loss) (attach Form 8825)		2	
	3a	Other gross rental income (loss)	3a		
	b	Expenses from other rental activities (attach statement)	3b		
	c	Other net rental income (loss). Subtract line 3b from line 3a		3c	
	4	Interest income		4	6,716.
	5	Dividends: a Ordinary dividends		5a	
		b Qualified dividends	5b		
	6	Royalties		6	
	7	Net short-term capital gain (loss) (attach Schedule D (Form 1120-S))		7	
	8a	Net long-term capital gain (loss) (attach Schedule D (Form 1120-S))		8a	1,400.
	b	Collectibles (28%) gain (loss)	8b		
	c	Unrecaptured section 1250 gain (attach statement)	8c		
	9	Net section 1231 gain (loss) (attach Form 4797)		9	
	10	Other income (loss) (see instructions) Type:		10	
Deductions	11	Section 179 deduction (attach Form 4562)		11	3,500.
	12a	Charitable contributions		12a	
	b	Investment interest expense		12b	
	c	Section 59(e)(2) expenditures Type:		12c	
	d	Other deductions (see instructions) Type:		12d	
Credits	13a	Low-income housing credit (section 42(j)(5))		13a	
	b	Low-income housing credit (other)		13b	
	c	Qualified rehabilitation expenditures (rental real estate) (attach Form 3468, if applicable)		13c	
	d	Other rental real estate credits (see instrs) Type:		13d	
	e	Other rental credits (see instructions) Type:		13e	
	f	Biofuel producer credit (attach Form 6478)		13f	
	g	Other credits (see instructions) Type:		13g	
International	14	Attach Schedule K-2 (Form 1120-S), Shareholders' Pro Rata Share Items—International, and check this box to indicate you are reporting items of international tax relevance ☐			
Alternative Minimum Tax (AMT) Items	15a	Post-1986 depreciation adjustment		15a	-2,308.
	b	Adjusted gain or loss		15b	
	c	Depletion (other than oil and gas)		15c	
	d	Oil, gas, and geothermal properties – gross income		15d	
	e	Oil, gas, and geothermal properties – deductions		15e	
	f	Other AMT items (attach statement)		15f	
Items Affecting Shareholder Basis	16a	Tax-exempt interest income		16a	
	b	Other tax-exempt income		16b	
	c	Nondeductible expenses		16c	1,099.
	d	Distributions (attach stmt if required) (see instrs)		16d	100,000.
	e	Repayment of loans from shareholders		16e	
	f	Foreign taxes paid or accrued		16f	

BAA SPSA0134 09/14/22 Form **1120-S** (2022)

Form 1120-S (2022) STRAIGHT EDGE, INC. 95-4145770 Page **4**

Schedule K	**Shareholders' Pro Rata Share Items** *(continued)*		**Total amount**
Other Information	**17a** Investment income	**17a**	6,716.
	b Investment expenses	**17b**	
	c Dividend distributions paid from accumulated earnings and profits	**17c**	
	d Other items and amounts (attach statement) SEE STATEMENT 2		
Reconciliation	**18** **Income (loss) reconciliation.** Combine the amounts on lines 1 through 10 in the far right column. From the result, subtract the sum of the amounts on lines 11 through 12d and 16f	**18**	77,691.

Schedule L Balance Sheets per Books	Beginning of tax year		End of tax year	
Assets	**(a)**	**(b)**	**(c)**	**(d)**
1 Cash		67,939.		49,210.
2a Trade notes and accounts receivable	80,573.		91,222.	
b Less allowance for bad debts	( )	80,573.	( )	91,222.
3 Inventories		612,171.		600,523.
4 U.S. government obligations				
5 Tax-exempt securities (see instructions)				
6 Other current assets (attach stmt) SEE ST 3		9,200.		9,200.
7 Loans to shareholders				
8 Mortgage and real estate loans				
9 Other investments (attach statement) SEE ST 4		10,500.		9,750.
10a Buildings and other depreciable assets	46,777.		50,277.	
b Less accumulated depreciation	(33,176.)	13,601.	(41,928.)	8,349.
11a Depletable assets				
b Less accumulated depletion	( )		( )	
12 Land (net of any amortization)				
13a Intangible assets (amortizable only)				
b Less accumulated amortization	( )		( )	
14 Other assets (attach stmt)				
15 Total assets		793,984.		768,254.
Liabilities and Shareholders' Equity				
16 Accounts payable		86,230.		84,900.
17 Mortgages, notes, bonds payable in less than 1 year				
18 Other current liabilities (attach stmt)				
19 Loans from shareholders		586,463.		585,471.
20 Mortgages, notes, bonds payable in 1 year or more				
21 Other liabilities (attach statement) SEE ST 5		2,000.		2,000.
22 Capital stock		15,000.		15,000.
23 Additional paid-in capital				
24 Retained earnings		104,291.		80,883.
25 Adjustments to shareholders' equity (att stmt)				
26 Less cost of treasury stock		( )		( )
27 Total liabilities and shareholders' equity		793,984.		768,254.

SPSA0134 09/14/22 Form **1120-S** (2022)

Form 1120-S (2022) STRAIGHT EDGE, INC. 95-4145770 Page 5

Schedule M-1 Reconciliation of Income (Loss) per Books With Income (Loss) per Return

Note: The corporation may be required to file Schedule M-3. See instructions.

1 Net income (loss) per books	76,592.	5 Income recorded on books this year not included on Schedule K, lines 1 through 10 (itemize): a Tax-exempt interest $	
2 Income included on Schedule K, lines 1, 2, 3c, 4, 5a, 6, 7, 8a, 9, and 10, not recorded on books this year (itemize):			
3 Expenses recorded on books this year not included on Schedule K, lines 1 through 12 and 16f (itemize): a Depreciation $ b Travel and entertainment $ 1,099.	1,099.	6 Deductions included on Schedule K, lines 1 through 12, and 16f, not charged against book income this year (itemize): a Depreciation $	
		7 Add lines 5 and 6	0.
4 Add lines 1 through 3	77,691.	8 Income (loss) (Schedule K, line 18). Subtract line 7 from line 4	77,691.

Schedule M-2 Analysis of Accumulated Adjustments Account, Shareholders' Undistributed Taxable Income Previously Taxed, Accumulated Earnings and Profits, and Other Adjustments Account (see instructions)

	(a) Accumulated adjustments account	(b) Shareholders' undistributed taxable income previously taxed	(c) Accumulated earnings and profits	(d) Other adjustments account
1 Balance at beginning of tax year	104,291.			
2 Ordinary income from page 1, line 21	73,075.			
3 Other additions SEE STATEMENT 6	8,116.			
4 Loss from page 1, line 21	( )			
5 Other reductions SEE STATEMENT 7	(4,599.)			( )
6 Combine lines 1 through 5	180,883.			
7 Distributions	100,000.			
8 Balance at end of tax year. Subtract line 7 from line 6	80,883.			

SPSA0134 09/14/22 Form **1120-S** (2022)

SCHEDULE D (Form 1120-S)

Department of the Treasury Internal Revenue Service

Capital Gains and Losses and Built-in Gains

Attach to Form 1120-S.
Use Form 8949 to list your transactions for lines 1b, 2, 3, 8b, 9, and 10.
Go to *www.irs.gov/Form1120S* for instructions and the latest information.

OMB No. 1545-0123

2022

Name	Employer identification number
STRAIGHT EDGE, INC.	95-4145770

Did the corporation dispose of any investment(s) in a qualified opportunity fund during the tax year? ☐ **Yes** ☒ **No**
If "Yes," attach Form 8949 and see its instructions for additional requirements for reporting your gain or loss.

Part I Short-Term Capital Gains and Losses – Generally Assets Held One Year or Less (see instructions)

See instructions for how to figure the amounts to enter on the lines below. This form may be easier to complete if you round off the cents to whole dollars.	(d) Proceeds (sales price)	(e) Cost (or other basis)	(g) Adjustments to gain or loss from Form(s) 8949, Part I, line 2, column (g)	(h) Gain or (loss) Subtract column (e) from column (d) and combine the result with column (g)
1a Totals for all short-term transactions reported on Form 1099-B for which basis was reported to the IRS and for which you have no adjustments (see instructions). However, if you choose to report all these transactions on Form 8949, leave this line blank and go to line 1b				
1b Totals for all transactions reported on Form(s) 8949 with **Box A** checked				
2 Totals for all transactions reported on Form(s) 8949 with **Box B** checked				
3 Totals for all transactions reported on Form(s) 8949 with **Box C** checked				

4 Short-term capital gain from installment sales from Form 6252, line 26 or 37	4	
5 Short-term capital gain or (loss) from like-kind exchanges from Form 8824	5	
6 Tax on short-term capital gain included on line 23 below	6	( )
7 **Net short-term capital gain or (loss).** Combine lines 1a through 6 in column (h). Enter here and on Form 1120-S, Schedule K, line 7 or 10	7	

Part II Long-Term Capital Gains and Losses – Generally Assets Held More Than One Year (see instructions)

See instructions for how to figure the amounts to enter on the lines below. This form may be easier to complete if you round off the cents to whole dollars.	(d) Proceeds (sales price)	(e) Cost (or other basis)	(g) Adjustments to gain or loss from Form(s) 8949, Part II, line 2, column (g)	(h) Gain or (loss) Subtract column (e) from column (d) and combine the result with column (g)
8a Totals for all long-term transactions reported on Form 1099-B for which basis was reported to the IRS and for which you have no adjustments (see instructions). However, if you choose to report all these transactions on Form 8949, leave this line blank and go to line 8b	6,200.	4,800.		1,400.
8b Totals for all transactions reported on Form(s) 8949 with **Box D** checked				
9 Totals for all transactions reported on Form(s) 8949 with **Box E** checked				
10 Totals for all transactions reported on Form(s) 8949 with **Box F** checked				

11 Long-term capital gain from installment sales from Form 6252, line 26 or 37	11	
12 Long-term capital gain or (loss) from like-kind exchanges from Form 8824	12	
13 Capital gain distributions (see instructions)	13	
14 Tax on long-term capital gain included on line 23 below	14	( )
15 **Net long-term capital gain or (loss).** Combine lines 8a through 14 in column (h). Enter here and on Form 1120-S, Schedule K, line 8a or 10	15	1,400.

BAA For Paperwork Reduction Act Notice, see the Instructions for Form 1120-S. **Schedule D (Form 1120-S) 2022**

SPSA0301L 09/27/22

Schedule D (Form 1120-S) 2022 STRAIGHT EDGE, INC. 95-4145770 Page **2**

Part III **Built-in Gains Tax** (See instructions **before** completing this part.)

16	Excess of recognized built-in gains over recognized built-in losses (attach computation statement)	**16**	
17	Taxable income (attach computation statement)	**17**	
18	Net recognized built-in gain. Enter the smallest of line 16, line 17, or line 8 of Schedule B	**18**	
19	Section 1374(b)(2) deduction	**19**	
20	Subtract line 19 from line 18. If zero or less, enter -0- here and on line 23	**20**	
21	Enter 21% (0.21) of line 20	**21**	
22	Section 1374(b)(3) business credit and minimum tax credit carryforwards from C corporation years	**22**	
23	**Tax.** Subtract line 22 from line 21 (if zero or less, enter -0-). Enter here and on Form 1120-S, page 1, line 22b	**23**	

Schedule D (Form 1120-S) 2022

Form **1125-A** (Rev. November 2018) Department of the Treasury Internal Revenue Service

Cost of Goods Sold

► Attach to Form 1120, 1120-C, 1120-F, 1120S, or 1065.
► Go to *www.irs.gov/Form1125A* for the latest information.

OMB No. 1545-0123

Name	Employer identification number
STRAIGHT EDGE, INC.	95-4145770

1	Inventory at beginning of year	1	612,171.
2	Purchases	2	520,241.
3	Cost of labor	3	
4	Additional section 263A costs (attach schedule)	4	
5	Other costs (attach schedule) SEE STATEMENT 8	5	42,192.
6	**Total.** Add lines 1 through 5	6	1,174,604.
7	Inventory at end of year	7	600,523.
8	**Cost of goods sold.** Subtract line 7 from line 6. Enter here and on Form 1120, page 1, line 2 or the appropriate line of your tax return. See instructions	8	574,081.

9a Check all methods used for valuing closing inventory:

(i) ☐ Cost

(ii) ☒ Lower of cost or market

(iii) ☐ Other (Specify method used and attach explanation.) ► ____________

b Check if there was a writedown of subnormal goods ► ☐

c Check if the LIFO inventory method was adopted this tax year for any goods (if checked, attach Form 970) ► ☐

d If the LIFO inventory method was used for this tax year, enter amount of closing inventory computed under LIFO **9d**

e If property is produced or acquired for resale, do the rules of section 263A apply to the entity? See instructions ☐ Yes ☒ No

f Was there any change in determining quantities, cost, or valuations between opening and closing inventory? If "Yes," attach explanation ☐ Yes ☒ No

BAA For Paperwork Reduction Act Notice, see instructions. Form **1125-A** (Rev. 11-2018)

CPCZ0401L 09/26/18

671121

Schedule K-1 (Form 1120-S) **2022**

Department of the Treasury
Internal Revenue Service

For calendar year 2022, or tax year

beginning / / ending / /

☐ Final K-1 ☐ Amended K-1 OMB No. 1545-0123

Shareholder's Share of Income, Deductions, Credits, etc.

See separate instructions.

Part I Information About the Corporation

A Corporation's employer identification number

95-4145770

B Corporation's name, address, city, state, and ZIP code

STRAIGHT EDGE, INC.
3855 TAMPA AVE.
TARZANA, CA 91356

C IRS Center where corporation filed return

E-FILE

D Corporation's total number of shares

Beginning of tax year 0

End of tax year..................... 0

Part II Information About the Shareholder

E Shareholder's identifying number

123-45-6789

F Shareholder's name, address, city, state, and ZIP code

MATTHEW T. COLLINS
4865 TROY ST.
LOS ANGELES, CA 90001

G Current year allocation percentage .... 100 %

H Shareholder's number of shares

Beginning of tax year 0

End of tax year..................... 0

I Loans from shareholder

Beginning of tax year .... $ 586,463.

End of tax year................... $ 587,621.

FOR IRS USE ONLY

Part III Shareholder's Share of Current Year Income, Deductions, Credits, and Other Items

1	Ordinary business income (loss)	73,075.	13	Credits	
2	Net rental real estate income (loss)				
3	Other net rental income (loss)				
4	Interest income	6,716.			
5a	Ordinary dividends				
5b	Qualified dividends		14	Schedule K-3 is attached if checked .... ☐	
6	Royalties		15	Alternative minimum tax (AMT) items	
			A		-2,308.
7	Net short-term capital gain (loss)				
8a	Net long-term capital gain (loss)	1,400.			
8b	Collectibles (28%) gain (loss)				
8c	Unrecaptured section 1250 gain				
9	Net section 1231 gain (loss)		16	Items affecting shareholder basis	
			C		1,099.
10	Other income (loss)		D		100,000.
			17	Other information	
			A		6,716.
11	Section 179 deduction	3,500.	AC		951,214.
12	Other deductions		V*	STMT	

18 ☐ More than one activity for at-risk purposes*

19 ☐ More than one activity for passive activity purposes*

*See attached statement for additional information.

BAA For Paperwork Reduction Act Notice, see the Instructions for Form 1120-S. www.irs.gov/Form1120S **Schedule K-1 (Form 1120-S) 2022**

SHAREHOLDER 1

SPSA0412 07/08/22

Statement A—QBI Pass-through Entity Reporting (Schedule K-1, Box 17, Code V)

S corporation's name: STRAIGHT EDGE, INC.	**S corporation's EIN:** 95-4145770
Shareholder's name: MATTHEW T. COLLINS	**Shareholder's identifying number:** 123-45-6789

	STRAIGHT EDGE, INC.		
Shareholder's share of:	☐ PTP ☐ Aggregated ☐ SSTB	☐ PTP ☐ Aggregated ☐ SSTB	☐ PTP ☐ Aggregated ☐ SSTB
QBI or qualified PTP items subject to shareholder-specific determinations:			
Ordinary business income (loss)	73,075.		
Rental income (loss)			
Royalty income (loss)			
Section 1231 gain (loss)			
Other income (loss)			
Section 179 deduction	3,500.		
Other deductions			
W-2 wages	78,020.		
UBIA of qualified property	50,277.		
Section 199A dividends			

Shareholder's share of:	☐ PTP ☐ Aggregated ☐ SSTB	☐ PTP ☐ Aggregated ☐ SSTB	☐ PTP ☐ Aggregated ☐ SSTB
QBI or qualified PTP items subject to shareholder-specific determinations:			
Ordinary business income (loss)			
Rental income (loss)			
Royalty income (loss)			
Section 1231 gain (loss)			
Other income (loss)			
Section 179 deduction			
Other deductions			
W-2 wages			
UBIA of qualified property			

SHAREHOLDER 1

BAA For Paperwork Reduction Act Notice, see the Instructions for Form 1120-S. SPSA1515 12/15/22 **Statement A (Form 1120-S) (2022)**

Form **1125-E**
(Rev October 2016)
Department of the Treasury
Internal Revenue Service

Compensation of Officers

► Attach to Form 1120, 1120-C, 1120-F, 1120-REIT, 1120-RIC, or 1120S.
► Information about Form 1125-E and its separate instructions is at *www.irs.gov/form1125e.*

OMB No. 1545-0123

Name	Employer identification number
STRAIGHT EDGE, INC.	95-4145770

Note: Complete Form 1125-E only if total receipts are $500,000 or more. See instructions for definition of total receipts.

1 (a) Name of officer	(b) Social security number	(c) Percent of time devoted to business	Percent of stock owned		(f) Amount of compensation
			(d) Common	(e) Preferred	
MATTHEW T. COLLINS	123-45-6789	100 %	100 %	%	50,000.
		%	%	%	
		%	%	%	
		%	%	%	
		%	%	%	
		%	%	%	
		%	%	%	
		%	%	%	
		%	%	%	
		%	%	%	
		%	%	%	
		%	%	%	
		%	%	%	
		%	%	%	
		%	%	%	
		%	%	%	
		%	%	%	
		%	%	%	
		%	%	%	
		%	%	%	

2 Total compensation of officers	50,000.
3 Compensation of officers claimed on Form 1125-A or elsewhere on return	
4 Subtract line 3 from line 2. Enter the result here and on Form 1120, page 1, line 12 or the appropriate line of your tax return	50,000.

BAA For Paperwork Reduction Act Notice, see separate instructions. Form **1125-E** (Rev 10-2016)

CPCA2101L 08/18/16

Form **4562**

Department of the Treasury
Internal Revenue Service

Depreciation and Amortization
(Including Information on Listed Property)

Attach to your tax return.

Go to *www.irs.gov/Form4562* for instructions and the latest information.

OMB No. 1545-0172

2022

Attachment Sequence No. **179**

Name(s) shown on return: STRAIGHT EDGE, INC.

Identifying number: 95-4145770

Business or activity to which this form relates: FORM 1120S

Part I Election To Expense Certain Property Under Section 179

Note: If you have any listed property, complete Part V before you complete Part I.

1	Maximum amount (see instructions)	1	1,080,000.
2	Total cost of section 179 property placed in service (see instructions)	2	3,500.
3	Threshold cost of section 179 property before reduction in limitation (see instructions)	3	2,700,000.
4	Reduction in limitation. Subtract line 3 from line 2. If zero or less, enter -0-	4	0.
5	Dollar limitation for tax year. Subtract line 4 from line 1. If zero or less, enter -0-. If married filing separately, see instructions	5	1,080,000.

6 (a) Description of property	(b) Cost (business use only)	(c) Elected cost
5-YEAR OFFICE EQUIPMENT	3,500.	3,500.

7	Listed property. Enter the amount from line 29	7	0.
8	Total elected cost of section 179 property. Add amounts in column (c), lines 6 and 7	8	3,500.
9	Tentative deduction. Enter the **smaller** of line 5 or line 8	9	3,500.
10	Carryover of disallowed deduction from line 13 of your 2021 Form 4562	10	0.
11	Business income limitation. Enter the smaller of business income (not less than zero) or line 5. See instrs	11	123,075.
12	Section 179 expense deduction. Add lines 9 and 10, but don't enter more than line 11	12	3,500.
13	Carryover of disallowed deduction to 2023. Add lines 9 and 10, less line 12	13	0.

Note: Don't use Part II or Part III below for listed property. Instead, use Part V.

Part II Special Depreciation Allowance and Other Depreciation (Don't include listed property. See instructions.)

14	Special depreciation allowance for qualified property (other than listed property) placed in service during the tax year. See instructions	14	
15	Property subject to section 168(f)(1) election	15	
16	Other depreciation (including ACRS)	16	

Part III MACRS Depreciation (Don't include listed property. See instructions.)

Section A

17	MACRS deductions for assets placed in service in tax years beginning before 2022	17	5,252.
18	If you are electing to group any assets placed in service during the tax year into one or more general asset accounts, check here ☐		

Section B – Assets Placed in Service During 2022 Tax Year Using the General Depreciation System

(a) Classification of property	(b) Month and year placed in service	(c) Basis for depreciation (business/investment use only – see instructions)	(d) Recovery period	(e) Convention	(f) Method	(g) Depreciation deduction
19a 3-year property						
b 5-year property						
c 7-year property						
d 10-year property						
e 15-year property						
f 20-year property						
g 25-year property			25 yrs		S/L	
h Residential rental property			27.5 yrs	MM	S/L	
			27.5 yrs	MM	S/L	
i Nonresidential real property			39 yrs	MM	S/L	
				MM	S/L	

Section C – Assets Placed in Service During 2022 Tax Year Using the Alternative Depreciation System

(a) Classification of property	(b)	(c)	(d)	(e)	(f)	(g)
20a Class life					S/L	
b 12-year			12 yrs		S/L	
c 30-year			30 yrs	MM	S/L	
d 40-year			40 yrs	MM	S/L	

Part IV Summary (See instructions.)

21	Listed property. Enter amount from line 28	21	
22	**Total.** Add amounts from line 12, lines 14 through 17, lines 19 and 20 in column (g), and line 21. Enter here and on the appropriate lines of your return. Partnerships and S corporations – see instructions	22	5,252.
23	For assets shown above and placed in service during the current year, enter the portion of the basis attributable to section 263A costs	23	

BAA For Paperwork Reduction Act Notice, see separate instructions. FDIZ0812L 06/28/22 Form **4562** (2022)

2022	FEDERAL STATEMENTS	PAGE 1
CLIENT STRAIGHT	STRAIGHT EDGE, INC.	95-4145770
1/26/23		03:05PM

STATEMENT 1
FORM 1120S, LINE 19
OTHER DEDUCTIONS

AUTO AND TRUCK EXPENSE	$	3,981.
BANK CHARGES		892.
COMMISSIONS		10,856.
COMPUTER & INTERNET		11,023.
DUES AND SUBSCRIPTIONS		110.
INSURANCE		5,295.
MACHINE PREP		3,800.
MEALS		1,100.
OFFICE EXPENSE		6,394.
OUTSIDE SERVICES		34,610.
POSTAGE		1,961.
PROFFESIONAL SERVICES		225.
SALES COMMISSIONS		14,483.
SECURITY & ALARM		924.
SHOP SUPPLIES		12,610.
TELEPHONE		15,894.
TRAVEL		5,821.
UTILITIES		3,971.
WARRANTY EXPENSE		1,850.
TOTAL	$	135,800.

STATEMENT 2
FORM 1120S, SCHEDULE K, LINE 17D
OTHER ITEMS AND AMOUNTS

GROSS RECEIPTS FOR SECTION 448(C)	$	951,214.

STATEMENT 3
FORM 1120S, SCHEDULE L, LINE 6
OTHER CURRENT ASSETS

	BEGINNING	ENDING
PREPAID RENT	$ 7,000.	$ 7,000.
PURCHASE DEPOSITS	2,200.	2,200.
TOTAL	$ 9,200.	$ 9,200.

STATEMENT 4
FORM 1120S, SCHEDULE L, LINE 9
OTHER INVESTMENTS

	BEGINNING	ENDING
SECURITIES	$ 10,500.	$ 9,750.
TOTAL	$ 10,500.	$ 9,750.

2022 **FEDERAL STATEMENTS** **PAGE 2**

CLIENT STRAIGHT **STRAIGHT EDGE, INC.** **95-4145770**

1/26/23 03:05PM

STATEMENT 5
FORM 1120S, SCHEDULE L, LINE 21
OTHER LIABILITIES

	BEGINNING	ENDING
ACCURED TAXES	$ 1,500.	$ 1,500.
REFUNDABLE CUSTOMER DEPOSITS	500.	500.
TOTAL	$ 2,000.	$ 2,000.

STATEMENT 6
FORM 1120S, SCHEDULE M-2, COLUMN A, LINE 3
OTHER ADDITIONS

INTEREST INCOME	$ 6,716.
LONG-TERM CAPITAL GAIN	1,400.
TOTAL	$ 8,116.

STATEMENT 7
FORM 1120S, SCHEDULE M-2, COLUMN A, LINE 5
OTHER REDUCTIONS

DISALLOWED MEALS AND ENTERTAINMENT	$ 1,099.
SECTION 179 EXPENSE	3,500.
TOTAL	$ 4,599.

STATEMENT 8
FORM 1125-A, LINE 5
OTHER COSTS

FREIGHT	$ 42,192.
TOTAL	$ 42,192.

INDEX

A

C

D

E

G

I

R

S